MASTERING NETWORKS
AN INTERNET LAB MANUAL

Jörg Liebeherr
University of Virginia

Magda El Zarki
University of California, Irvine

PEARSON
Addison
Wesley

Boston San Francisco New York
London Toronto Sydney Tokyo Singapore Madrid
Mexico City Munich Paris Cape Town Hong Kong Montreal

Executive Editor	*Susan Hartman Sullivan*
Assistant Editor	*Galia Shokry*
Marketing Manager	*Nathan Schultz*
Senior Production Supervisor	*Jeffrey Holcomb*
Copyeditor	*Norma Emory*
Proofreader	*Holly McLean-Aldis*
Indexer	*Bruce Tracy*
Composition and Art	*Gillian Hall, The Aardvark Group*
Text and Cover Designer	*Leslie Haimes*
Cover Image	*© 2003 Masterfile*
Prepress and Manufacturing	*Caroline Fell*

Access the latest information about Addison-Wesley titles from our World Wide Web site:
http://www.aw.com/computing

Many of the designations used by manufacturers and sellers to distinguish their products are claimed as trademarks. Where those designations appear in this book, and Addison-Wesley was aware of a trademark claim, the designations have been printed in initial caps or all caps.

The programs and applications presented in this book have been included for their instructional value. They have been tested with care, but are not guaranteed for any particular purpose. The publisher does not offer any warranties or representations, nor does it accept any liabilities with respect to the programs or applications.

ISBN 0-201-78134-4

1 2 3 4 5 6 7 8 9 10-PHT-06 05 04 03

Table of Contents

Preface

Welcome to the first edition of *Mastering Networks: An Internet Lab Manual*. This book is a guide to study the protocols of the Internet through a sequence of lab exercises. In addition to an in-depth study of the Internet protocols in real network settings, you will gain hands-on experience working on networking equipment and acquire useful networking skills. By putting computer networking into practice, this Internet Lab Manual illustrates how network protocols work and how networked systems interact.

Many networking courses teach networking concepts at a relatively abstract level. This book takes a lab-oriented approach, which emphasizes how networking concepts are applied in a real network. We believe that hands-on lab exercises lead to a deeper understanding of the principles of network protocols. The general organization of the labs is inspired by lab courses in the sciences: Students gain insight and understanding of the material through guided observations and measurements. In the Internet Lab Manual, networks take the place of test tubes, network traffic takes the place of chemicals, and protocol analyzers take the place of scales. Whereas experiments in a science lab can give insights into the laws of nature, the lab exercises in this book focus on the principles of network protocols.

Two trends have motivated the development of this Internet Lab Manual:

1. The explosive growth of the Internet in recent years has created a need for scientists and engineers who can maintain, tune, debug, and innovate the Internet infrastructure. The Internet Lab Manual aims to prepare the next generation of Internet engineers for the challenges of maintaining and participating in an ever-evolving and ever-growing Internet.

2. Many traditional courses in networking do not provide direct access to networking equipment and software. Increasingly, however, the need for hands-on experience is seen as essential for a high-quality education in networking. The Internet Lab Manual tries to meet the demand for creating lab-oriented courses in networking by offering an extended set of lab exercises that cover a broad range of topics.

This book tries to simplify the setup and organization of a lab course in computer networking by relying on a fixed set of equipment that can be maintained with little effort. By following an open lab approach, where lab exercises can be completed without supervision, the Internet Lab Manual can be taught with a relatively low overhead for administering and supervising lab activities.

WHO IS THE TARGET AUDIENCE FOR THE INTERNET LAB MANUAL?

This book is suitable for a second course in computer networking at the undergraduate or graduate level. It is assumed that students have some knowledge of basic concepts in computer networking, such as layering, addressing, routing, and multiplexing. A conceptual understanding of algorithms for routing, flow control, error control, and congestion control will be helpful, but it is not required. The lab exercises can be offered in conjunction with a lecture course, or they can be offered as a course without a lecture component. The Internet Lab Manual can also be used to supplement an introductory networking course. This book may also be of interest to computer and engineering professionals who are seeking to study Internet protocols in more detail. The lab exercises do not assume familiarity or prior knowledge of Linux or IOS.

WHAT THE INTERNET LAB MANUAL DOES NOT OFFER

The primary purpose of the Internet Lab Manual is the study of networking protocols in operation. The lab exercises do not try to turn students into experts in configuring or troubleshooting networks. The approach of the Internet Lab Manual gives priority to insight and learning over skill development. The knowledge of router configuration provided in the labs is just enough so that the lab exercises can be completed. Details of system administration or router configurations can be learned in certification courses and professional training programs that already exist outside of universities and colleges. Having said this, with the experience gained from the lab exercises, students will become knowledgeable and comfortable with configuring IP networks.

The Internet Lab Manual does not use tools for simulation or emulation of networks. While these tools have an important place in networking education, the Internet Lab Manual avoids using them, as they insert a layer of abstraction between students and the network they study. The Internet Lab Manual also does not use sophisticated network configuration tools, since they tend to direct the focus towards learning the configuration tools and away from the study of protocols. Labs are organized so that students can understand all aspects of the configuration of a lab experiment and can complete the lab setup themselves with a feeling of being in complete control of the network equipment.

Finally, the Internet Lab Manual does not have a network-programming component, such as socket-programming exercises or modifications of network protocols or algorithms in the Linux kernel. Adding such a component would be very useful, but it would justify the creation of a separate and more advanced course.

HOW THE LAB MANUAL WAS CREATED

Versions of the Internet Lab Manual have been taught at the University of Virginia (UVA) and at the University of California, Irvine (UCI) since 1999. Over the years, several hundred students have completed all or parts of the exercises in the Internet Lab Manual. The labs have been revised and extended over the years: Many of the labs in this book have gone through 30 or more revisions before they took their current form.

The main source of inspiration for the Internet Lab Manual is the book *TCP/IP Illustrated, Version 1*, by W. Richard Stevens, which was first published in 1994 and has been used by a whole generation of students, researchers, and professionals to study the details of the Internet protocols. The unique aspect of *TCP/IP Illustrated* is that, rather than describing what protocols do, it uses the *tcpdump* protocol analyzer tool to describe observations of protocols in action. The *Internet Lab Manual* takes essentially the same approach. The main difference is that, instead of reading about experiments and observations of protocol behavior, students do the experiments themselves. Instead of *tcpdump*, the Internet Lab Manual employs a state-of-the-art software protocol analyzer tool, called *ethereal*.

A second influence for this book is the lab manual developed by Shiv Panwar and Jeong-dong Ryoo at Polytechnic University, which contains lab exercises on routed and switched networks, following the basic approach of the *TCP/IP Illustrated* book.

HARDWARE AND SOFTWARE REQUIREMENTS FOR THE LAB

The exercises in the Internet Lab Manual are designed for a set of equipment, henceforth referred to as the Internet Lab, which consists of Cisco routers, Linux PCs, Ethernet hubs, and some additional cabling equipment. Most of the software packages needed for the Linux PCs are included in recent Linux distributions, and the remaining software can be downloaded from the Lab Manual web site. All software required for the Linux PCs is provided under the GNU Public License or similar licenses. This means that the software can be obtained without cost and that there is no restriction on distributing the software.

The setup of equipment is explained in detail in the Introduction chapter. The equipment of the Internet Lab is housed in a 19-inch rack. Dependent on the size of the class, multiple racks with Internet Labs may be made available. Access to the Internet Lab can be maximized by placing the equipment racks in a public computer room. The Internet Lab is not connected to the Internet, thereby avoiding security issues and preventing interference with the production network.

OVERVIEW OF THE LABS

The Internet Lab Manual consists of a set of 10 labs, as shown in Figure 0. Each lab covers a separate topic related to the Internet architecture and its protocols. The first five labs comprise core material. These core labs include exercises that relate to addressing of hosts and networks, forwarding of IP routers, the dynamics of routing protocols, and the behavior of transport protocols. The arrows in Figure 0 show how the topics of the core labs relate to each other. The first three labs build on each other and should be taken as a sequence. Labs 4 and 5 assume knowledge of the previous labs, but their order can be switched. Labs 6 through 10 are advanced labs. These labs assume that students have completed all of the core labs. The advanced labs each cover a self-contained topic and do not require completion in a specific sequence.

- **Lab 1, "Introduction to the Internet Lab"**
  This lab gives an overview of the Internet Lab equipment. The lab exercises introduce important procedures used in all labs, such as saving data for the lab reports and traffic capture with the ethereal tool. The lab also covers basic Linux commands, providing enough information so that Linux novices can conduct the lab exercises.

- **Lab 2, "Single-Segment IP Networks"**
  This lab shows how to configure a network interface for IP networking and what can happen when a network has configuration errors. Another subject of study is the address translation of IP addresses to MAC addresses using ARP. The final lab exercise exposes students to security problems of common Internet applications.

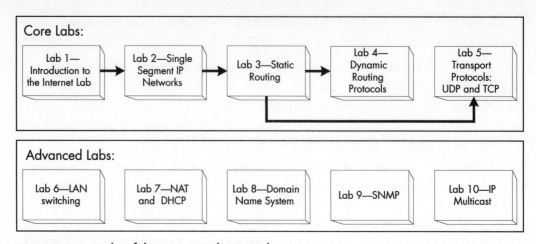

FIGURE 0. Labs of the Internet Lab Manual

- **Lab 3, "Static Routing"**
  Lab 3 introduces the concepts of IP forwarding and routing between IP networks. The lab exercises show how to set up a Linux PC and a Cisco router as an IP router and reveals the similarities of IP forwarding and routing tables on a Linux PC and a Cisco router. Students learn how to interpret and manually edit routing-table entries in a network with multiple IP networks and IP routers. The lab exposes some of the pitfalls of static routing, such as the possibility of routing loops. Since this is the first lab that uses the Cisco routers, there is a component that shows how to access the console port of a Cisco router from a Linux PC and how to issue configuration commands on a Cisco router.

- **Lab 4, "Dynamic Routing Protocols"**
  The lab explores the following routing protocols of the Internet: RIP, OSPF, and BGP. The goal of the lab is to observe the dynamics of routing protocols and to study convergence properties after changes to the network topology. One of the experiments illustrates the count-to-infinity problem in the distance vector routing protocol RIP. A lab exercise with the routing protocol OSPF explores the advantages of hierarchical routing. Finally, an exercise with the interdomain routing protocol BGP shows how to set up an autonomous system and explores routing between autonomous systems.

- **Lab 5, "Transport Layer Protocols: UDP and TCP"**
  The topics covered in Lab 5 consist of the transport protocols of the Internet, TCP and UDP. One exercise compares the performance of data transmissions with TCP and UDP. The majority of the lab exercises are devoted to an in-depth study of the various aspects of TCP, such as connection management, flow control, retransmissions, and congestion control.

- **Lab 6, "LAN Switching"**
  This lab covers LAN switching in Ethernet networks. The lab exercises show how packets are forwarded between LANs and how the paths of packets between source and destination are determined. The lab exercises illustrate the difference between Ethernet hubs and an Ethernet switches, as well as the differences between an

Ethernet switch and an IP router. The lab explores the operation of the spanning tree protocol that achieves loop-free routing between interconnected LANs.

- **Lab 7, "Network Address Translation (NAT) and Dynamic Host Configuration Protocol (DHCP)"**
  This lab has three parts. In the first part, the lab exercises explore how network address translation permits IP routers to pass traffic between private networks and the public Internet. The second part of the lab studies dynamic assignment of IP addresses with DHCP. In the last part, network address translation and DHCP are combined to investigate a network configuration that is found in many small office and home (SOHO) networks with dial-up or broadband access to an Internet service provider.

- **Lab 8, "The Domain Name System"**
  This lab studies DNS, a distributed database that performs a translation of domain names to IP addresses, and vice versa. The focus of the lab is on the interaction between resolvers and name servers. The lab exercises work with the BIND software distribution, a widely used reference implementation of DNS. The lab also explores the name server hierarchy and the setup of a DNS root server.

- **Lab 9, "Simple Network Management Protocol (SNMP)"**
  Lab 9 explores SNMP, the network management framework of the Internet, which offers facilities for managing and monitoring network resources on the Internet. The lab exercises investigate the components of the SNMP framework, including SNMP agents, SNMP managers, MIBs, and the SNMP protocol itself. Particular attention is given to the security features of different versions of SNMP.

- **Lab 10, "IP Multicast"**
  This lab is about IP multicast, the network layer mechanisms in the Internet that support data transmission from a sender to multiple receivers. The lab exercises include multicast group management with IGMP and IP multicast forwarding. The lab also covers the multicast routing protocols PIM-SM and PIM-DM and explores their dynamic behavior.

STRUCTURE OF THE LABS

All labs of the Internet Lab Manual are structured in a similar fashion. Each lab has three phases: a prelab, a lab session, and a lab report.

1. **Pre-laboratory Assignment (Prelab).** These are exercises to be completed in advance of the associated lab session. Each prelab provides a set of URLs with pointers to study material and a question sheet about this material. The prelabs ask students to acquire background knowledge that is needed during the lab exercises. The preparations in the prelabs also help to reduce the risk of making configuration errors and inadvertently damaging the hardware or software configuration in the Internet Lab.

2. **Lab Session.** These are lab exercises that are performed on the equipment of the Internet Lab. All lab exercises can be completed without supervision. The time to complete a lab session should be three hours on the average, but may vary depending on the experience and skill of the individual students and, of course, on the difficulty or complexity of the exercises themselves. The activities during the lab session are

not necessarily graded, but students must have completed all exercises of a lab session to complete a lab report.

Each lab is broken up into parts with corresponding lab exercises, which ask students to complete a network configuration and then perform experiments on the configured network. Students collect traffic measurements and/or take notes that describe the experiments. A floppy disk symbol (as shown in the margin) indicates that data needs to be saved to files. Students are responsible for saving collected data and for taking notes. Before leaving the lab session, all files with collected data need to be copied to floppy disks, for use in the lab report.

Here are a few additional things to consider:

- The equipment of the Internet Lab is not connected to the Internet. Therefore, notes, textbook, and other materials should be brought to the lab session.

- Students need to bring floppy disks to the lab session for saving data.

- Each lab has an anonymous feedback sheet. The feedback can be used by the instructor to improve the setup and organization of the labs.

- Since students have administrative (root) privileges on the Internet Lab equipment, students are asked to exercise caution when modifying the configuration of the Internet Lab equipment.

3. **Lab Reports.** After each lab session, students prepare lab reports that summarize and analyze the findings from the lab session. A notepad symbol (as shown in the margin) indicates an assignment for the lab report. The lab reports should be submitted as a typewritten document.

The lab report should not include unnecessary data that has no direct bearing to the answers in the lab report. Saved data should be included in the report only if it is requested in the lab report and if it is used to answer a question. Filtering the relevant measurements for the answers of the lab report is part of the analysis.

SUPPLEMENTAL MATERIAL

The following instructor supplements are only available to qualified instructors. Please contact your local Addison-Wesley Sales Representative, or send e-mail to aw.cse@aw.com, for information about how to access them. These supplements should greatly simplify the setup and installation of the Internet Lab equipment:

- **Equipment list for the Internet Lab:** We provide a detailed description for the equipment needed to set up an Internet Lab.

- **Configuration of PCs and routers:** We include instructions for installing the Red Hat distribution of Linux on the PCs. The instructions do not assume a lot of expertise with Linux. We also provide a script that performs the configuration of the PCs and a list of configuration commands for the Cisco routers.

- **PowerPoint Slides:** The website provides PowerPoint slides that cover the topics of all 10 labs.

- **Instructor's Manual with Solutions:** This manual contains teaching hints, sample syllabi, and sample quizzes to be used in the classroom.

ACKNOWLEDGMENTS

Since work began on the Internet Lab Manual in 1999, many people have contributed to the development of the lab exercises and have provided help and feedback.

In the past two years, Jianping Wang, Koji Noguchi, Hoan Tran, and Sun Woo Kim have provided substantial help with designing and testing lab exercises. We are very grateful for their contributions to this book project. We also thank former graduate students Vinod Balakrishnan and Nicolas Christin, who contributed to earlier versions of the lab exercises.

Jörg Liebeherr thanks Kevin Thompson and Vint Cerf for initiating the establishment of the Virginia Internet Teaching Lab (VINTLab) in 1999. The creation of the VINTLab was the starting point for lab-oriented networking education at UVA.

We want to thank the students who have completed some or the entire lab exercises in this book and for the feedback that they provided. These are the students of ICS 156 at UCI and the students of CS 551, CS 458, and CS 757 at UVA. We want to thank Jim Kurose and his students, who were early adaptors of the Internet Lab Manual and who provided feedback that led to the improvement of the labs. A special thanks to Anthony Bellissimo for extensive comments.

We thank Yvan Pointurier and Jianping Wang for developing the *msend* and *mreceive* programs used in Lab 10.

We want to thank the reviewers of the book: Christos Papadopoulos (University of Southern California), Mario Gerla (Univeristy of California, Los Angeles), Anthony Barnard (University of Alabama, Birmingham), John Cigas, Kostas Pentikousis (Stony Brook University), Melody Moh (San Jose State University), Victor Frost (University of Kansas/ITTC), and Zhi-li Zhang (University of Minnesota) for their constructive comments to improve this book.

We thank the editorial and production staff at Addison Wesley for their work on the creation of this book.

Finally, we want to express our gratitude to our editor Susan Hartman Sullivan for encouraging us to pursue this book project, and for patience with us when we, time and again, fell behind schedule.

Jörg Liebeherr
University of Virginia
Charlottesville, Virginia, USA

Magda El Zarki
University of California, Irvine
Irvine, California, USA

June 2003

●●●○ INTRODUCTION

This introduction provides an overview of the hardware and software environment of the Internet Lab. In Section 1 we describe the different network devices and cables that will be used throughout the Internet Lab Manual. All network exercises in the Internet Lab are run from computer systems that run the Linux operating system. In Section 2 we provide an overview of Linux and discuss basic commands that are used throughout the Internet Lab Manual. Section 3 discusses the traffic analysis tools *tcpdump* and *ethereal*. These tools are used to capture and display network traffic and are essential for studying network protocols. Section 4 provides an overview of the Internet Operating System (IOS), the operating system of Cisco routers, and covers basic features of the command language used to configure Cisco routers.

CONTENTS

1. OVERVIEW OF THE INTERNET LAB HARDWARE

The Internet Lab consists of a set of routers, PCs, and Ethernet hubs. The setup of the Internet Lab equipment should be similar to that in Figure 1. The Internet Lab is completely isolated from the Internet. By not connecting the Internet Lab to an operational network, the Internet Lab manual can ask you to perform tasks that would otherwise cause significant disruptions, such as unplugging network cables, or would raise security concerns, such as capturing and studying network traffic. In a real network, the majority of tasks that you perform in the lab exercises are restricted to network engineers and administrators.

1.1. DESCRIPTION OF THE HARDWARE

The Internet Lab has four PCs, which are labeled as *PC1*, *PC2*, *PC3*, and *PC4*. All PCs have the Linux Red Hat operating system installed. Each PC has a floppy drive, a serial port, and two 10/100 Mbps Ethernet interface cards (NICs). The back of each PC is similar to Figure 2. Each PC has ports to connect a keyboard, a mouse, a monitor, a parallel port, one or more serial ports, and ports to connect audio devices. In addition, each PC has two network interface cards with Ethernet ports. In Figure 2 the network interface cards are labeled as *eth0* and *eth1*. The serial ports, assuming that the PC has two such ports, are labeled as *ttyS0* and *ttyS1*. These labels refer to the names that the Linux operating system uses to identify the Ethernet cards or serial ports. For example, when you assign an IP address to an Ethernet interface card in Linux, you need to specify the name of the interface.

The PCs are controlled from a single KVM (keyboard-video-mouse) switch, which connects a keyboard, monitor, and mouse to the PCs. The KVM switch gives you control over all four PCs from a single keyboard, monitor, and mouse. The KVM switch has buttons that select to which PC the keyboard, monitor, and mouse are connected. With the KVM switch, you can access only one PC at a time.

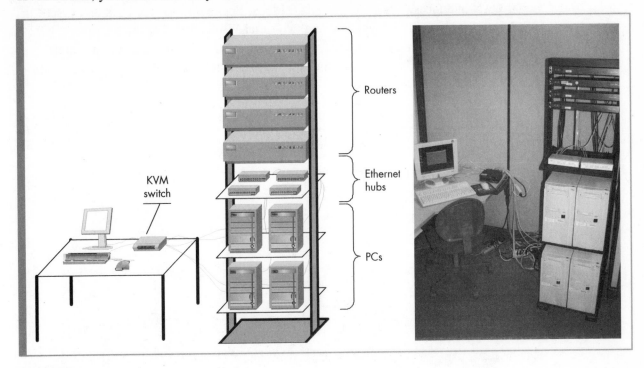

FIGURE 1.

The Internet Lab equipment.

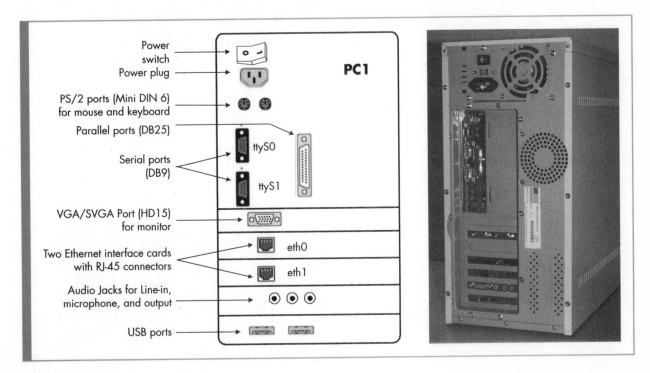

FIGURE 2.

Ports in the back of a PC.

The Internet Lab has four Cisco routers, labeled as *Router1, Router2, Router3,* and *Router4.* Each router has two Ethernet interfaces and one or more serial wide area network (WAN) interfaces. The Ethernet interfaces operate at 10 or 100 Mbps, and the serial WAN interfaces have a rate of up to 2 Mbps. Figure 3 shows the back of a Cisco 2514 router, with two Ethernet ports, and two serial WAN ports. The routers run the IOS, the operating system of Cisco routers, which has its own command and configuration language for routers. The version of the operating system used in the Internet Lab is IOS 12.0 or a more recent version.

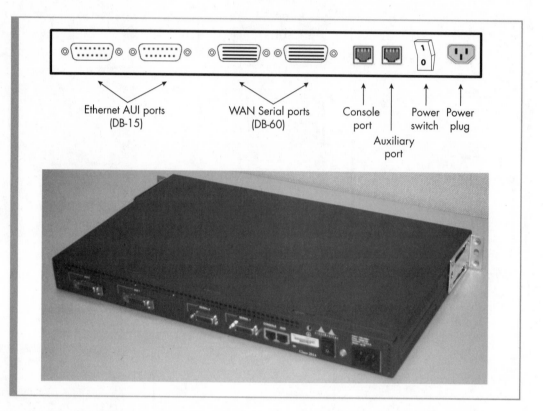

FIGURE 3.

Cisco 2514 router with two Ethernet ports and two serial ports.

Each of the four Ethernet hubs in the lab has at least four ports (see Figure 4). The hubs have a datarate of 10 Mbps, 100 Mbps or dual speed at 10/100 Mbps. PCs and routers that connect to the same Ethernet hub form an Ethernet local area network (LAN), also called an *Ethernet segment.*

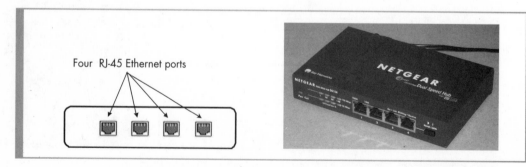

FIGURE 4.

Ethernet hub with four ports.

The Internet Lab has many different types of cables and connectors. One type of cables connects the keyboard, video, and mouse ports of the PCs to the KVM switch. Other cables connect the Ethernet interface cards of the PCs and routers to the Ethernet hubs. Last are two types of serial cables: one to connect a PC to the console port of a router and the other to connect two serial WAN interfaces of the Cisco routers.

1.2. WIRING A TWISTED PAIR ETHERNET NETWORK

Most network experiments in the Internet Lab are done over Ethernet networks, which is the dominant networking technology for local area networks. The Ethernet equipment in the Internet Lab uses the physical layers 10BaseT and 100BaseTX, currently the most widely used physical layers for Ethernet. 10BaseT and 100BaseTX have a data rate of 10 Mbps and 100 Mbps, respectively. The cables that connect 10BaseT or 10Base100TX Ethernet interface cards are unshielded twisted pair (UTP) cables with RJ-45 connectors, as shown in Figure 5. We will often to refer to these cables as *Ethernet cables*.

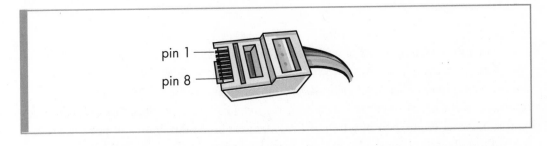

pin 1
pin 8

FIGURE 5.
UTP cable with RJ-45 connector.

Setting up a 10BaseT and 100BaseTX Ethernet network configuration is relatively easy. Given a set of PCs, routers, and Ethernet hubs, all that is needed is to connect PCs and hubs with Ethernet cables. However, there are a few things to consider when wiring an Ethernet network. First is the quality grade of the UTP cables. For 100BaseTX Ethernet, a cable must satisfy the Category 5 (Cat 5) rating of the Telecommunication Industry Association standard for wiring commercial buildings. A Cat 5 cable has four pairs of twisted wires, even though 10BaseT and 100BaseTX Ethernet use only two of the four-wire pairs.

A second issue to consider when wiring an Ethernet network is that Ethernet cables come in two types: *straight-through cables* and *crossover cables*. The difference between these two types is the assignment of pins of the RJ-45 connector to the wires of the Cat 5 UTP cable. In Figure 5, we show an RJ-45 connector with 8 pins. The assignment of pins to the wires is shown in Figure 6. In a straight-through cable, the pins of the RJ-45 connectors at both ends of the cable are connected to the same wire. A crossover cable switches pins 1 and 6 and pins 2 and 3, which corresponds to switching the transmit and receive pins. Since it is easy to confuse straight-through cables and crossover cables, it is good practice to clearly label the different types of cables.

To determine if an Ethernet cable is straight-through or crossover, simply hold the RJ-45 connectors of both cable ends next to each other (with the connector end pointing away from you) and compare how the colored wires are connected to the pins of the RJ-45 connectors. Since the plastic shielding of each wire has a different color, you can determine the difference between a straight-through cable and a crossover cable. In a straight-through cable, colors appear in the same sequence. In a crossover cable the positions of pins 1 and 3 and 2 and 6 are reversed.

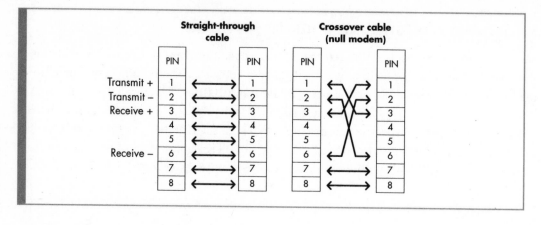

FIGURE 6.

Pin connection for straight-through and crossover Ethernet. Ethernet uses only pins 1, 2, 3, and 6.

To connect a PC or Cisco router to an Ethernet hub, you need to use a straight-through cable. When connecting two PCs, two routers, or two hubs with an Ethernet cable, you must use a crossover cable. Likewise, when connecting two hubs, you must use a crossover cable. There is one special case: Some hubs have a port labeled as *uplink port*. If you connect an uplink port of a hub to a regular port of another hub, you need to use a straight-through cable. Figure 7 illustrates these scenarios. In Figure 7(a) devices are connected to a hub using a straight-through cable. In Figure 7(b) devices are connected directly with crossover cables, and in Figure 7(c), hubs are connected to each other, with and without an uplink port.

The last issue to consider when wiring an Ethernet network is that some Ethernet interfaces may not have RJ-45 connectors. Some Ethernet interfaces (e.g., those on Cisco 2500 series routers) have 15-pin AUI ports on their Ethernet interfaces as shown in Figure 3. In that case, an AUI/RJ-45 transceiver, as shown in Figure 8, is needed. The transceiver is a small device with an AUI interface on one side and an RJ-45 port on the other side.

1.3. WIRING A SERIAL CONNECTION FROM A PC TO A ROUTER

Most routers have a *console port* that can be used to configure the router from a remote terminal. The console port is an asynchronous serial port that provides an interface for sending and receiving ASCII characters. In the Internet Lab, routers are generally accessed via the console port. This is done by connecting a serial cable from a serial port of a PC to the console port of a router, as shown in Figure 9, and by executing a terminal emulation program on the PC that sends and receives characters over the serial port. On the Linux PCs, we use the terminal emulation program *kermit* to access the routers. *kermit* can send commands to a router and can display the output from a router on a PC.

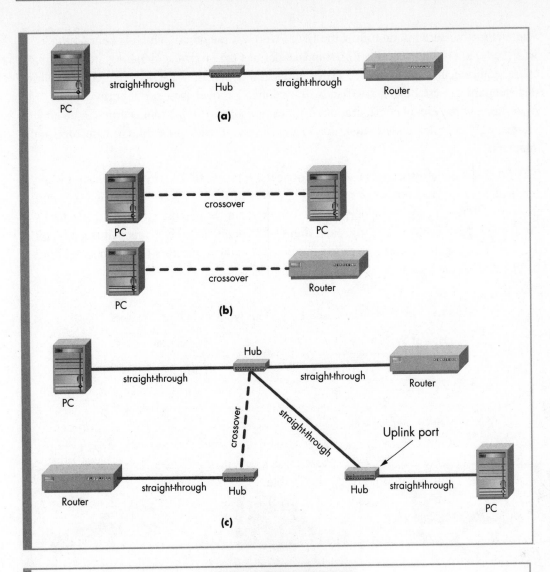

FIGURE 7.

Wiring an Ethernet network with straight-through and crossover cables.

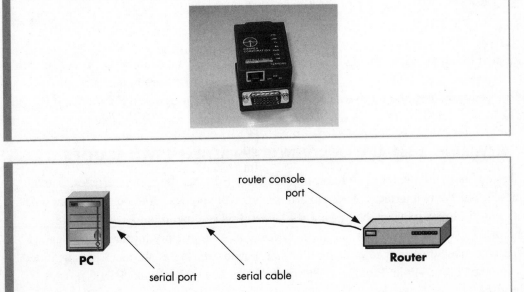

FIGURE 8.

Two AUI/RJ-45 transceivers—the top one shows the RJ-45 end; the bottom one shows the AUI end.

FIGURE 9.

Connecting a PC to a router with a serial cable.

The majority of serial ports follow the EIA/TIA 232-C standard, which is commonly referred to as *RS-232*. The RS-232 standard defines the electrical signaling, connectors, cable requirements, and other properties of a serial connection. Devices that comply with this standard can establish a low-bandwidth connection over their serial ports without requiring any additional configuration. Still, establishing a serial connection can be an interestingly complex undertaking, due to the variety of available cables, connectors, and adapters.

The RS-232 standard specifies a 25-pin connector, called DB-25. However, since most applications of serial connections use only a subset of the available 25 pins, RS-232 connectors with fewer pins are widely used. Among the most popular types of connectors are the DB-9 connector with 9 pins and the RJ-45 connector with 8 pins. All three types are shown in Figure 10. Table 1 shows the type of serial connectors found on serial ports of PCs and on the console ports of some Cisco routers.

TABLE 1. Connectors used on various types of PCs and routers.

Type of System	Connector
Recent PCs (post-1995)	DB-9
Cisco 2500, 2600	RJ-45
Cisco 7000, 7200	DB-25

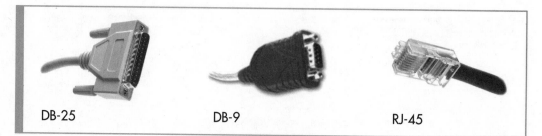

FIGURE 10.
Serial connectors.

DB-25   DB-9   RJ-45

Most of the time, cables for RS-232 serial connections use a cable with eight wires, such as the cables used for Ethernet. Three different types of wiring are in use: straight-through, crossover, and rollover. The wiring options are illustrated in Figure 6 and Figure 11. Most recent Cisco routers require rollover wiring to access the console port.

1.4. WIRING A SERIAL WAN CONNECTION BETWEEN TWO ROUTERS

The routers in the Internet Lab have, in addition to Ethernet network interfaces, one or more serial WAN interfaces. These interfaces are synchronous serial ports that can operate in full-duplex mode at the rates of a T1 line (1.544 Mbps) or an E1 line (2.048 Mbps). The connectors of the interfaces have a Cisco proprietary format and are called DB-60 connectors. Instead of using Ethernet, traffic over these interfaces is transmitted using the Point-to-Point Protocol (PPP) or the High Level Data Link (HDLC) protocol.

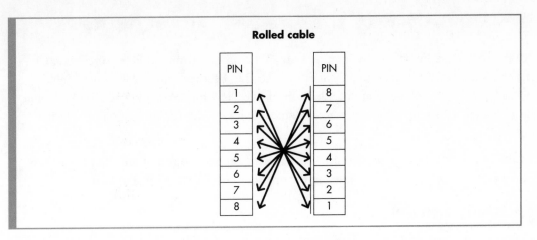

FIGURE 11.
Wiring of a rollover
serial cable.

In the Internet Lab, the serial WAN interfaces will be used as shown in Figure 12. Two serial WAN interfaces are connected with a proprietary crossover cable with two DB-60 connectors.

In real networks, serial WAN interfaces are used as shown in Figure 13. Two routers in remote locations can be connected by leasing a T1 line from a telecommunications network provider, which provides a dedicated capacity of 1.544 Mbps. Typically, the T1 service is accessed via a UTP cable with RJ-45 connectors. A router sends traffic over the leased T1 line, by connecting one of its serial interfaces to a data service unit/channel service unit (DSU/CSU), which can be thought of as a digital modem for a serial WAN connection.

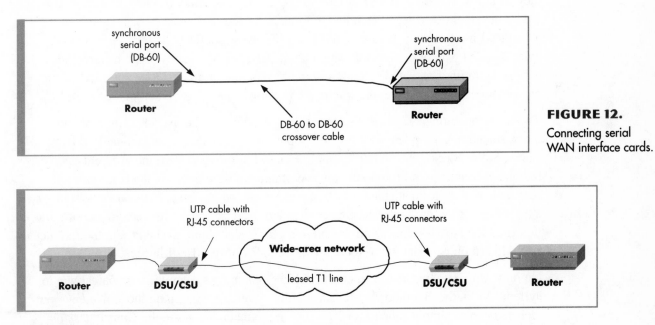

FIGURE 12.
Connecting serial
WAN interface cards.

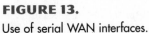

FIGURE 13.
Use of serial WAN interfaces.

2. AN OVERVIEW OF THE INTERNET LAB SOFTWARE

All network experiments in the Internet Lab are controlled from the PCs. Since the PCs run the Red Hat Linux operating system, you need to become familiar with the Linux operating system. This section provides a brief overview for newcomers to Linux. If you have worked on Linux before, you may want to quickly browse this section or skip it entirely.

At the end of this section, we discuss some Internet applications that are used extensively in the Internet Lab exercises. These are the applications *Telnet*, *FTP*, and *ping*.

2.1. LINUX AND UNIX

Linux is a clone of the Unix operating system. Unix was developed in the late 1960s at Bell Laboratories. A Unix operating system consists of a kernel and a set of common utility programs. The kernel is the core of the operating system, which manages the computer hardware and provides essential facilities, such as the control of program executions, memory management, file systems, and mechanisms for exchanging data with attached devices, other programs, or a network. The utility programs include a *shell*, a command line interface for Unix systems, and numerous commands, compilers, and other programs.

Since its inception, many different versions of Unix-like operating systems have been developed, including AIX (developed by IBM), HP-UX (by HP), SunOS and Solaris (by Sun Microsystems), and many others. By the early 1990s, when PCs had become fast enough to run full Unix-like operating systems, Unix versions for PCs started to emerge; they included, FreeBSD, NetBSD, OpenBSD, and Linux. Linux is a new branch of Unix, whose development was initiated by the Finnish computer science student Linus Torvalds. Linux software is distributed freely. Even the source code for Linux is available. Bundled with other free software, particularly, the GNU software, which includes editors, compilers, and applications, and the X Windows graphical user interface, Linux has become an alternative to the Microsoft Windows operating system platform for PCs.

The Linux operating system is distributed by organizations that package Linux with other, sometimes proprietary, software. Popular Linux distributions include Red Hat Linux, SuSE, Slackware, Mandrake, and Debian. For the most part, the different distributions of Linux are quite similar. However, there are differences in the configuration files, that is, the files that contain system parameters, which are read when the system or a server on the system is started. Since many lab exercises deal with changing configuration files, the lab experiments are bound to a certain distribution. The PCs in the Internet Lab will run on Red Hat 9.0 or more recent versions of Red Hat Linux.

On most Unix systems, a user interacts with the operating system via a graphical window system. Virtually all window systems for Unix systems are based on the *X Windows system*, sometimes simply called *X* or *X11*. In the lab manual, we use the *Gnome desktop* with the *Enlightenment window manager*, one of the popular desktop environments for Linux, that is based on X11. However, all labs can be completed with any window manager or desktop environment for X11.

Next we describe some features of Linux and show how to perform a set of basic tasks.

2.1.1. Logging in

Linux is a multiuser operating system: Multiple users can work on the same system at the same time. Linux uses accounts to administer access to the system. Before you can work on a Linux system you must provide an account name (*login name*) and a password. This process is referred to as logging in. Each Linux system has a special account, with login name *root*. The root account is reserved for administrative tasks. The root user, often called *root*, can access all files and all programs, delete all files, create or delete accounts, and change configuration files. In short, the root user can do anything on a Linux system.

Most lab exercises require that you make changes to the configuration of the Linux system or run programs that require the privileges of the root user. Therefore, whenever you access the PCs in the Internet Lab, you log in as the root user. A risk of logging in as root is that a single inadvertent action may render the system useless and may require a new installation of the operating system. Some actions may even damage the hardware of the system. Therefore, whenever you are logged in as root, exercise caution when deleting files, so that you do not delete a file that is needed by the Linux kernel.

When you log in to a Linux Red Hat system that has the Gnome desktop environment installed, you see a window as shown in Figure 14. Other X11 window managers or desktop environments would show a similar window. To log in as root, type *root* in the *Login* field and press the Enter key. When prompted for the password, type the root password and press the Enter key. If the password is correct, you will see a desktop similar to the one shown in Figure 15. You must know the root password to log in as the root user. If you have done the installation of Linux yourself, you have selected a root password during the installation procedure. Otherwise, someone must have given the root password to you.

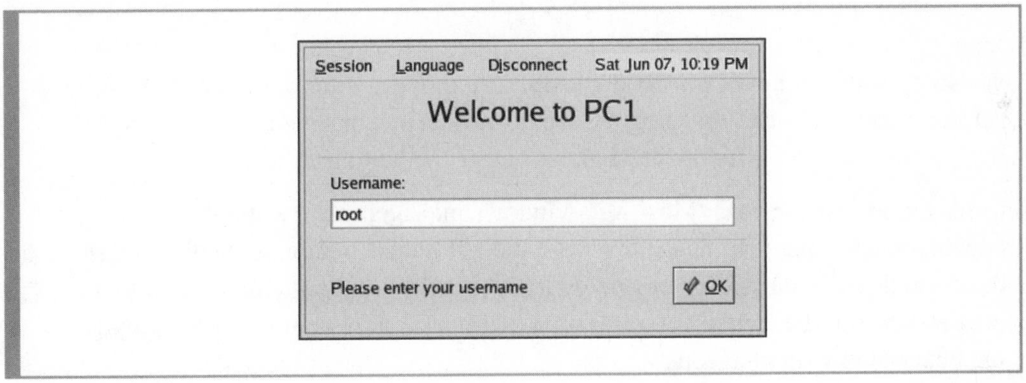

FIGURE 14.
Login Window.

2.1.2. Navigating the Desktop

The following are a few tasks that you need to be able to perform in the Gnome desktop environment:

- **Opening a terminal window:** To use the command line interface of Linux you need to create a *terminal window*. A new terminal window is created by clicking the right button of the mouse in the main window, and then selecting (left-click the mouse) New Terminal in the displayed menu (as shown in Figure 15). The center of the desktop in Figure 15 shows a terminal window.

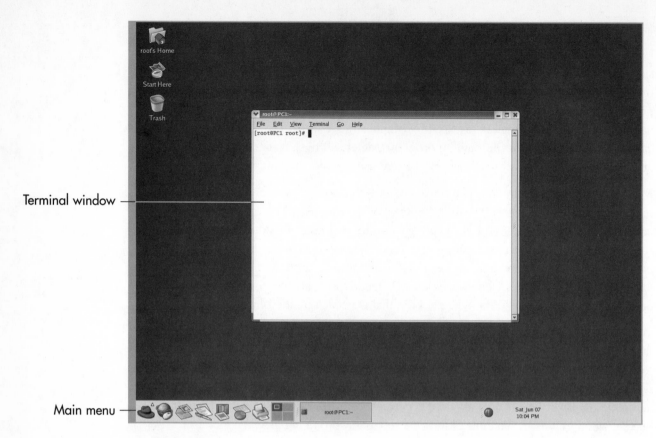

Terminal window

Main menu

FIGURE 15.
Snapshot of a Gnome Desktop.

- **Working with windows on the desktop:** You move a window on the desktop by selecting its top bar and dragging the window to its new position. You can hide, maximize, or close a window by clicking one of the buttons in its top bar.

- **Cutting and pasting text:** Most X11 windows managers have a simple feature for copying and pasting text. Select text with the left mouse button, move the mouse to the desired position in the same or a different window, and paste the copied text by pressing the middle mouse button. With a two-button mouse, you can paste by pushing both buttons simultaneously.

- **Logging out:** At the end of each lab session, you must log out of the root account. In the Gnome desktop, you log out by clicking on the main menu button (see Figure 15). In the displayed menu, shown in Figure 16(a), select *Log out*. This will display a window on the desktop as shown in Figure 16(b). Selecting the *Logout* button logs you out of the root account.

- **Getting help:** The Gnome desktop has an online help system. The system is started by clicking on the main menu button (see Figure 15), and selecting Help in the displayed menu.

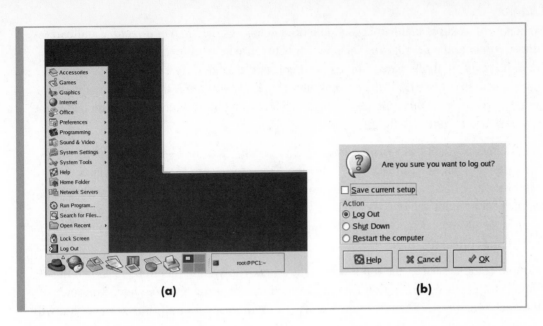

FIGURE 16.

Logging out in Gnome.

2.1.3. The Linux File System

Like most operating systems, Linux organizes files as a hierarchical tree of directories. Figure 17 shows a snapshot of the directory hierarchy of Linux. The directory at the top of the hierarchy, which is denoted by a slash (/), is called the *root directory*.

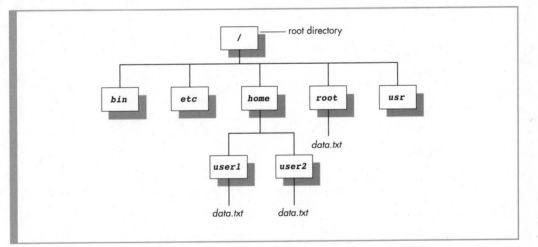

FIGURE 17.

Snapshot of a Linux directory hierarchy.

Each file and directory in a Linux file system is uniquely identified by a *pathname*. Pathnames can be absolute or relative. Absolute pathnames start at the root directory. The absolute pathname of the root directory is a slash (/). In the file hierarchy in Figure 17, the absolute pathname of directory *home* in the root directory is */home*, that of directory *user1* in */home* is */home/user1*, and the absolute pathname of file *data.txt* in */home/user1* is */home/user1/data.txt*.

Pathnames that do not begin with a slash are relative pathnames and are interpreted relative to a *current (working) directory*. For example, if the current directory is */home*, then the pathname *user1/data.txt* refers to the absolute pathname */home/user1/data.txt*.

When using relative pathnames, a single dot (.) denotes the *current directory* and two dots (..) denote the *parent directory*, which is the directory immediately above the current directory. With the parent directory, it is feasible to identify each file with relative pathnames. In Figure 17, if the current directory is */home/user1*, the relative pathname .. refers to directory */home*, the pathname ../.. refers to the root directory, and the pathname ../user2/data.txt refers to the file */home/user2/data.txt*.

Each Linux account has a *home directory*. For regular accounts—that is, accounts that are different from the root account—the home directories are located in */home*. So, */home/user1* is the home directory for an account with login *user1*. The home directory of the root account is */root*. When a new terminal window is created, the current directory in the terminal window is the home directory. Since you log in as root in the Internet Lab, this is directory */root*.

A more complete list of the top levels in the Linux file system hierarchy is shown in Figure 18. Linux configuration files are located in directories */etc*, */usr/etc*, */var*, and their subdirectories. Whenever you modify the configuration of a Linux system, you will work on files in these directories.

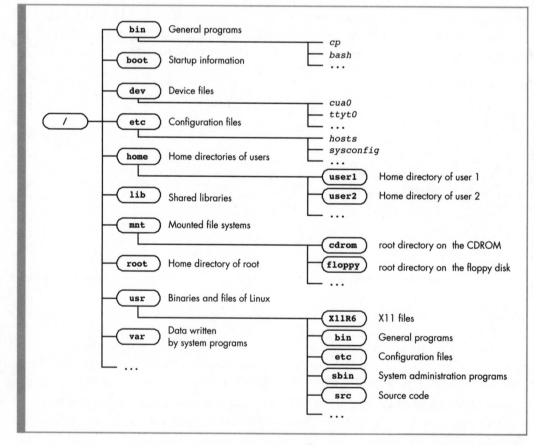

FIGURE 18.

Main directories of the hierarchical Linux directory structure. Directories are shown as boxes and file names are shown in italics.

Each file and each directory has an owner. A regular user owns only the home directory and all files created by the user. The root is the owner of all other files on the system.

In Linux, each file has a set of access permissions. The permissions are read (*r*), write (*w*), and execute (*x*) and give, respectively, permission to read the contents of a file, modify the file, or execute the file as a program. Permissions are set by the owner of a file. Linux specifies access permissions separately for the owner of the file, a user group that is associated with the file, and the set of all users. So, the owner of a file can set the permissions so that all users can read the files, but only the owner can modify the file. The root user can ignore all access permissions and can even change the ownership of files. Since the exercises in the Internet Lab are done from the root account, access permissions are not important for the Internet Lab. The downside of not having to worry about access permissions is that there is no protection against accidentally deleting or corrupting files.

When using a floppy disk or a CD-ROM on a Linux system, the media can be attached to the directory tree of the Linux system. Linux expects that the external media have been formatted with a hierarchical file system that is recognized by Linux, complete with root directory. The process of adding an external file is illustrated in Figure 19. The figure shows a file system on a floppy disk that is mounted to an existing Linux file system. After mounting the floppy disk, the files on the floppy disk are available through the pathname */mnt/floppy*. The commands for mounting a floppy disk are discussed in Lab 1.

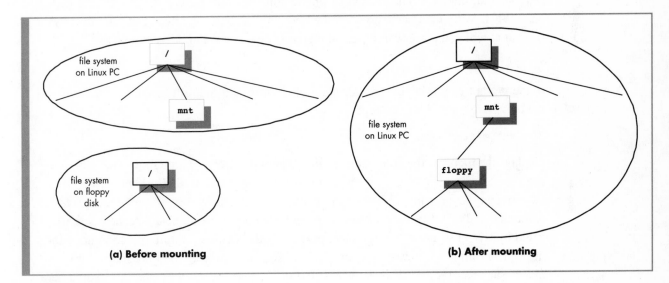

(a) Before mounting   **(b) After mounting**

FIGURE 19.
Mounting a file system on a floppy disk.

2.1.4. Linux Devices and Network Interfaces

In Linux, hardware devices such as disks, the keyboard, and the mouse are represented by *device files*, which reside in the directory */dev*. For example, the mouse of a PC is represented by the device file */dev/mouse*. With device files, communication with an external device is similar to reading and writing from and to a file. When data is written to or read from a device file, Linux communicates with a device driver that is associated with the device file. The device driver communicates with and controls a hardware device. In the Internet Lab, you will work with a number of different device files. For example, you will access the serial ports of the PCs via device files */dev/ttyS0* or */dev/ttyS1,* and the floppy disk drive will be accessed via */dev/fd0.*

The software abstraction through which the Linux kernel accesses networking hardware is that of a *network interface.* For example, when assigning an IP address to an Ethernet interface card, you manipulate the configuration parameters of the network interface that represents the Ethernet card. Just like other devices, each network interface is associated with a device driver. In most Unix-like operating systems, a network interface is implemented as a device file. This is different in Linux, where network interfaces are internally defined in the kernel. As a result, networking hardware is handled slightly differently from other hardware. In Linux, the names of network interfaces for Ethernet hardware are *eth0* for the first Ethernet interface card and *eth1* for the second Ethernet interface card. There is a special network interface, the *loopback interface*, with name *lo*. The loopback interface is not connected to a real device but is a virtual interface, which allows a PC to send messages to itself.

2.1.5. Linux Shell and Commands

The command line interface of the Linux operating system is called a shell. A shell is a program that interprets and executes Linux commands that are typed in a terminal window. Whenever you create a new terminal window, a shell is started. The shell displays a prompt at which the user can type commands. The prompt can be as simple as

```
%
```

or the prompt can be set to provide additional information. For example, in the terminal window in Figure 15, the prompt

```
39: PC1@/root =>
```

displays the name of the computer and the current directory. Throughout this book, we use the prompts `%`, or `PC1%` if we want to indicate that this is a shell prompt at PC1. When you type a command at the prompt and press the Enter key, the shell interprets the command and, if it is a valid Linux command, executes the command. A shell is terminated by typing `exit` at the command prompt. If the shell is running in a terminal window, the terminal window disappears. Linux offers a variety of shell programs with names such as *sh*, *csh*, *ksh*, *tcsh*, and *bash*. For the purposes of the material covered here, the differences between these shell programs are not relevant.

Next, we review some basic Linux commands that are typed in at a shell prompt. Commands in Linux have a common format: a command name, which may be followed by a set of options and arguments. For example, in the command `ls -l data.txt`, `ls` is the command, `-l` is an option that further specifies the command, and `data.txt` is an argument. Options are generally preceded by a – (dash), and multiple options can be specified in a single command.

The only built-in help feature of a Linux system is the online manual pages for Linux commands, called the *man pages*. The man pages offer detailed information on a command; however, they provide a lot of detail that is not always helpful for new users of Linux. Desktop environments, such as Gnome, provide additional help information.

GETTING HELP

man *cmd*

> Displays the on-line manual pages. For example, the command man ls displays the manual pages of the command ls.

When you log in to a PC in the Internet Lab you may find that changes to the Linux system from a previous lab are still in effect. Restarting (*rebooting*) the operating system removes all temporary configuration changes. Therefore at the beginning of each lab you should always reboot the Linux PCs.

REBOOTING LINUX

reboot

> Stops and restarts the Linux operating system. Rebooting removes all temporary changes to the operating system. When system configuration files have been modified, the changes are effective after the system reboots.
>
> Do not reboot Linux by powering the PC off and on. This can leave the file system in an inconsistent state.

halt

> Stops Linux without restarting.

Note: In the Gnome desktop environment, you can reboot the system following the instructions for logging out. When you arrive at the window shown in Figure 16, simply select Shut Down or Restart the computer.

Since all files in Linux are organized as a tree of directories, you need to become familiar with navigating and manipulating the directory tree with the commands shown.

DIRECTORY COMMANDS

pwd

> Prints the absolute path of the current directory.

cd *dirpath*

cd

> Changes the current directory to the relative or absolute pathname of the directory *dirpath*. If no directory is given, the command changes the current directory to the home directory. For example, the command cd /usr/bin changes to directory */usr/bin*, the command cd .. changes to the parent directory, and the command cd without a parameter changes, if you are logged in as root, to directory /root.

mkdir *dirname*

> Creates a new directory with name *dirname* in the current directory. For example, the command mkdir xyz creates a new directory with name *xyz*.

rmdir *dirname*

> Deletes the directory *dirname* from the current directory. A directory cannot be deleted when it still contains files or subdirectories. Thus, before deleting a directory, you must delete all its files and subdirectories first.

Before discussing the commands to list and manipulate files, we introduce the *wildcard characters* * (star) and ? (question mark). The wildcard character * matches any sequence of zero or more characters, and ? matches any single character. Wildcard characters are useful to describe multiple files in a concise manner. For example, the text string *A*.txt* matches all file names that start with an *A* and end with *.txt* (e.g., *ABC.txt*, *A.txt*, and *Ab.txt*). The text string *A?.txt* matches all file names that are two characters long and start with *A* (e.g., *Ab.txt* and *A1.txt*).

FILE COMMANDS

`ls`

`ls` *dirname*

> Lists information about files and directories in the current directory. If the command has a directory name as argument, then the command lists the files in that directory. The `ls` command has several options. The most important is `ls-l`, which displays extensive information on each file, including the access permissions, owner, file size, and time when the file was last modified.
>
> For example, `ls /` lists all files and directories in the root directory; `ls AB*` lists all files and directories in the current directory that start with *AB*; `ls-l ..` prints detailed information on each file and directory in the parent directory of the current directory.

`mv` *fname newfile*

`mv` *fname dirname*

> The first renames a file or directory with name *fname* as *newfile*. The second moves a file or directory to the directory *dirname*. If the destination file (*newfile*) exists, then the content of the file is overwritten, and the old content of *newfile* is lost. If the first argument is a file name and the second argument is a directory name (*dirname*), the file is moved to the specified directory.
>
> For example, `mv data.txt text.txt` simply renames file *data.txt*, and `mv * /root` moves all files from the current directory to directory */root* (and gives an error message if the current directory is */root*).

`cp` *fname newfile*

`cp` *fname dirname*

> Copies the content of file *fname* to *newfile*. If a file with name *newfile* exists, the content of that file is overwritten. If the second argument is a directory, then a copy of *fname* is created in directory *dirname*.
>
> For example, `cp *.txt /tmp` creates a copy of all files that end with *.txt* in directory */tmp*.

`rm` *fname*

> Removes a file. Once removed, the file cannot be recovered. For example, `rm *` removes all files in the current directory.

Note: Linux may not issue a warning when a file is overwritten or when a file is removed. When you use the option `-i`, Linux asks for confirmation before overwriting or deleting files. We strongly recommend that you use `cp -i` instead of `cp`, `mv - i` instead of `mv`, and `rm -i` instead of `rm`. Many shells are configured to always use the `-i` option.

An important thing to have in mind is that Linux does not have an `undo` command that reverses the effects of a previously issued command.

In many lab exercises you need to modify the content of configuration files. Here, you may find the listed commands helpful.

COMMANDS TO VIEW AND MODIFY TEXT FILES

`more` *fname*
> Displays the contents of file *fname*, one page at a time. The display can be scrolled with the Page Up and Page Down keys. Keyboard controls are Space Bar or `f` for the next page, `b` for the previous page, and `q` to end the display.

`cat` *fname*
> This is similar to the `more` command, but the file is displayed without stopping at the end of each page.

`gedit` *fname*
`gedit`
> This command opens the file *fname* in the text editor *gedit*. A new text file can be written by running `gedit` without an argument. A text editor is used to view or modify the content of a text file.

Linux has a wide variety of editors that can be used to modify text files. Widely used text editors in Linux include *vi*, *emacs*, and *pico*. We recommend the *gedit* editor if you have never worked with a text editor on an Unix-like system, since it has an intuitive graphical user interface. To edit the file */etc/hosts* with *gedit*, simply type

```
PC1% gedit /etc/hosts
```

The user interface of *gedit* is shown in Figure 20. To modify the file simply click on a location in the text window and type text. You can press Ctrl-C for copying highlighted text and Ctrl-V for pasting text.[1] To save the changes, click the *Save* button. To exit the application, select *File: Quit*.

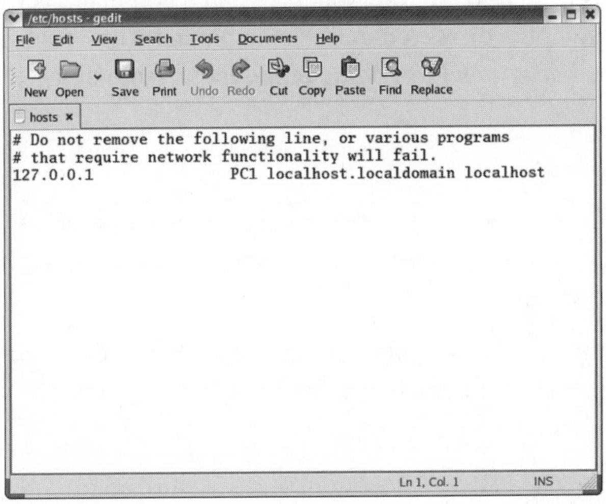

FIGURE 20.
The *gedit* text editor.

---

[1] To enter Ctrl-C, hold down the Ctrl key and then press the C key.

Many lab experiments ask you to save data that is displayed in a terminal window to a file. You can redirect the output of a terminal window to a file with the commands shown.

REDIRECTING THE OUTPUT OF COMMANDS

`cmd > fname`		The output of `cmd` is written to file `fname`. The file is created if it doesn't already exist, and its contents are overwritten if the file exists. For example, the command `ls > mlist.txt` writes a listing of the current directory in file *mylist.txt*.
`cmd >> fname`		The >> operator *appends* the output of command `cmd` to the end of file `fname`.
		For example, the command, `ls >> mlist.txt` appends a listing of the current directory to file *mylist.txt*.

`cmd | tee fname`
`cmd > fname & tail -f fname`

Both commands have the effect that the output of command `cmd` is displayed in the terminal window and also written to file `fname`. The file is created if it does not exist, or the content is overwritten if the file exists.

For example, the command `ls | tee mylist.txt` displays the listing of the current directory on the screen, and writes a listing of the current directory to file *mylist.txt*.

In Linux, each terminal window can run multiple commands at the same time. Also, it is possible to stop a command temporarily and resume it at a later time. In each terminal window, one command can be run as a *foreground process* and multiple commands can be run as *background processes*. When a command is issued from the prompt, say

`% gedit`

the command `gedit` is started in the foreground. When a command is running in the foreground, no shell prompt is displayed until the command is finished. The same command can be run in the *background* by adding an `&` (ampersand) at the end of the command, as follows:

`% gedit &`

If a command is executed in the background, the shell prints a prompt for the next command without any delay. Using background commands, you can run multiple commands from a single terminal window.

You can switch a command that is running in the foreground to the background and vice versa. Switching a command from the foreground to the background is done as follows:

`% gedit`

then press Ctrl-Z followed by

`% bg`
`%`

Here, `gedit` is the command in the foreground. Pressing Ctrl-Z stops the command, and `bg` resumes the stopped command in the background. To switch a command from the background to the foreground, type

```
% jobs
```

The command `jobs` lists all commands that are currently running in the background or are stopped (e.g., with Ctrl-Z. The command

```
% fg %1
```

resumes the first command in the foreground. See the set of Linux commands that control the execution of commands.

CONTROL OF COMMANDS

`Ctrl-C`
     Pressing Ctrl-C terminates the command running in the foreground.

`Ctrl-Z`
     Pressing Ctrl-Z *stops* the command running in the foreground.

`cmd &`
     Executes the command `cmd` in the background.

`jobs`
     Lists all background and stopped commands of the current user and assigns a number to each command.

`fg %n`
`fg`
     Resumes the *n*th command of the user (as listed by the command `jobs`). If no number is given, the command refers to the command that was last running, started, or stopped.

`bg %n`
`bg`
     Resumes the *n*th command of the user that is stopped or running in the background. If no number is given, the command refers to the command that was last running, started, or stopped.

`kill %n`
     Terminates the *n*th command of the user.

`pkill cmd`
     Terminates a process that executes the command with name *cmd*.

2.2. APPLICATIONS

We next describe some of the software tools and applications that are used throughout the Internet Lab manual. These are the remote terminal application *Telnet*, the file transfer protocol *FTP*, and *ping*.

2.2.1. Running a *Telnet* Session

Telnet is a remote login protocol for executing commands on a remote host. To establish a *Telnet* session to a host with name PC2 at IP address 10.0.1.12, simply type the command `telnet 10.0.1.2`. Assuming that a *Telnet* server is running at PC2, you are prompted for a login name and a password. If the login is successful, you see a shell prompt from PC2 and can issue Linux commands. A *Telnet* session is terminated by typing `exit` at the command prompt. Figure 21 shows the output from a short *Telnet* session from PC1 to PC2.

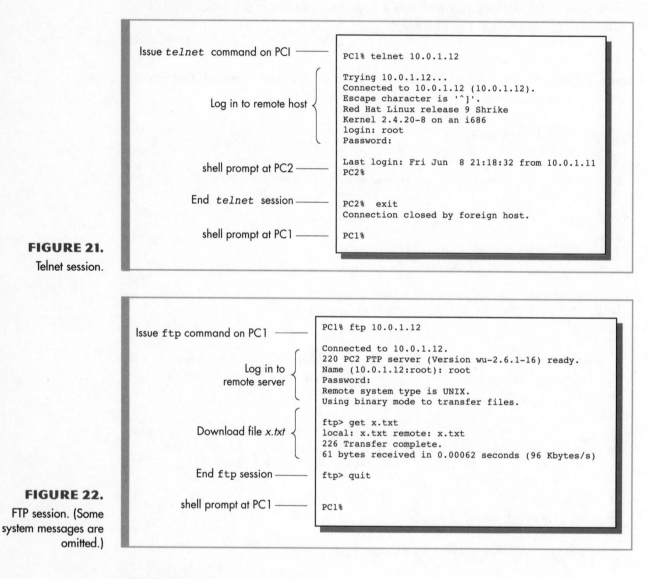

FIGURE 21.

Telnet session.

2.2.2. Running an FTP Session

The File Transfer Protocol (*FTP*) is used for copying files between computer systems. An *FTP* session from PC1 to PC2, where PC2 has IP address 10.0.1.12, is initiated by typing the command *ftp 10.0.1.2* (see Figure 22). Similar as in *Telnet*, the user at PC1 is prompted by PC2 for a login name and a password. If the login is successful, the user at PC1 sees a command prompt: `ftp>`. The *FTP* prompt accepts a limited set of commands, which can be used to download files from PC2 to PC1 or to upload files from PC1 to PC2. The command `get` is used to download a file, and the command `put` is used to upload a file. See the list of the most important *FTP* commands.

FTP COMMANDS

`ls`

Lists the content of the current directory on the remote FTP server. After logging in, the current directory is the home directory of the user.

`!ls`

Lists the content of the current directory on the local system.

`cd dirname`

Changes the current directory at the remote system to `dirname`.

`lcd dirname`

Changes the current directory at the local system to `dirname`.

`binary`
`ascii`

FTP transfers files either as text files or as binary files. The default mode is to transfer files as binary files, which is suitable for JPEG images or a compiled program. Before transferring a text file, the transfer mode must be switched to ASCII mode with the command `ascii`. The command `binary` switches back to binary mode.

`get fname`
`get fname fname2`

Downloads the file with name `fname` from the current remote directory to the current local directory. If a file with name `fname` exists in the local directory, it is overwritten without issuing a warning. If the command has a second filename as argument (`fname2`), the downloaded file is renamed as `fname2` on the local system.

`mget fname`

Downloads multiple files if `fname` uses wildcard characters. For example, the command `mget *.txt` downloads all files that end with *.txt*.

`put fname fname2`

Uploads file `fname` from the current local directory to the current remote directory. If a file with name `fname` exists in the remote directory, it is overwritten without issuing a warning. If the command has a second filename as argument (`fname2`), the downloaded file is renamed as `fname2` on the remote system.

`mput fname`

Uploads multiple files if `fname` uses wildcard characters. For example, the command `mput *.txt` uploads all files that end with *.txt*.

`quit`

Ends the FTP session.

`help`

Lists all available commands.

2.2.3. ping

One of the most simple, but also most effective, tools to debug IP networks is the `ping` command. `ping` tests whether a given IP address is reachable. `ping` sends a short packet to an IP address and waits for a response from that IP address (see Figure 23). The packets that are issued during a ping are ICMP Echo Request and ICMP Echo Response messages.[2] The `ping` command sends an ICMP Echo Request message to an interface with the specified IP address and expects an ICMP Echo Reply message in return.

---

[2]ICMP packets are covered in Lab 2.

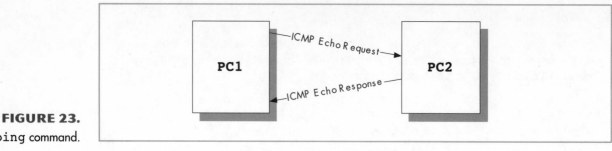

FIGURE 23.

ping command.

When issuing a ping command, a Linux system measures and displays the time between the transmission of the ICMP Echo Request and the return of the ICMP Echo Response. However, the main information provided by ping is not the time to receive a response, but whether a certain host is reachable at all. In most cases, if a ping command between two machines is successful, most Internet applications are likely to run without problems.

ping is the single most important tool of a network engineer to troubleshoot problems in a network configuration. Whenever you change the network setup in the Internet Lab, the ping command can be useful to test the network configuration.

PING COMMANDS

ping *IPaddress*

Issues a ping command for the host with the given IP address. The system will issue one *ICMP Echo Request* packet with a size of 56 bytes every second. The command is stopped by pressing Ctrl-C.

ping -c *num IPaddress*

The command stops after sending *num* ICMP Echo Requests and receiving *num* ICMP Echo Response packets, where *num* is a number.

ping -f *IPaddress*

The sender transmits *ICMP Echo Reply* messages as quickly as possible.

ping -i *num IPaddress*

The sender waits for *num* seconds between transmissions of *ICMP Echo Request* messages. The default value is 1 second.

ping -n *IPaddress*

With this option, the output uses numeric IP addresses and does not display symbolic names of hosts.

ping -R *IPaddress*

With this option, the traversed route of the ICMP messages is displayed. The display is limited to the IP addresses of the first nine hops of the route.

ping -s *num IPaddress*

The number of data bytes in the *ICMP Echo Request* is set to *num* bytes. The default value is 56 bytes.

ping -v *IPaddress*

Displays a verbose output.

3. NETWORK PROTOCOL ANALYZERS

To make observations of the behavior of network protocols, we need to have tools that can monitor network traffic and present the traffic in a human readable form. Tools that capture and display traffic on a network interface card are referred to as *network protocol analyzers* or *packet sniffers*. In the Internet Lab we extensively use two network protocol analyzers: *tcpdump* and *ethereal*.

Network protocol analyzers set the network interface card into a mode, called *promiscuous mode*, in which the card captures all traffic that passes by the interface card. An Ethernet interface in promiscuous mode can capture the traffic transmitted by all systems that are connected to the same Ethernet hub. Because of the involved security issues, the use of network protocol analyzers is generally restricted to the root user.

The software architecture of a network protocol analyzer on a Linux system with an Ethernet card is shown in Figure 24. The network protocol analyzer is running as an application that communicates with a component in the Linux kernel, called the *Linux socket filter*. The Linux socket filter acts as an agent between the protocol analyzer and the Ethernet device driver. It sets the Ethernet device driver in a mode where it obtains a copy of all incoming traffic from the network and all outgoing traffic to the network. The socket filter processes the traffic and passes the traffic to the network protocol analyzer, which displays the traffic to the user.

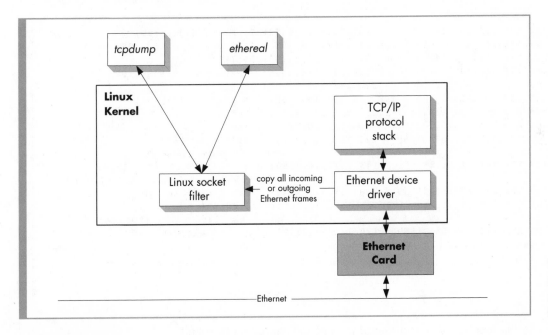

FIGURE 24.

Implementation of network protocol analyzers in Linux.

3.1. *TCPDUMP*

tcpdump, which was developed in the early 1990s at the Lawrence Berkeley National Laboratory, is started by running the command

```
% tcpdump
```

An example of the output of *tcpdump* is shown in Figure 25. The figure depicts the output for an FTP session. The output from *tcpdump* is displayed in the terminal window where the program was started.

tcpdump displays one line for each transmitted or received Ethernet frame. In each line, *tcpdump* displays a timestamp and information that is derived from the protocol headers contained in the Ethernet frame. The timestamp 16:54:51.340712 corresponds to 4:54 PM and 51.340712 seconds. The fractions of a second after the second digit may not be very accurate, since the system clocks on most PCs are reliable only for times that exceed 10–50 milliseconds. If the Ethernet frame is an IP datagram with UDP or TCP payload, then *tcpdump* displays information on the source and the destination of the frame. For example, the entry in Line 1 of Figure 25 128.143.137.144.1555 > 128.143.137.11.53 indicates that the sender of the IP datagram is IP address 128.143.137.144 at port 1555 and the destination is 128.143.137.11 at port 53. Even if a frame does not contain an IP datagram, *tcpdump* attempts to interpret the payload. For example, in Figure 25, Lines 7 and 8 show that the payload of the frame is an ARP packet. *tcpdump* displays, in addition to IP addresses, information from other protocol headers, such as TCP, UDP, routing protocols, and other protocols. In Figure 25, Lines 1–6 display information from DNS messages, and Lines 9–13 display information from TCP segment headers.

```
%tcpdump
1.  16:54:51.340712 128.143.137.144.1555 > 128.143.137.11.53: 1+ A? neon.cs. (25)
2.  16:54:51.341749 128.143.137.11.53 > 128.143.137.144.1555: 1 NXDomain* 0/1/0 (98) (DF)
3.  16:54:51.342539 128.143.137.144.1556 > 128.143.137.11.53: 2+ (41)
4.  16:54:51.343436 128.143.137.11.53 > 128.143.137.144.1556: 2 NXDomain* 0/1/0 (109) (DF)
5.  16:54:51.344147 128.143.137.144.1557 > 128.143.137.11.53: 3+ (38)
6.  16:54:51.345220 128.143.137.11.53 > 128.143.137.144.1557: 3* 1/1/2 (122) (DF)
7.  16:54:51.350996 arp who-has 128.143.71.21 tell 128.143.137.144
8.  16:54:51.351614 arp reply 128.143.71.21 is-at 0:e0:f9:23:a8:20
9.  16:54:51.351712 128.143.137.144.1558 > 128.143.71.21.21: S 607568:607568(0)
                                                  win 8192 <mss 1460> (DF)
10. 16:54:51.352895 128.143.71.21.21 > 128.143.137.144.1558: S 3964010655:3964010655(0)
                                                  ack 607569 win 17520 <mss 1460> (DF)
11. 16:54:51.353007 128.143.137.144.1558 > 128.143.71.21.21: . ack 1 win 8760 (DF)
12. 16:54:51.365603 128.143.71.21.21 > 128.143.137.144.1558: P 1:60(59)
                                                  ack 1 win 17520 (DF) [tos 0x10]
13. 16:54:51.507399 128.143.137.144.1558 > 128.143.71.21.21: . ack 60 win 8701 (DF)
```

    Timestamp   Source IP address and destination IP address   Packet headers from other protocols

FIGURE 25.

Output of tcpdump.

The list opposite shows different uses of the *tcpdump* command.

When the *tcpdump* tool is started with the command

```
% tcpdump -n -i eth0
```

it displays all packets that are captured on network interface *eth0*. Instead of capturing all traffic and then searching through the output for the data of interest, you can limit the

USES OF THE TCPDUMP COMMAND

`tcpdump  -i interface`

Specifies that *tcpdump* is started on the given interface. This option should be used on systems with multiple network interfaces. For example, `tcpdump -i eth0` starts *tcpdump* on interface `eth0`.

`tcpdump  -n`

With the `-n` option, *tcpdump* does not print host names, but prints the IP addresses in the packet. We recommend to always set the `-n` option, since resolving host names from the IP addresses may have the undesirable effect that *tcpdump* sends DNS messages, that is, *tcpdump* may generate traffic on its own.

`tcpdump  -x`

With this option, the first 68 bytes of the captured packet are displayed in hexadecimal form.

`tcpdump -l`

Buffers the output to the terminal window and enables to save output to a file. When saving the output of *tcpdump* to file `fname`, use the command

`tcpdump  -l  |  tee  fname`

or

`tcpdump  -l  > fname &  tail  -f  fname`

Note: Multiple options can be used in the same command line. For example, the command `tcpdump -i eth0 -n -x - t -vv` enables all of the preceding options.

amount of traffic captured by *tcpdump* by specifying a filter expression in the command line. With a filter expression, only the traffic that matches the filter expression is captured and displayed. For example, the command

`% tcpdump -n host 10.0.1.12`

captures IP datagrams from or to IP address 10.0.1.12 and ignores traffic with different addresses. A list of filter expressions that may be useful in the exercises of the Internet Lab is shown in Table 2.

The filter expressions can be combined using negation (`not`), concatenation (`and`), or alternation (`or`) to form complex filter expressions. In filter expressions with multiple operators, negation has the highest precedence. Concatenation and alternation have equal precedence and are interpreted from left to right. For example, the command

`% tcpdump -n not \icmp or src host 10.0.1.12 and ip multicast`

displays IP datagrams that are not ICMP messages or that come from host 10.0.1.12 and, in addition, have an IP multicast destination address. A different precedence of the operators can be enforced with parentheses. For example, each of the following three filter expressions yields a different result:

```
not \icmp or host 10.0.1.2  and \tcp
not \(\icmp or host 10.0.1.2\)  and \tcp
not \icmp or \(host 10.0.1.2  and \tcp\).
```

TABLE 2. Filter expressions for *tcpdump* filters.

Expression	Description
`dst host 10.0.1.2`	IP destination address field is 10.0.1.2.
`src host 10.0.1.2`	IP source address field is 10.0.1.2.
`host 10.0.1.2`	IP source or destination address field is 10.0.1.2.
`src net 10.0.1.0/24`	IP source address matches the network address 10.0.1.0/24.
`dst net 10.0.1.0/24`	IP destination address matches the network address 10.0.1.0/24.
`net 10.0.1.0/24`	IP source or destination address matches the network address 10.0.1.0/24.
`dst port 80`	Destination port is 80 in TCP segment or UDP datagram.
`src port 80`	Source port is 80 in TCP segment or UDP datagram.
`port 80`	Destination or source port is 80 in TCP segment or UDP datagram.
`src and dst port 80`	Destination and source port is 80 in TCP segment or UDP datagram.
`tcp port 80`	Destination or source port is 80 in TCP segment.
`udp port 80`	Destination or source port is 80 in UDP datagram.
`Less 200`	Packet size is not longer than 200 bytes.

`icmp`
`tcp`
`udp`
`ospf`
	IP protocol field is set to the number for ICMP, TCP, UDP, or OSPF.

`ip proto 17`	IP protocol number is set to 17.
`broadcast`	Ethernet broadcast packet
`ip broadcast`	IP broadcast packet
`multicast`	Ethernet multicast packet
`ip multicast`	IP multicast packet
`ip` `arp`	Ethernet payload is IP or ARP.

If an address or number is not specified by a keyword, then the most recent keyword is assumed. For example,

```
host 10.0.1.2 and 10.0.1.3
```

is short for

```
host 10.0.1.2  and  host 10.0.1.3
```

It is possible to access specific fields in protocol headers and select packets based on the values of protocol header fields. This is done with expressions of the form *proto[offset : size]* which select bytes *offset*+1, *offset*+2, ..., *offset*+*size* from the header of protocol *proto*. For example, 'ip[2:2]' selects the third and fourth byte in the IP header which contains the total length field. The expression 'ip[2:2]>576' selects IP datagrams that are longer than 576 bytes. The *tcpdump* expression that displays these IP datagrams is

```
% tcpdump -n 'ip[2:2]>576'
```

Note that the expression is put in quotes (' '). If a selection specifies a protocol header, packets that do not have such a protocol header are simply ignored. Table 3 shows examples for selecting packets based on the contents of protocol headers. Single bits can be

TABLE 3. Selection of packets based on protocol header contents.

Expression	Description
tcp[0] > 4	The first byte of the TCP header is greater than 4.
ip[2] <= 0xf	The third byte of the IP header does not exceed 15.
udp[0:2] == 1023	The first 2 bytes of the UDP header are equal to 1023.
ip[0] & 0xf > 5	IP headers that are longer than 20 bytes (i.e., IP headers with options). The expression 'ip[0]' selects the first byte from the IP packet, and 'ip[0]& 0xf' filters the 4 lower-order bits in the first byte. The expression 'ip[0] & 0xf > 5' selects all IP packets with an IP header length larger than 5. Since the IP header field expresses multiples of 4 bytes, these are packets with an IP header longer than 20 bytes.
ip[6:2] & 0x1fff == 0	IP packets with a fragment offset field is of 0 (i.e., unfragmented IP packets or the first fragment of a fragmented IP packet). The expression 'ip[6:2]' selects the 7th and 8th byte from an IP header, and 'ip[6:2] & 0x1fff' filters the last 13 bits from these 2 bytes.
tcp[13] & 3 != 0	TCP headers with the SYN flag or the FIN flag set. The expression 'tcp[13] & 3' selects the 2 least-significant bits from the 14th byte in the TCP header. These bits hold the SYN flag and the FIN flag. The expression is not 0, if at least one of the bits is set.

tested using a *bitwise and* operator (&) and a *comparison* operator (>, <, >=, <=, =, !=). For example, `'ip[0] & 0x80 > 0'` selects packets where the first bit of the IP header is set. Also, a selection can be combined with any other filter expression. For example,

```
% tcpdump -n 'ip[2:2]>576' and not host 10.0.1.2
```

selects all IP datagrams longer than 576 bytes that do not have IP address 10.0.1.2 as their source or destination IP address.

3.2. ETHEREAL

ethereal is a protocol analyzer with a graphical user interface, which recognizes a large number of protocols. *ethereal* is the main tool for capturing traffic in the Internet Lab. *ethereal* is started from a terminal window with the command

```
% ethereal
```

The command displays a window as shown in Figure 26. The traffic capture is started by selecting *Capture:Start* in the main menu of the window. Once the traffic capture is started, the *ethereal* window displays the traffic in three different views. The first view shows a summary of the captured packets, one line for each packet. One of these packets can be highlighted, by clicking on the corresponding line. In Figure 26, the first packet is highlighted. The second view shows the protocol header details from the highlighted packet. Packet headers can be expanded and hidden. In Figure 26, the Ethernet header is expanded and the other headers are hidden. The third view shows the hexadecimal and ASCII representation of the packet headers and the data. The traffic captured by *ethereal* can be saved to a file by selecting *File:Print* in the main menu.

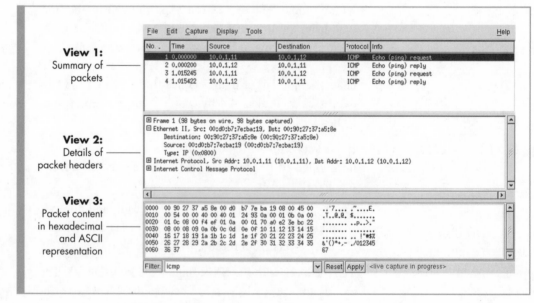

FIGURE 26.
ethereal window.

As in *tcpdump*, a user can limit the traffic to be captured. In *ethereal*, this is done by setting a *capture filter*. In addition, for traffic that is already captured, a user can display a subset of the captured traffic by specifying a *display filter*.

Capture filters: A capture filter specifies the type of traffic that is captured by *ethereal*, similarly to filters in *tcpdump*. In fact, capture filters in *ethereal* are written using the same syntax as *tcpdump* filters. A capture filter can be set in the command line when *ethereal* is started or in the capture window before a traffic capture is initiated. The following command is used to set a capture filter from the command line:

```
% ethereal -i interface -f filter
```

where `interface` is a network interface and `filter` is a capture filter expression. The capture filter expression is written using the same syntax as for *tcpdump* filters. If no capture filter is specified, *ethereal* captures all traffic.

Alternatively, the interface and the capture filter can be set from the *Capture Options* window of *ethereal*, which is opened by selecting *Capture:Start* in the main window and by typing in the interface name and the desired filter expression in the appropriate boxes. The *Capture Options* window of *ethereal* is shown Figure 27. Here, the interface is set to *eth0* and the capture filter is set to host 10.0.1.12.

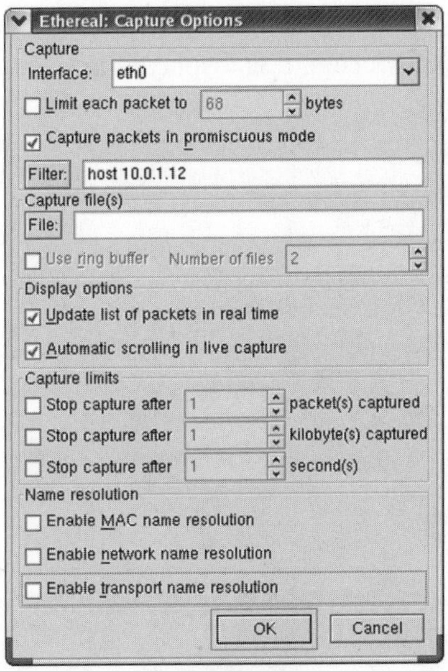

FIGURE 27.

Setting a capture filter in *ethereal*.

Display filters: A display filter specifies the type of traffic that is displayed in the main window of *ethereal* but does not restrict the amount of traffic that is captured. An advantage of using display filters is that it is possible to change display filters after packets have been captured. The syntax for setting display filters is different from the syntax for setting capture filters. Also, display filters cannot be set from the command line. A display filter is set by typing a display filter expression at the bottom of the main window in *ethereal*, next to the label *Filter*. At the bottom of Figure 26, the display filter expression `icmp` restricts the display of traffic to ICMP messages. In Figure 28, we see that the display filter is set to `ip.dst==10.0.1.12`, which selects all IP packets with the destination IP address 10.0.1.12. When the filter is applied by pressing Enter, only packets that match the filter are displayed in the main window. The *Reset* button next to the *Filter* box removes the filter.

FIGURE 28.

Setting a display filter
in *ethereal*.

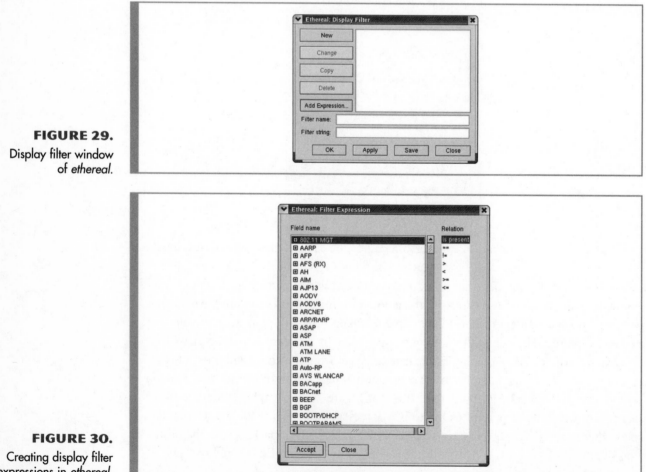

Filter: ip.dst == 10.0.1.12   ☑ Reset Apply <live capture in progress>

The syntax for display filters is different from that for capture filters. In Table 4 and 5 we show *ethereal* display filters that correspond to the *tcpdump* filters (and *ethereal* capture filters) from Table 2 and Table 3. Display filters have a separate keyword for each header field of a protocol and are generally easier to read. The keywords for a particular header field can be obtained from the manual page of *ethereal*.

ethereal offers interactive help for writing display filters. The help is activated by clicking on the *Filter* button, located in the bottom left corner of the *ethereal* main window (see Figures 26 and 28). This pops up the *Display Filter* window (see Figure 29). Then, clicking on the *Add Expression* button pops up the *Filter Expression* window (see Figure 30). Now, the desired filter expression can be built by selecting a protocol and a protocol field. Once a filter expression is constructed, it is displayed in the main window of *ethereal*.

FIGURE 29.

Display filter window
of *ethereal*.

FIGURE 30.

Creating display filter
expressions in *ethereal*.

TABLE 4. Display filter expressions in *ethereal* (compare with Table 2).

Expression	Description
`ip.dst==10.0.1.2`	IP destination address field is 10.0.1.2.
`ip.src==10.0.1.2`	IP source address field is 10.0.1.2.
`ip.addr==10.0.1.2`	IP source or destination address field is 10.0.1.2.
`ip.src==10.0.1.0/24`	IP source address matches the network address 10.0.1.0/24.
`ip.dst==10.0.1.0/24`	IP destination address matches the network address 10.0.1.0/24.
`ip.addr== 10.0.1.0/24`	IP source or destination address matches the network address 10.0.1.0/24.
`tcp.dstport == 80 or udp.dstport == 80`	Destination port is 80 in TCP segment or UDP datagram.
`tcp.srcport==80 or udp.srcport==80`	Source port is 80 in TCP segment or UDP datagram.
`tcp.port==80 or udp.port==80`	Destination or source port is 80 in TCP segment or UDP datagram.
`(tcp.srcport==80 and tcp.dstport==80) or (udp.srcport==80 and udp.dstport==80)`	Destination and source port is 80 in TCP segment or UDP datagram.
`tcp.port==80`	Destination or source port is 80 in TCP segment.
`udp.port==80`	Destination or source port is 80 in UDP datagram.
`eth.len <= 200`	Packet size is not longer than 200 bytes.
`icmp` `tcp` `udp` `ospf`	IP protocol field is set to the number for ICMP, TCP, UDP, or OSPF (see later example) or one can use the protocol name. (Since `icmp`, `tcp`, and `udp` are keywords in *tcpdump*, an escape character (\) must be placed in front of these keywords.)
`ip.proto==17`	IP protocol number is set to 17.
`eth.dst== ff:ff:ff:ff:ff:ff`	Ethernet broadcast packet
`eth.dst[0]==1`	Ethernet multicast packet
`ip.dst==224.0.0.0/4`	IP multicast packet
`ip` `arp`	Ethernet payload is IP or ARP.

TABLE 5. More display filter expressions in *ethereal* (compare with Table 3).

Expression	Description
`tcp[0] > 4`	The 1st byte of the TCP header is greater than 4.
`ip[2] <= f`	The 3rd byte of the IP header does not exceed 15.
`udp[0:2] == 3:ff`	The 1st two bytes of the UDP header are equal to 1023. **Note:** When selecting bytes from a header, each byte is written as a hexadecimal number, and bytes are separated by a colon.
`ip.hdr_len > 20`	IP headers that are longer than 20 bytes (i.e., IP headers with options)
`ip.frag_offset == 0`	IP packets with a fragment offset field of 0 (i.e., unfragmented IP packets or the first fragment of a fragmented IP packet)
`tcp.flags.syn==1 or` `tcp.flags.fin==1`	TCP headers with the SYN flag or the FIN flag set

4. CISCO INTERNET OPERATING SYSTEM (IOS)

Just like a general purpose computer, routers run an operating system. The operating system generally is started (*booted*) when a router is powered up. Since routers do not have hard disk drives, the operating system is stored on a flash memory card or nonvolatile RAM (NVRAM). This section gives an overview of the Internet Operating System (IOS), the operating system of Cisco routers. The Cisco routers in the Internet Lab run IOS version 12.0 or higher.

In the Internet Lab, routers are generally accessed from the PC via the console port, as discussed in Section 1.2. Once the connection is made, the terminal emulation program *kermit* can be started on a PC to send commands to and receive the output from the router. In the Internet Lab, PC1 is connected to Router1, PC2 to Router2, and so on.

If one of the interfaces of a router has an IP address configured, an alternative method to access a router is to use *telnet* or *secure shell* (*ssh*) to establish a terminal window to the IP address of the configured interface. However, this works only if the router has an interface with a valid IP address.

Once a connection is established, a router shows a command prompt or asks for a login password. After a successful login, a user types commands, similarly as in a Linux shell. Each router manufacturer has its own command line interface, and the syntax for router commands can be very different across different types of routers. Here we discuss the command line interface of Cisco IOS.

4.1. THE CISCO IOS COMMAND MODES

The command line interface of IOS has a rich syntax. There are hundreds of configuration commands, and some commands have numerous options. Unlike a Linux shell, the command line interface of IOS runs in different modes, and each command requires a certain mode. The Internet Lab features only the most common command modes and, for each command mode, uses only a small subset of available commands. The command modes used in the Internet Lab are the *user EXEC mode*, the *privileged EXEC mode*, the *global configuration mode*, the *interface configuration mode*, and the *router configuration mode*.

Each command mode has a different prompt, and a user can derive the current command mode from the command prompt. The user EXEC mode is indicated by an angle bracket (>), the privileged EXEC mode by the pound sign (#), and the configuration modes by an abbreviation of the configuration mode, followed by the pound sign, for example, `(config)#`, `(config-if)#`, and `(config-router)#`. Typing a question mark (?) in any command mode generates a list of all available commands in the current mode.

Table 6 presents a summary of the command modes. Figure 31 illustrates the available transitions between different command modes, and which commands need to be issued. For example, changing from the privileged EXEC mode to the global configuration mode is done with the command `configure terminal`. Typing `exit` in this mode returns to the privileged EXEC mode. As shown in Figure 31, it is not feasible to switch arbitrarily from one command mode to another. For example, the global configuration mode cannot be entered from the user EXEC mode.

TABLE 6. Cisco IOS command modes.

IOS Command Mode	Role of Command Mode	Command Prompt
User EXEC mode	• Limited command set (e.g., `ping`, `telnet`, `traceroute`) • No change of system parameters	`Router1 >`
Privileged EXEC mode	• Manage configuration files • Examine state of router • Access control with password (enable secret)	`Router1#`
Global configuration mode	• Change systemwide configuration parameters	`Router1(config)#`
Interface configuration mode	• Modify configuration of a specific interface	`Router1(config-if)#`
Router configuration mode	• Modify configuration of a specific routing protocol	`Router1(config-router)#`

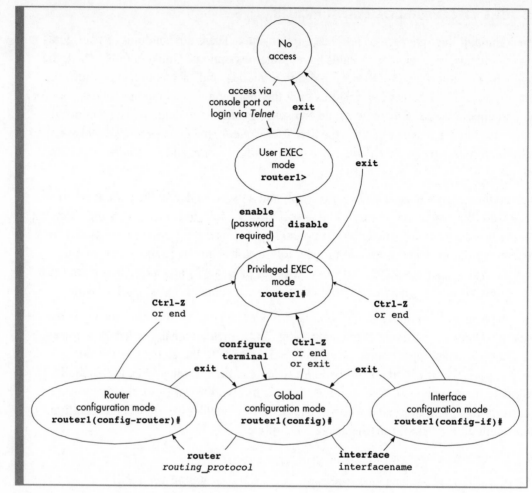

FIGURE 31.

The Cisco IOS command modes.

4.1.1. User EXEC Mode

The user EXEC mode is entered when the router is accessed via the console port or via *Telnet*.[3] The command prompt of the user EXEC mode is

`Router1>`

where `Router1` is the name that is assigned to the router. The user EXEC mode offers only a small set of commands, such as `ping`, `Telnet`, and `traceroute`. Configuration parameters cannot be read or modified in this mode. Typing

`Router1>exit`

logs the user off.

4.1.2. Privileged EXEC Mode

To change or view configuration information of a Cisco router, a user must enter a system administrator mode. In IOS, the system administrator mode is called the *privileged*

---

[3]Entering the user EXEC mode over a serial connection may require a login password, and entering this mode with *Telnet* always requires a login password.

EXEC mode. In the privileged EXEC mode, a user has rights similar to the root account on a Linux system. The privileged EXEC mode is used to read configuration files, reboot the router, and set operating parameters. To modify the configuration of a router, a user must proceed from the privileged EXEC mode to the global configuration mode and, from there, to other configuration modes.

Entering the privileged EXEC mode requires you to type a password, called the *enable secret*. The privileged EXEC mode is entered from the user EXEC mode by typing the command

```
Router1>enable
Password : <enable secret>
```

Typing the correct password displays the following command prompt:

```
Router1#
```

To change the command mode back to the user EXEC mode, the user types

```
Router1#disable
```

Typing `exit` logs the user off.

4.1.3. Global Configuration Mode

The global configuration mode is used to modify systemwide configuration parameters, such as routing algorithms and routing tables. The global configuration mode can be entered only from the privileged EXEC mode. This is done by typing

```
Router1#configure terminal
```

No additional password is required to enter this mode. The argument `terminal` tells the router that the configuration commands will be entered from a terminal. The alternatives are to issue configuration commands from a configuration file or from a remote machine via a file transfer. The command prompt in the global configuration mode is

```
Router1(config)#
```

Global configuration commands include commands that enable or disable IP forwarding and that set static routing table entries. For example, the command

```
Router1(config)#ip routing
```

enables IP forwarding on the router, and the command

```
Router1(config)#ip route 20.0.1.0  255.255.255.0 10.1.1.1
```

adds a network route for destination address 20.0.1.0/24 via gateway 10.1.1.1 to the routing table. Typing Ctrl-Z as in

```
Router1(config)#Ctrl-Z
```

changes from the global configuration to the privileged EXEC mode.

4.1.4. Interface Configuration Mode

To modify the configuration parameters of a specific interface, for example, the IP address, a user must enter the interface configuration mode. The interface configuration mode for a network interface, which is entered from the global configuration mode, is entered by typing the keyword `interface` followed by the interface name.

In IOS, each network interface is associated with a name, which specifies an interface type, a slot number, and a port number. Examples of interface types that are used in the Internet Lab are a serial WAN interface (serial), 10 Mbps Ethernet (Ethernet), and 100 Mbps Ethernet (FastEthernet). Other types of interfaces are FDDI Token Ring (FDDI), and Asynchronous Transfer Mode (ATM). The slot number indicates the slot into which the interface card is inserted. The port number identifies a port on the interface card. For example, on a Cisco 2611 or Cisco 2611XM, the interface name `Ethernet0/0` identifies port 0 on a 10 Mbps Ethernet card, which is located in slot 0 of the router. `Ethernet0/1` identifies port 1 on the same card. On routers that have a fixed number of interfaces and do not have a slotted chassis, the slot number is omitted. For example, on a Cisco 2514 router, which has two Ethernet interfaces and two serial WAN interfaces, as shown in Figure 3, the interface names are `Ethernet0`, `Ethernet1`, `Serial0`, and `Serial1`. Throughout this book, we use the syntax for interface cards for slotted router chassis. For other routers, such as Cisco 2500 series routers, the names of the interfaces need to be changed appropriately. IOS assigns interface names automatically without intervention by a user. The privileged EXEC command `show protocols` or `show interfaces` lists the names of all interfaces on a router.

The interface configuration mode for the network interface on port 1 of a 10 Mbps Ethernet card inserted in slot 0 of the router is entered with the command

```
Router1(config)#interface Ethernet0/1
```

The command prompt of the interface configuration mode is

```
Router1(config-if)#
```

To return to the global configuration mode, one types

```
Router1(config-if)#exit
```

When a global configuration command is typed in the interface configuration mode, then IOS changes to the global configuration command.

4.1.5. Router Configuration Mode

The router configuration mode is used to configure the parameters for a specific routing protocol. When entering the router configuration mode, the name of the routing protocol must be specified as an argument. IOS supports numerous routing protocols, including the Routing Information Protocol (RIP), Open Shortest Path First (OSPF), Border Gateway Protocol (BGP), and many more. The command to enter the router configuration mode for the routing protocol RIP from the global configuration mode is

```
Router1(config)#router rip
```

The command prompt for the router configuration protocol is

```
Router1(config-router)#
```

Typing

```
Router1(config-if)#exit
```

changes to the global configuration mode.

4.2. IOS COMMANDS FOR INTERFACE CONFIGURATION

We next discuss the IP configuration of a network interface in IOS. Consider a router with a 10 Mbps Ethernet (Ethernet) interface card with two ports that is located in slot 0 of the router, with names `Ethernet0/0` and `Ethernet0/1`. The following sequence of IOS commands configures port 0 with IP address 10.0.2.1/24 and port 1 with IP address 10.0.3.1/24. In addition, the commands enable IP forwarding on the router.

```
Router1> enable
Password: <enable secret>
Router1# configure terminal
Router1(config)# no ip routing
Router1(config)# ip routing
Router1(config)# interface Ethernet0/0
Router1(config-if)# no shutdown
Router1(config-if)# ip address 10.0.2.1 255.255.255.0
Router1(config-if)# interface Ethernet0/1
Router1(config-if)# no shutdown
Router1(config-if)# ip address 10.0.3.1 255.255.255.0
Router1(config-if)# end
```

The first two commands change to the privileged EXEC mode and, from there, to the global configuration mode. The command `no ip routing`, which is the command to disable IP forwarding, is used to reset the contents of the routing table and other related information. The next command, `ip routing`, enables IP forwarding on the router. Then, the interface configuration mode is entered for interface `Ethernet0/0`. The command `no shutdown` enables the interface, and the command `ip address 10.0.3.1 255.255.255.0` sets the IP address to 10.0.3.1/24. The commands to configure the second interface are similar. Note that the interface configuration mode for interface `Ethernet0/1` is entered without returning to the global configuration mode. The last command (end) returns to the privileged EXEC mode.

The list summarizes the IOS commands for enabling IP forwarding and for configuring IP addresses.

IOS MODE: GLOBAL CONFIGURATION

`ip routing`
  Enables IP forwarding.

`no ip routing`
  Disables IP forwarding. This command also deletes the content of the routing table.

IOS MODE: INTERFACE CONFIGURATION

`no shutdown`
Enables network interface.

`shutdown`
Disables a network interface.

`ip address IPaddress netmask`
Sets the IP address and netmask of an interface to `Ipaddress` and `netmask`.

The routers in the Internet Lab have two Ethernet interfaces, of type Ethernet or FastEthernet, and one or more serial WAN interfaces of type serial. The names of the interfaces depend on the types of routers used. The interface names of a router are displayed with the privileged EXEC command `show interfaces` or `show protocols`. For example, on a Cisco 2611 router, where a FastEthernet card with two ports is inserted in slot 0 and a serial card with two ports is inserted in slot 1, the interface names are:

`FastEthernet0/0, FastEthernet0/1, Serial1/0, Serial1/1`

On routers with fixed interface cards, the interface names do not list a slot number. For example, on a Cisco 2514, the interface names are:

`Ethernet0, Ethernet1, Serial0, Serial1`

4.3. IOS COMMANDS TO DISPLAY THE CONFIGURATION AND OTHER INFORMATION

IOS maintains two configuration files, which are called *startup configuration* and *running configuration*. The configuration files consists of a sequence of IOS commands. The startup configuration is kept in a file on NVRAM and contains the IOS commands that are executed when IOS is rebooted. To reboot IOS, one can turn the power switch off and then on again. Alternatively, a reboot of IOS is initiated when typing the privileged EXEC command `reload`. When IOS is booted up, the running configuration is set to the startup configuration. The running configuration stores the currently active configuration of the router, and issuing IOS configuration commands modifies the running configuration. The running configuration is kept in RAM and is lost when the router is powered off or when IOS is rebooted. To make changes to the running configuration permanent, the command `copy running-config starting-config` can be used to save the running configuration as the startup configuration.

The commands that display the configuration files are entered from the privileged EXEC mode and are shown in the list.

In addition to configuration files, various commands are available to display information about the router. Some of the most frequently used ones are listed.

IOS MODE: PRIVILEGED EXEC

```
write term
show running-config
```
Displays the current configuration of the router. The two commands produce identical results.

```
show config
show startup-config
```
Displays the startup configuration of the router. The two commands produce identical results.

```
reload
```
Forces a reboot of IOS. This command discards the running configuration and reloads the startup configuration.

```
copy running-config starting-config
```
Saves the current configuration as the startup configuration. The new startup configuration will be used the next time IOS is rebooted.

IOS MODE: PRIVILEGED EXEC

```
show version
```
Displays the version of IOS.

```
show protocols
```
Displays the IP configuration of the interfaces of the router. Also indicates if IP forwarding is enabled or disabled.

```
show ip route
```
Displays the routing table.

```
show ip cache
```
Displays the routing cache.

```
show interfaces
show interfaces interfacename
```
Displays information about all network interfaces. When an interface name is given as argument, for example, `Ethernet0/1`, information is displayed only for the specified interface.

```
show ip arp
```
Displays the contents of the ARP cache.

The `show protocols` command gives a concise overview of the IP configuration of the interfaces of the router.

```
router1#show protocols
Global values:
   Internet Protocol routing is enabled
Ethernet0 is up, line protocol is up
   Internet address is 10.0.2.1/24
```

```
Ethernet1 is up, line protocol is up
   Internet address is 10.0.3.1/24
Serial0 is administratively down, line protocol is down
Serial1 is administratively down, line protocol is down
```

From this output, we can tell that IP forwarding is enabled on the router, that the Ethernet interfaces `Ethernet0` and `Ethernet1` are configured with IP addresses, and that the serial interfaces are currently not used. More information about the interfaces can be displayed with the `show interfaces` command.

4.4. NAVIGATING THE IOS COMMAND LINE INTERFACE

IOS provides a few features that make typing commands more convenient. We already mentioned that typing a question mark (?) in a given command mode generates a list of all available commands in the current command mode. For example,

```
Router1(config-if)#?
```

lists the available commands in the interface configuration mode. Since IOS commands can be executed only in a certain command mode, this command helps to determine if a command can be executed in the current mode. The question mark can also be used to determine the list of available options of a command. For example,

```
Router1#configure ?
```

lists all options that are available for the command `configure`.

When typing commands or the names of network interfaces, it is sufficient to type just enough characters so that IOS can interpret the input without ambiguity. The following shows how some abbreviations are interpreted:

```
conf        configure
w t         write terminal
int e0/0    interface Ethernet0/0
```

When the Tab key (`<Tab>`) is typed in the command line interface, IOS attempts to complete the command. Command completion is successful only if enough characters are typed so that the prefix can be completed without ambiguity. Here are some examples of command line completions:

```
conf <Tab>            configure
conf <Tab> t <Tab>    configure terminal
```

An interesting feature of IOS, is that putting a no in front of some commands often creates a valid command. For example, if a certain command enables a feature of a router, adding a no in front of that command disables the same feature. Sometimes it is the other way around, that is, the command to enable a feature uses the command to disable the feature preceded by a no. A set of examples follows:

Enable IP forwarding:	`ip routing`
Disable IP forwarding:	`no ip routing`
Add a routing table entry:	`ip route 10.0.2.0 255.255.255.0 10.0.3.1`
Delete a routing table entry:	`no ip route 10.0.2.0 255.255.255.0 10.0.3.1`
Disable a network interface:	`shutdown`
Enable a network interface:	`no shutdown`

Introduction to the Internet Lab

OBJECTIVES

- Overview of the equipment

- Saving your data

- Navigating your way around Linux

- Working with protocol analyzers: *tcpdump, ethereal*

CONTENTS

PRELAB 1

1. **Man pages:** The PCs run the Linux operating system, a Unix-like operating system. This assignment asks you to review some Unix commands. Manual pages (*man pages*) exist on every lab machine. You can also find the man pages online at

   `http://www.tcpip-lab.net/links/manual.html`

   On this web page, select the operating system "Red Hat Linux/i386 7.3". For each of the following commands, type the name of the command as a search term. The search will return the appropriate man page.

   Read the man pages of the following commands:

man	mv	rmdir
pwd	cp	chmod
ls	rm	kill
more	mkdir	ping
tcpdump		

2. **ethereal:** The man page for *ethereal*, a network analyzer tool, can be found on every lab machine. You can also read about the *ethereal* network analyzer at the website

   `http://www.tcpip-lab.net/links/ethereal.html`

   Read the introduction and the manual pages of *ethereal*.

QUESTION SHEET FOR PRELAB 1

Answer the questions in the space provided below each one. Use extra sheets of paper if needed and attach them to this document. Submit the answers to the prelab with your lab report.

Name (please print):_____

1. What will happen if you type `man  man` in Linux?

2. How can you use the command `ls` to find out about the size of file */etc/lilo.conf*?

3. What happens if you have two files with names *file1* and *file2* and you type `mv file1 file2`? Which option of `mv` issues a warning in this situation?

4. What is the command that you issue if you are in directory / and want to copy the file */mydata* to directory */labdata*?

5. What is the command that you issue if you are in directory / and want to copy all files and directories under directory */mydirectory* to directory */newdirectory*?

6. What happens if you type the command `rm  *` in a directory?

7. What is the command that you issue if you want to delete all files and directories under the directory */mydirectory*?

LAB 1

In Lab 1, you will acquaint yourself with the equipment of the Internet Lab, the Linux operating system, and some traffic measurement tools.

NOTE:

- Before you get started, please reboot the Linux PCs by typing the `reboot` command at the root prompt.
- Do not switch the KVM switch while a Linux PC is rebooting, otherwise the keyboard and mouse will not work properly.
- Save your files to a floppy disk before the end of the lab. You will need the files when you prepare your lab report.

SETUP FOR LAB 1

- All four Linux PCs will be connected to a single Ethernet segment via a single hub as shown in Figure 1.1.

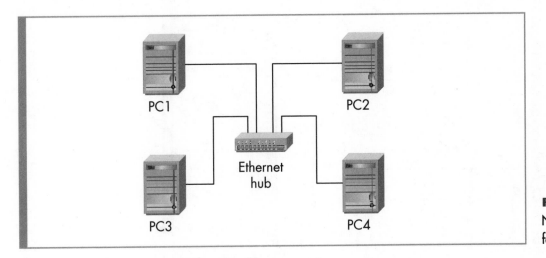

FIGURE 1.1.
Network configuration for Lab 1.

- IP addresses for the Linux PCs are preconfigured as shown in Table 1.1.

TABLE 1.1. IP addresses for Lab 1.

Linux PC	IP Addresses of Ethernet Interface *eth0*
PC1	10.0.1.11/24
PC2	10.0.1.12/24
PC3	10.0.1.13/24
PC4	10.0.1.14/24

- The notation 10.0.1.11/24 means that the IP address is 10.0.1.11 and the network prefix is 24 bits long. A network prefix of 24 bits corresponds to a netmask set to 255.255.255.0. With this netmask, all hosts are on the 10.0.1.0/24 network.

PART 1. BECOMING FAMILIAR WITH THE EQUIPMENT

The equipment that you are working with in the lab has a setup similar to Figure 1.2 and described in detail in Section 1 of the Introduction.

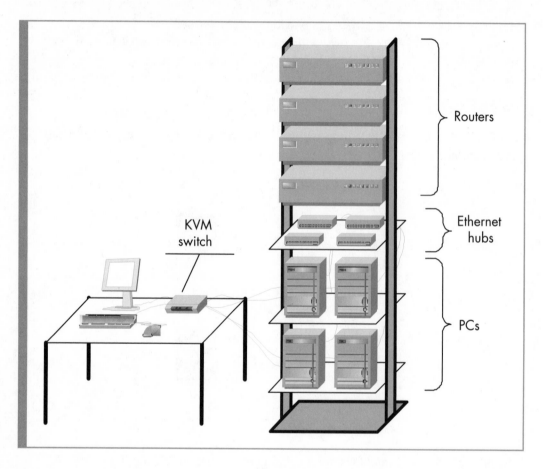

FIGURE 1.2.
Internet Lab
equipment.

Please take a few minutes to compare the following description with the actual equipment:

- A 19" rack that houses most of the equipment.

- Four Linux PCs, which are labeled as PC1, PC2, PC3, and PC4. The PCs have the Linux Red Hat operating system version 9.0 or later installed. All four Linux PCs have floppy drives and CD-ROM drives. Each Linux PC has two Ethernet network interface cards (NICs) installed, which are labeled *eth0* and *eth1*.

- Four Cisco routers, which are labeled as *Router1*, *Router2*, *Router3*, and *Router4*.

- The Cisco routers have either a slotted chassis where network interface cards are inserted into the slots of the chassis (e.g., Cisco 2600 series routers), or a fixed set of network interfaces (e.g., Cisco 2500 series routers). Regardless of the type of chassis, each Cisco router in the Internet Lab has at least two Ethernet interfaces and at least one serial interface.

- Four Ethernet hubs, each with at least four ports. The data rates of the ports are 10 Mbps, 100 Mbps, or dual speed at 10/100 Mbps.

- A monitor, a keyboard, a mouse, and a KVM (keyboard-video-mouse) switch. The KVM switch connects the keyboard, monitor, and mouse to the four Linux PCs. The KVM switch gives you control over all four Linux PCs from one keyboard, one monitor, and one mouse, but you can access only one computer at a time.[1]

- Ethernet cables. Note that there are two kinds: straight-through Ethernet cables and crossover Ethernet cables. The crossover cables should be color-coded or labeled. Otherwise, use the description in Section 1 of the Introduction to identify whether an Ethernet cable is straight-through or crossover. In Lab 1, only straight-through Ethernet cables are used.

EXERCISE 1(A).
Using the KVM switch, logging in to a Linux PC, and exploring the desktop.

The steps of logging into a Linux system are explained in Section 2.1.1 of the Introduction. Use the instructions to log in as the root user. Note that you need to have the root password.

1. Set the KVM switch to PC1 (the first light or the number 1 should light up). Log in as root.

2. Use the KVM switch to switch to PC3 (the third light or the number 3 should light up) and log in as root.

3. Explore the desktop environment of PC3.

4. Use the instructions in Section 2.1.2 of the Introduction and create a terminal window. Recall that all Linux commands are typed from a terminal window.

5. Set the KVM switch to PC1 and reboot PC1 by typing `reboot` on the command line at the `PC1%` prompt in the terminal window:

```
PC1% reboot
```

EXERCISE 1(B).
Setup of the network.

In Lab 1 the four Linux PCs must be connected to an Ethernet hub as shown in Figure 1.1. All Linux PCs are attached to the same Ethernet hub.

1. Attach each Linux PC to the same Ethernet hub with (straight-through) Ethernet cables. Connect the Ethernet interface with label *eth0* of each Linux PC to one of the hubs using an Ethernet cable.

---

[1]Please note that when rebooting a Linux PC, do not switch the KVM switch to another Linux PC. You have to wait unitl the Linux PC is fully booted before you can make the switch. A Linux PC needs a monitor, a keyboard, and a mouse to reboot. Switching before it is done will cause the process to hang and you will have to start again.

> **NOTE:**
>
> Make sure that you do not use an uplink port of the Ethernet hub. Uplink ports, which are described in Section 1.2 of the Introduction, are used to interconnect. If the Linux PC is properly connected, the status light of the connected port displays a green light.

2. When you reboot the Linux PCs, the IP addresses of the computers are configured as shown in Table 1.1. The IP addresses listed in the table are associated with the Ethernet card of the Linux PC, which is labeled *eth0*. In this lab, the second Ethernet card of the Linux PCs, labeled *eth1*, is not used.

EXERCISE 1(C).
Testing connectivity between computers.

After connecting the four Linux PCs to the Ethernet hub, all four computers should be able to communicate with one another. The following steps verify that the Linux PCs are properly connected. The test consists of running a remote terminal session between two Linux PCs, using the *Telnet* application.

1. Set the KVM switch to PC1. Start a *Telnet* session from PC1 to PC2, by typing

```
PC1% telnet 10.0.1.12
```

If you see a login prompt from PC2, PC1 and PC2 are connected to the network. When the login prompt appears, type `Ctrl-]`, then `quit`, to terminate the connection.

2. Set the KVM switch to PC3. Start a *Telnet* session from PC3 to PC4 by typing

```
PC3% telnet 10.0.1.14
```

If you see a login prompt from PC4, PC3 and PC4 are connected to the network. When the login prompt appears, type `Ctrl-]`, then `quit`, to terminate the connection.

PART 2. USING THE LINUX OPERATING SYSTEM

Here you explore the Linux system by trying out commands that are typed in a terminal window. Some basic Linux commands are reviewed next. See the man pages for a more detailed description.

EXERCISE 2.
Using Linux commands.

Review the Linux commands discussed in Section 2 of the Introduction. If you are not familiar with Linux or other Unix-like systems, try out some Linux commands by performing the following tasks on PC1:

1. Create a terminal window.

2. Change to the home directory of the root account.

3. Create a directory *test* in that directory (unless a directory already exists).

4. Copy the file */etc/hosts* to directory *test*.

5. Change the current directory to directory *test*.

6. Change the name of file *hosts* to *hostfile*.

7. List the content of directory *test*.

8. Edit file *hostfile* with *gedit*. Run *gedit* in the background.

9. Switch *gedit* to run in the foreground.

10. Change the content of the *hostfile* in the editor and save the results. Quit the editor.

11. List the content of *hostfile*.

12. Remove all files in directory *test*.

13. Remove directory *test*.

PART 3. SAVING YOUR DATA

Most lab exercises ask you to save data that is displayed on your monitor to a file. The purpose of this exercise is to make you familiar with some methods to save data to a file.

> **NOTE:**
>
> Whenever you create a file, place the file in the directory */labdata*. Since other students will most likely purge the files in this directory, please remember to save your files to a floppy disk at the end of your lab session.

Here are three methods to save data to a file on a Linux system. The methods are described in more detail in Section 2.1.5 of the Introduction.

1. Save data to a file with the redirection operators: Linux provides an easy way for redirecting the output of a command to a file via the redirection operators > and >>.

2. View and save data at the same time: You can view data on the monitor and save data to a file at the same time. For example, to display the output of command `ls` in a terminal window, and also to file with name *fname*, you can use the command

```
PC1% ls | tee fname
```

or

```
PC1% ls > fname & tail -f fname.
```

3. Save data with a text editor (with copy and paste): If you have experience with a Unix-like operating system, you may have your favorite text editor (e.g., *vi*, *emacs*, *pico*, etc.). If you have never edited a file on a Unix-like system, we recommend the *gedit* editor. To edit a file with name *fname* using *gedit*, simply type

```
PC1% gedit fname
```

If you use the text editor *gedit*, you can copy text by highlighting the text and pressing Ctrl-C. Then paste the text by pressing Ctrl-V. If you are using a different text editor you may use the copy and paste features of the X11 window manager (see Section 2.1.2 of the Introduction) to copy data to a file.

EXERCISE 3.
On PC1 try each of the preceding methods to save data to a file.

Save the output of the command `ls -l /etc` to a file named *labdata/etcfile_x*, where *x* refers to the method used for saving: 1 for method 1, 2 for method 2, and so on.

PART 4. COPYING FILES TO A FLOPPY DISK

In all labs you need the data saved in the lab sessions to complete the lab report. Since the equipment of the Internet Lab is not connected to the Internet, the most convenient way to transfer your saved data is with a 1.44MB floppy disk. This part of the lab acquaints you with the basic commands for accessing a floppy drive on a Linux system.

A REVIEW OF USING FLOPPY DISKS IN LINUX

If you want to save data to an unformatted floppy disk, you first need to format the disk. Before you can use a formatted floppy disk on a Linux system, you must *mount* the floppy disk. Once a floppy disk is mounted, you can use it exactly like a hard drive, that is, you can list files (`ls`), copy files (`cp`), rename files (`mv`), and so on. When you are done with a floppy disk, you must *unmount* the floppy disk before you remove it from the drive.

1. **Test if a floppy disk is in use:** If there is a floppy disk in the floppy drive, first make sure that the floppy disk is currently not in use. You can do this by typing

    ```
    PC1% df
    ```

    If you see the line */dev/fd0 ... /mnt/floppy*, then unmount the floppy drive by typing

    ```
    PC1% umount /mnt/floppy
    ```

2. **Formatting a floppy disk (for new disks):** Use the command `mkfs` (*make file system*) to format a new floppy disk. Formatting erases any content on the floppy disk, and there is no means to recover the data that was previously on the disk. The syntax for formatting a floppy is

    ```
    PC1%  mkfs -t msdos /dev/fd0
    ```

    The option `-t msdos` enforces compatibility with Microsoft Windows systems. The file parameter `/dev/floppy` specifies the floppy disk drive. An alternative command to format a floppy disk is

    ```
    PC1% mformat a:
    ```

    This command formats a floppy disk in drive *a:* with the MS-DOS FAT16 file system, a file format that is compatible with Microsoft Windows systems.

3. **Mounting:** Before you can use a formatted floppy disk, you must "mount" the file system on the floppy disk. The command for mounting a floppy disk is

```
PC1% mount   /mnt/floppy
```

The files on the floppy disk are now accessible from the directory /mnt/floppy.

4. **Using the file system:** After mounting you can perform any read and write operation on the floppy disk. Everything that you read from or write to directory /mnt/floppy will be read from or written to the floppy disk. You can copy files to and from this directory, add or delete subdirectories or files, or make this directory the current directory.

5. **Unmounting:** Before you remove the floppy disk from the floppy drive, you must first "unmount" the file system on the floppy disk. If you skip this step, you will likely lose data and ruin the floppy disk! When you unmount a disk, the current working directory should not be /mnt or any of its subdirectories. If necessary, change the current working directory with the cd command. The command for unmounting is

```
PC1% umount /mnt/floppy
```

Note the spelling of the command. (It is *umount* and not *unmount*.) You can safely eject the floppy disk after you have unmounted the file system.

> **NOTE:**
>
> In the event that the system has trouble unmounting the floppy drive, try using these optional arguments with the umount command
> ```
> PC1% umount -f /mnt/floppy
> PC1% umount -l /mnt/floppy
> ```

The following describes an alternative method to work with floppy disks on a Linux system. This method does not require you to run the mount and umount commands, but it offers only a limited set of commands to read from or write to a floppy disk.

mmd *dirname*
  Creates a subdirectory with name *dirname*. Example:
  ```
PC1% mmd a:/labdata01
```

mdir
mdir *dirname*
  Lists the contents of a directory on the floppy disk. If no argument is given, the command lists the root directory on the floppy disk. Example:
  ```
PC1% mdir a:/labdata01
```

mcd
mcd *dirname*
  Changes the working directory on the floppy disk. If no name is given, it changes to the topmost level (root directory on the floppy disk). Example:
  ```
PC1% mcd a:/labdata01
```

```
mcopy fname newfile
mcopy fname [ fnames ... ]dirname
    Copy MS-DOS files to and from the floppy drive.  Example:
    PC1% mcopy /labdata a:/

mmove fname newfile
mmove fname dirname
    Move or rename an existing MSDOS file or subdirectory within the floppy disk.
    Example:
    PC1% mmove a:/myfile a:/labdata01

mdel fname
    Deletes file. Example:
    PC1% mdel a:/labdata01/myfile

mdeltree dirname
    Removes a directory and all files and subdirectories from an MS-DOS file system.
    Example:
    PC1% mdeltree a:/labdata01

mtype fname
    Displays the contents of file fname. Example:
    PC1% mtype a:/labdata01/myfile
```

EXERCISE 4(A).
Saving data to a floppy disk.

1. Use the previous commands to save the file */labdata/etcfile_1*, on PC1 from Exercise 3 to a floppy disk.

2. On PC1, run the command

```
PC1% df
```

to obtain a list of all file systems currently mounted on your system. Save the output of the command to a file and save the file to the floppy disk.

Lab Report Attach the files you saved to your lab report.

EXERCISE 4(B).
Convention for saving data on floppy disks.

Instead of using one floppy disk for each Linux PC, we recommend that you use the *FTP* application (see Section 2.2.2 of the Introduction) to copy files to a single Linux PC that contains your floppy disk. We recommend the following convention for saving data from the Linux PCs.

> **CONVENTION FOR SAVING DATA ON FLOPPY DISKS:**
>
> **1.** During the lab exercises, save files on each Linux PC in directory */labdata*.
> **2.** At the end of a lab session, use a floppy in only one Linux PC (e.g., PC1).
> **3.** Use the file transfer protocol FTP for copying saved files from the other Linux PCs to PC1.

The following steps illustrate the convention:

1. On each Linux PC, create a file */labdata/etcfile_1* as described in Exercise 3.

2. On PC1, create new directories, one for each remote Linux PC: */labdata/PC2*, */labdata/PC3*, and */labdata/PC4*.

3. Use *FTP* to copy the file */labdata/etcfile_1* from PC2.

   ```
   PC1% cd /labdata/PC2
   PC1% ftp 10.0.1.12
   ```

   Log in as *root*.

   ```
   ftp> cd /labdata
   ftp> get etcfile_1
   ftp> quit
   ```

   Repeat Step 3 for PC3 and PC4.

4. Insert a floppy disk into the floppy drive of PC1. If necessary, format the disk, then mount it.

5. Copy all files under directory */labdata* to the floppy drive.

PART 5. LOCATING CONFIGURATION FILES IN LINUX

Linux has numerous configuration files that set the environment variables of the operating system. For example, if you want to set up your Linux PC as an IP router, you merely need to change a single line in one of the configuration files. Studying configuration files also provides a way of learning what network configuration options are available to you.

In all labs, you will use Red Hat Linux version 9.0 or later. A list of the most important network configuration files follows:

IMPORTANT:

Please do not modify configuration files unless asked to do so. Certain changes to the configuration files may require a reinstallation of the operating system.

NOTE:

Configuration files are fundamentally different across different versions of Unix-like operating systems (e.g., AIX, Solaris, Linux, FreeBSD). Sometimes the structure of configuration files changes between releases of the same Unix version. For example, the configuration files of different Linux distributions, such as Red Hat and Slackware, are quite different. Furthermore, the configuration files between different versions of the same Linux distribution can have significant differences.

`/etc/sysconfig/network`

This file defines global parameters of the network configuration, such as the host name, domain name, and IP address of the default gateway. It also includes a line to determine whether the Linux PC acts as a router or not.

`/etc/sysconfig/network-scripts/ifcfg-lo`
`/etc/sysconfig/network-scripts/ifcfg-eth0`
`/etc/sysconfig/network-scripts/ifcfg-eth1`

These files define the configuration of the network interfaces. There is one configuration file for each network interface. The files `ifcfg-eth0` and `ifcfg-eth1` are for the two installed Ethernet interface cards. The file `ifcfg-lo` is for the loopback interface.

`/etc/sysctl.conf`

This file specifies many kernel options related to the network configuration.

`/etc/hosts`

This file specifies the mapping between the host names and IP addresses for network devices. This file also determines the name of the local Linux system.

`/etc/sysconfig/static-routes`

This file contains the settings of the static routing table, which is set when booting the Linux PC. It may not exist or may be empty if no static routes have been previously assigned.

EXERCISE 5.
Using the more command.

1. On PC1, explore the preceding files using the `more` command

   `PC1% more /etc/hosts`

   Please do not make any changes to these files.

2. Save the content of the preceding files.

Lab Report

- Which files must be edited to change the name of a Linux PC (e.g., from PC1 to machine1)?

- Which files include information that determines whether a Linux PC performs IP forwarding?

- Attach the content of the file */etc/sysconfig/network-scripts/ifcfg-eth0* to your lab report.

PART 6. USING PING

One of the most basic, but also most effective, tools to debug IP networks is the `ping` command. The `ping` command tests whether another host or router on the Internet is reachable. The `ping` command sends an ICMP Echo Request datagram to an interface and expects an ICMP Echo Reply datagram in return. The different uses of the ping command are explained in Section 2.2.3 of the Introduction.

> **NOTE:**
>
> - On Linux systems, *ping* continues to send packets until you interrupt the command with the Ctrl-C keys.
> - When using *ping* on the Linux PCs, we recommend to always send at least two ICMP Echo Request packets. We have observed that the first ICMP Echo Request may often be dropped at the receiver. (Time Exceeded Type 11, Code 0 or 1). This occurs when the ICMP Echo Request packet does not reach its destination within a certain amount of time or number of hops, e.g., when waiting for an ARP Reply or ICMP Redirect. This is explained further in Labs 2 and 3.

EXERCISE 6.
Issuing ping commands.

1. From PC1, send five ping messages (using the **-c** option) to PC2. Save the output.

   ```
   PC1% ping -c 5 10.0.1.12
   ```

2. On PC2, issue a ping to the IP address of PC1. Also, issue a ping command to the *loopback* interface, 127.0.0.1. Limit the number of pings to five. Save the output.

Lab Report

- Include the output you saved in this exercise.

- Explain the difference between pinging the local Ethernet interface and the loopback interface. Specifically, on PC1, what is the difference between typing *ping 10.0.1.11* and *ping 127.0.0.1*. (This is a conceptual question on the role of the loopback interface. The response to the ping command does not provide you with the answer to this question.)

PART 7. BASICS OF TCPDUMP

tcpdump allows you to capture traffic on a network and display the packet headers of the captured traffic. *tcpdump* can be used to identify network problems or to monitor network activities. See Section 3 of the Introduction for more details on the tcpdump command and its use for network traffic analysis.

EXERCISE 7(A).
Simple *tcpdump* exercise.

Use *tcpdump* to observe the network traffic that is generated by issuing ping commands.

1. Switch to PC1. Start *tcpdump* so that it monitors all packets that contain the IP address of PC2, by typing

   ```
   PC1% tcpdump -n host 10.0.1.12
   ```

2. Open a new window and execute

```
PC1% ping -c 1 10.0.1.12
```

3. Observe the output of *tcpdump*. Save the output to a file.

> **NOTE:**
>
> If you use the `tee` or `tail` commands to simultaneously view and save the output from *tcpdump*, you need to use the `-l` option of *tcpdump*. For example,
>
> ```
> tcpdump -n -l > filename & tail -f filename
> tcpdump -n -l | tee filename
> ```
>
> It may be necessary to hit Ctrl-C to terminate the *tcpdump* session. It may sometimes be best to simply redirect the output of *tcpdump* straight to a file (e.g., `tcpdump > filename`) and view it afterward with the `more` command or a text editor.

Lab Report

Include the saved output in your lab report. Explain the meaning of each field in the captured data.

EXERCISE 7(B).
Another *tcpdump* traffic capture.

1. On PC1, start capturing packets using the *tcpdump* `-n` command.

2. Issue a ping to the nonexisting IP address 111.111.111.111:

```
PC1% ping -c 1 111.111.111.111
```

3. Issue a ping to the broadcast address 10.0.1.255 using the command

```
PC1% ping -c 2 -b 10.0.1.255
```

4. Save the outputs of *ping* and *tcpdump* to a file.

Lab Report

Include the saved output in your lab report and interpret the results. How many of the Linux PCs responded to the broadcast ping?

PART 8. BASICS OF ETHEREAL

ethereal is a network protocol analyzer with a graphical user interface. Using *ethereal*, you can interactively capture and examine network traffic, view summaries, and get detailed information for each packet. Section 3 of the Introduction provides more details on the use of *ethereal*.

EXERCISE 8.
Running *ethereal*.

This exercise walks you through the steps of capturing and saving network traffic with *ethereal*. The exercise is conducted on PC1.

1. **Starting *ethereal*:** On PC1, start *ethereal* by typing

   ```
   PC1% ethereal
   ```

   This displays the *ethereal* main window on your desktop as shown in Figure 1.3.

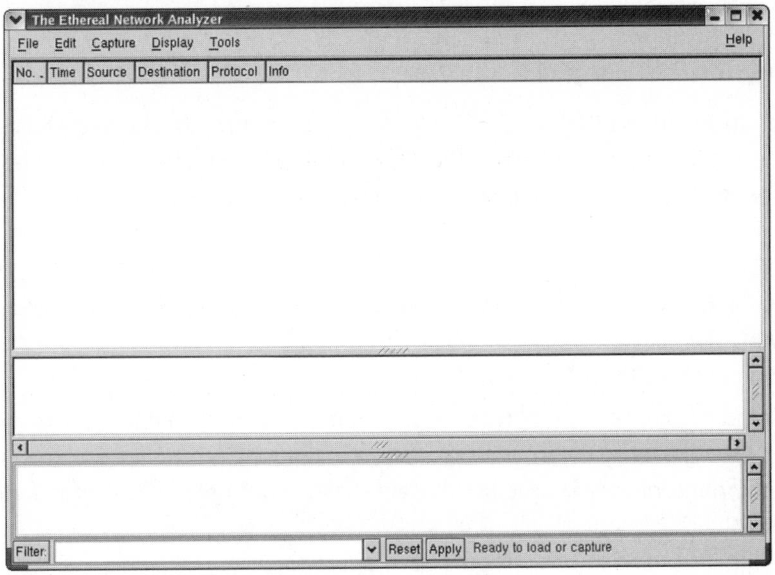

FIGURE 1.3.
ethereal main window.

2. **Selecting the capture options:** Use the instructions in Figure 1.4 to set the options of *ethereal* in preparation for capturing traffic. Use the same options in other labs, whenever *ethereal* is started.

Selecting capture preferences in *ethereal*:
1. From the main window, select *Capture:Start*.
2. This displays the *Capture Options* window.
3. Select *eth0* in *Interface*.
4. Select *Capture packets in promiscuous mode*.
5. Select *Update list of packets in real time*.
6. Select *Automatic scrolling in live capture*.
7. Unselect *Enable MAC name resolution*.
8. Unselect *Enable network name resolution*.
9. Unselect *Enable transport name resolution*.

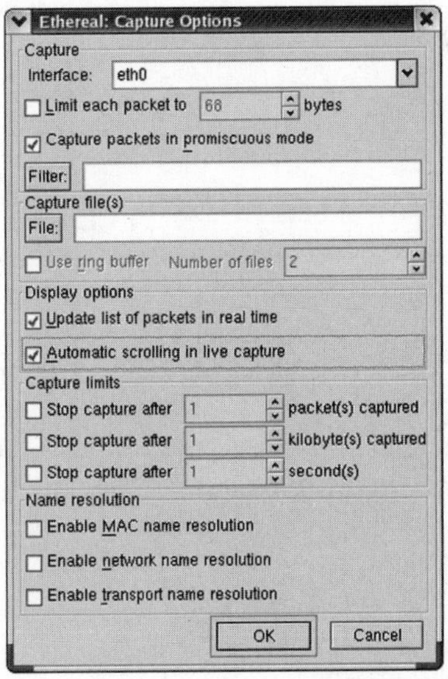

FIGURE 1.4.
General capture settings for *ethereal*.

3. **Starting the traffic capture:** Start the packet capture by clicking *OK* in the *Capture Options* window.

4. **Generating traffic:** In a separate window on PC1, execute a `ping` command to PC3.

   `PC1% ping -c 2 10.0.1.13`

   Observe the output in the *ethereal* main window.

   Click and highlight a captured packet in the *ethereal* window and view the headers of the captured traffic.

5. **Stopping the traffic capture:** Click *Stop* in the window *Ethernet Capture*.

6. **Saving captured traffic:** Save the results of the captured traffic as a plain text file. This is done by selecting *Print* in the *File* menu. When a *Print* window pops up, select the options and set a filename as shown in Figure 1.5.

Selecting print options in the *Print* window for saving captured traffic to plain text files:

1. Select the format *Plain Text*.

2. Select the *File* checkbox and type the filename in the field next to the *File* button.

3. Select *Print summary* if you want to save only some high-level information on each packet. *Print summary* is usually sufficient. Select *Print detail* and *Expand all levels* if you want to save all details of all packets at all levels.

4. Click the *OK* button to complete the save operation.

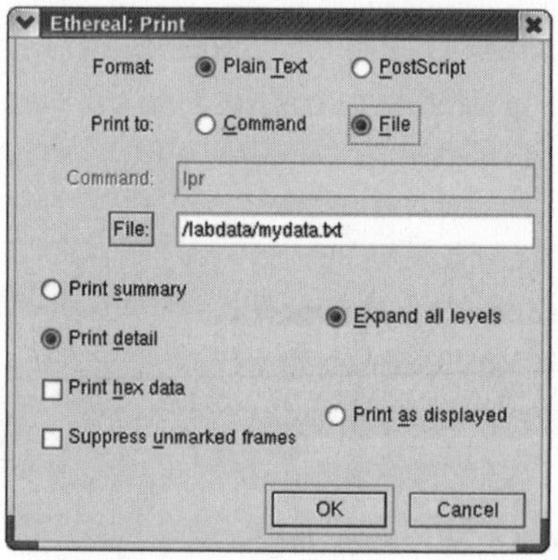

FIGURE 1.5.
Selecting print
options.

NOTE:

- In general, unless asked to do otherwise, always select the *Print summary* option when you include saved data in the lab report. This will help keep the length of the lab report reasonably small. If detailed information is required, you will be asked to save details of the captured traffic. In this case, select the *Print detail* option.

- If you select *Save* in the *File* menu, the captured data is saved in the format of a *libpcap* file. This format can be interpreted by both *tcpdump* and *ethereal*. Measurements saved in *libpcap* format can be analyzed at a later time. However, *libpcap* files are not plain text files and are not useful for preparing your report.

- Unless you have the *tcpdump* and/or *ethereal* tools available on a system outside of the Internet Lab, which allows you to view and save captured traffic as text at a later time, always save captured traffic in plain text format.

Lab Report

Include the file with the captured data in your lab report. Save the *details* of the captured traffic, using the *Print detail* option in the *Print* window. Describe the differences between the files saved by *tcpdump* (in Part 7) and by *ethereal* (in this part).

CHECKLIST FORM FOR LAB 1

Complete this checklist as you work through the laboratory exercises and attach the form to your lab report.

Name (please print):_____

☐ Prelab 1 question sheet

☐ Checkoff for Part 1   ☐ Checkoff for Part 6

☐ Checkoff for Part 2   ☐ Checkoff for Part 7

☐ Checkoff for Part 3   ☐ Checkoff for Part 8

☐ Checkoff for Part 4   ☐ Feedback sheet

☐ Checkoff for Part 5   ☐ Lab report

FEEDBACK FORM FOR LAB 1

- Complete this feedback form at the completion of the lab exercises and submit the form when submitting your lab report.

- The feedback is anonymous. *Do not put your name on this form* and keep it separate from your lab report.

- For each exercise, please record the following:

	Difficulty (–2, –1, 0, 1, 2) –2 = too easy 0 = just right 2 = too hard	Interest Level (–2, –1, 0, 1, 2) –2 = low interest 0 = just right 2 = high interest	Time to Complete (minutes)
Part 1. Becoming familiar with the equipment			
Part 2. Using the Linux operating system			
Part 3. Saving your data			
Part 4. Copying files to a floppy disk			
Part 5. Locating configuration files in Linux			
Part 6. Using *ping*			
Part 7. Basics of *tcpdump*			
Part 8. Basics of *ethereal*			

(continues on next page)

Please answer the following questions:

- What did you like about this lab?

- What did you dislike about this lab?

- Make a suggestion to improve the lab.

single-Segment IP Networks

OBJECTIVES

- How to configure a network interface for IP networking

- How to access IP statistics and settings with the `netstat` command

- How ARP works

- How hackers snoop passwords from the network

CONTENTS

PRELAB 2

1. **Network commands in Unix:** Go to the online hypertext man pages at

   `http://www.tcpip-lab.net/links/manual.html`

   and select the OS version Red Hat Linux/i386 7.3. Read the manual pages of the
   following commands:

   - `arp`
   - `ifconfig`
   - `netstat`

2. **IP addresses:** Read the article "Understanding IP Addressing: Everything You Ever
   Wanted to Know" by Chuck Semeria, at

   `http://www.tcpip-lab.net/links/ip_subnet.html`

3. *tcpdump:* Go to the online hypertext man pages at

   `http://www.tcpip-lab.net/links/manual.html`

   and select the OS version Red Hat Linux/i386 7.3 and read about the various
   optional arguments available for *tcpdump*.

4. *ethereal:* Go to the website

   `http://www.tcpip-lab.net/links/ethereal.html`

   and read about capture filters and display filters in *ethereal*.

QUESTION SHEET FOR PRELAB 2

Answer the questions in the space provided below each one. Use extra sheets of paper if needed and attach them to this document. Submit the answers with your lab report.

Name (please print):_____

1. Write the syntax for an `ifconfig` command that sets the IP address of the interface `eth0` to 128.143.2.3/16 with broadcast address 128.143.255.255.

2. Write the syntax of a `tcpdump` command that captures packets containing IP datagrams with a source or destination IP address equal to 10.0.1.12.

3. Write the syntax of a `tcpdump` command that captures packets containing ICMP messages with a source or destination IP address equal to 10.0.1.12.

4. Write the syntax of a `tcpdump` command that captures packets containing IP datagrams between two hosts with IP addresses 10.0.1.11 and 10.0.1.12, both on interface *eth1*.

5. Write a `tcpdump` filter expression that captures packets containing TCP segments with a source or destination IP address equal to 10.0.1.12.

6. Write a `tcpdump` filter expression that, in addition to the constraints in Question 5, only captures packets using port number 23.

7. Write the syntax for an `ethereal` command with capture filter so that all IP datagrams with a source or destination IP address equal to 10.0.1.12 are recorded.

8. Write the syntax for an `ethereal` display filter that shows IP datagrams with a destination IP address equal to 10.0.1.50 and frame sizes greater than 400 bytes.

9. Write the syntax for an `ethereal` display filter that shows packets containing ICMP messages with a source or destination IP address equal to 10.0.1.12 and frame numbers between 15 and 30.

10. Write the syntax for an `ethereal` display filter that shows packets containing TCP segments with a source or destination IP address equal to 10.0.1.12 and using port number 23.

11. Write an `ethereal` capture filter expression for Question 10.

LAB 2

In Lab 2 you become acquainted with IP configuration issues on a single Ethernet segment. The lab also exposes you to advanced issues in *tcpdump* and *ethereal*.

RECALL:

- Before you get started, please reboot the Linux PCs.
- During the lab, you need to save data to files. Save all files in the directory /labdata
- ave your files to a floppy disk before the end of the lab. You will need the files when you prepare your lab report

SETUP FOR LAB 2

- The setup for this lab is identical to that in Lab 1. All Linux PCs are connected to the same Ethernet segment by an Ethernet hub as shown in Figure 2.1.

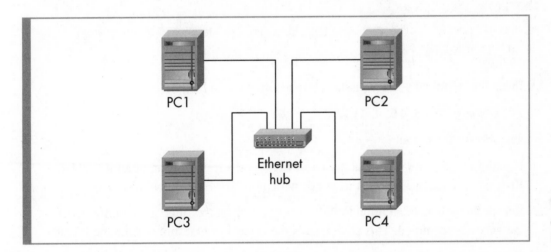

FIGURE 2.1.
Configuration for Lab 2.

- The IP addresses for the Linux PCs are configured as shown in Table 2.1. Whenever a Linux PC is rebooted, the IP addresses are set to the values displayed in the table.

TABLE 2.1. IP addresses for Lab 2.

Linux PC	IP Addresses of Ethernet Interface *eth0*
PC1	10.0.1.11/24
PC2	10.0.1.12/24
PC3	10.0.1.13/24
PC4	10.0.1.14/24

PART 1.   USING FILTERS IN TCPDUMP

In the first part of the lab, you explore *tcpdump* in more detail. In particular you learn how to write filter expressions so that *tcpdump* monitors only selected traffic flows on the network. See Section 3 in the Introduction for more details on the use of filters in *tcpdump*.

EXERCISE 1.
Writing filter expressions for *tcpdump*.

In this exercise, you explore the use of simple filter expressions with the `tcpdump` command. Save the output for your lab report.

1. On PC1, execute a `tcpdump` command with a filter that prints all packets with PC2 as source or destination. This command is the answer to Question 2 from the Prelab. Save the output of this *tcpdump* session to a file using the `tee` or `tail` commands discussed in Lab 1.

> **NOTE:**
>
> As in Lab 1, always use the –n option (i.e., `tcpdump  –n`) to prevent *tcpdump* from trying to resolve host names.

2. In another terminal window, issue a `ping` command to PC2 by typing

    `PC1% ping –c 5 10.0.1.12`

    and observe the output.

    Recall that the `ping` command to a host triggers the transmission of an ICMP Echo Request. The destination host responds with an ICMP Echo Reply message.

3. Repeat Steps 1–2. In addition to the existing filter, set the filter so that only ICMP messages are captured. This command is the answer to Question 3 from the Prelab.

Lab Report Include the saved data in your lab report.

PART 2.   USING FILTERS IN ETHEREAL

In this part of the lab, you experiment with filter expressions in *ethereal*. Recall that *ethereal* has two types of filters: capture filters and display filters. The filtering capabilities and options of *ethereal* are described in Section 3.2 of the Introduction.

NOTE:

Several command line options can be assigned when starting *ethereal*:

Capture filters: A capture filter specifies the traffic to be captured by the *ethereal* tool. A capture filter expression can be specified from the command line using the -f option or using the *ethereal* GUI, under the *Capture:Start* menu. The syntax for specifying the filter expression is the same syntax as used by *tcpdump*.

Display filters: By default, *ethereal* displays all captured packets. With a display filter, just the packets that meet the requirements of the filter are displayed. The display filter cannot be set from the command line. It must be entered in the *Filter* window at the bottom of the GUI. The syntax for setting the display filter is different from the syntax for setting a capture filter.

Setting an interface: When you run *ethereal* on a host with multiple network interfaces, you may specify the interface with the -i argument. For example, to start *ethereal* to capture traffic on interface *eth1*, type

```
ethereal -i eth1
```

If you do not specify an interface, the default is *eth0*. Alternatively, you can change the interface using the *ethereal* GUI, under the *Capture:Start* menu.

EXERCISE 2(A).
Setting capture filters in *ethereal*.

This exercise is a review of the traffic capture capabilities of *ethereal*. You are introduced to the notion of capture filters as a new feature.

1. Start *ethereal* on PC1 and set the same capture preferences as in Lab 1 and as shown again in Figure 2.2 for your convenience. You should always set these *same* preferences for all your experiments.

2. **Setting a capture filter:** In the window *Capture Options*, set a filter so that all packets that contain the IP address of PC2 are recorded. The filter is set in the *Filter* box under *Capture Options* (see Figure 2.2).

   The required filter expression is the answer to Question 7 from the Prelab.

3. Start the capture by clicking *OK* in the *Capture Options* window.

4. In another terminal window of PC1, issue a `ping` command to PC2:

   ```
   PC1% ping -c 2 10.0.1.12
   ```

5. Stop the capture process of *ethereal*.

6. **Saving captured traffic:** Save the results of the capture. This is done by selecting *Print* in the *File* menu as described in Lab 1. (As instructed in Lab 1, unless asked to save the details of captured frames, selecting the *Print summary* option is usually sufficient.)

Selecting capture preferences in *ethereal*:

1. From the main window, select *Capture:Start*.

2. This displays the *Capture Options* window.

3. Select *eth0* in *Interface*.

4. Select *Capture packets in promiscuous mode*.

5. Select *Update list of packets in real time*.

6. Select *Automatic scrolling in live capture*.

7. Unselect *Enable MAC name resolution*.

8. Unselect *Enable network name resolution*.

9. Unselect *Enable transport name resolution*.

FIGURE 2.2.
General capture settings for *ethereal*.

EXERCISE 2(B).
Working with display filters.

Next you set display filters, which allow you to select a subset of the captured data for display in the main window of *ethereal*.

1. In the *ethereal* main window on PC1 from Exercise 2(A), set the display options as shown in Figure 2.3.

Selecting diplay preferences in *ethereal*:

1. Select *Options* under *Display* menu.

2. Select *Automatic scrolling in live capture*.

3. Unselect *Enable MAC name resolution*.

4. Unselect *Enable network name resolution*.

5. Unselect *Enable transport name resolution*.

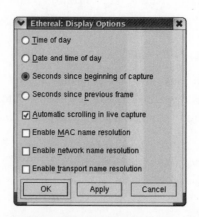

FIGURE 2.3.
Options for setting display preferences in *ethereal*.

2. To set the display filter, type the desired display filter in the field next to the *Filter* box, which is located at the bottom of the *ethereal* main window, as shown in Figure 2.4. Click the *Reset* button next to the *Filter* box to clear any existing filter.

Filter: ip.dst == 10.0.1.12 ▼ Reset Apply <live capture in progress>

FIGURE 2.4.
Filter box for setting display filters.

Enter a display filter so that all IP datagrams with destination IP address 10.0.1.12 are shown. Press Enter after typing the filter. Refer to Question 8 from the Prelab.

3. Observe the changes in the display panel of *ethereal*. Only packets with 10.0.1.12 in the IP destination address field are now being displayed.

4. Save the displayed data, by selecting *File:Print*. Note that the *Print* command saves only packets that are currently being displayed. If a display filter is used, the saved data is limited to the packets that match the display filter.

5. Repeat the previous exercise with a display filter that lists only IP datagrams with a source IP address equal to 10.0.1.12. Save the results.

Lab Report Include the saved data in your lab report.

EXERCISE 2(C).
More complex capture and display filters.

In this exercise, you learn how to use more sophisticated filters to restrict the packets being captured and displayed.

1. Start *ethereal* on PC1 and start to capture traffic using the same settings as in Exercise 2(A). *Do not set any capture or display filters!*

2. From a new terminal window on PC1, execute the `ping` command for PC2:

```
PC1% ping -c 5 10.0.1.12
```

3. At the same time, start a *Telnet* session from PC1 to PC2 in another terminal window by typing

```
PC1% telnet 10.0.1.12
```

and log in as *root*. After you log in successfully to PC2, log out with the command `exit`.

4. Stop the traffic capture of *ethereal*.

5. Apply a set of display filters to the captured traffic and save the output to a text file. Select the option *Print summary* in the *Print* window.

   a. Display packets that contain ICMP messages with the IP address of PC2 either in the IP destination address or IP source address. Refer to Question 9 from the Prelab. Save the output.

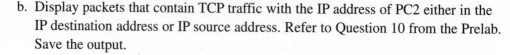

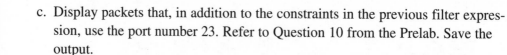

b. Display packets that contain TCP traffic with the IP address of PC2 either in the IP destination address or IP source address. Refer to Question 10 from the Prelab. Save the output.

c. Display packets that, in addition to the constraints in the previous filter expression, use the port number 23. Refer to Question 10 from the Prelab. Save the output.

Lab Report Include the saved data in your lab report.

PART 3. ARP—ADDRESS RESOLUTION PROTOCOL

This part of the lab explores the operation of the Address Resolution Protocol (ARP), which resolves a MAC address for a given IP address. The lab exercises use the Linux command `arp`, for displaying and manipulating the contents of the ARP cache. The ARP cache is a table that holds entries of the form `<IPaddress, MACaddress>`.

The most common uses of the `arp` command are listed.

COMMON USES OF THE ARP COMMAND

`arp -a`

Displays the content of the ARP cache.

`arp -d IPAddress`

Deletes the entry with the IP address *IPAddress*.

`arp -s IPaddress MACAddress`

Adds a static entry to the ARP cache that is never overwritten by network events. The MAC address is entered as 6 hexadecimal bytes separated by colons.

Example: `arp -s 10.0.1.12 00:02:2D:0D:68:C1`

TIME-OUTS IN THE ARP CACHE

The entries in an ARP cache have a limited lifetime. Entries are deleted unless they are refreshed. The typical lifetime of an ARP entry is 2 minutes, but much longer lifetimes (up to 20 minutes) have been observed. You may want to verify when your Linux system does remove ARP entries automatically after a certain amount of time.

REFRESHING THE ARP CACHE

In Linux you will observe that a host occasionally sends out ARP requests to interfaces that are already in the ARP cache.

Example: Suppose that a host with IP address 10.0.1.12 has an ARP cache entry:

`<10.0.1.11> is-at <00:02:83:39:2C:42>`

Then, this host occasionally sends a unicast ARP Request to MAC address 00:02:83:39:2C:42 of the form

`Who has 10.0.1.11? Tell 10.0.1.12`

to verify that the IP address 10.0.1.11 is still present before deleting the entry from the ARP cache.

EXERCISE 3(A).
A simple experiment with ARP.

1. On PC1, view the ARP cache with `arp -a` and delete all entries with the `-d` option.

2. Start *ethereal* on PC1 with a capture filter set to the IP address of PC2.

3. Issue a `ping` command from PC1 to PC2:

   `PC1% ping -c 2 10.0.1.12`

   Observe the ARP packets in the *ethereal* window. Explore the MAC addresses in the Ethernet headers of the captured packets.

   Direct your attention to the following fields:

   - The destination MAC address of the ARP Request packets

   - The Type field in the Ethernet headers of ARP packets and ICMP messages

4. View the ARP cache again with the command `arp -a`. Note that ARP cache entries get deleted fairly quickly (~2 minutes).

5. Save the results of *ethereal* to a text file, using the *Print detail* option.

Lab Report Use the saved data to answer the following questions:

- What is the destination MAC address of an ARP Request packet?

- What are the different values of the Type field in the Ethernet headers that you observed?

- Use the captured data to discuss the process in which ARP acquires the MAC address for IP address 10.0.1.12.

EXERCISE 3(B).
Matching IP addresses and MAC addresses.

Identify the MAC addresses of all interfaces connected to the network and enter them in Table 2.2. You can obtain the MAC addresses from the ARP cache of each PC. You can fill up the ARP cache at a host by issuing a `ping` command from that host to every other host on the network. Alternatively, you can obtain the MAC addresses from the output of the `ifconfig -a` command explained in Part 5.

TABLE 2.2. IP and MAC addresses.

Linux PC	IP Address of Ethernet Interface *eth0*	MAC Address of Ethernet Interface *eth0*
PC1	10.0.1.11/24	
PC2	10.0.1.12/24	
PC3	10.0.1.13/24	
PC4	10.0.1.14/24	

Lab Report Include the completed Table 2.2 in your lab report.

EXERCISE 3(C).
ARP requests for a nonexisting address.

Observe what happens when an ARP Request is issued for an IP address that does not exist.

1. On PC1, start *ethereal* with a capture filter set to capture packets that contain the IP address of PC1:

   ```
   PC1% ethereal -f 'host 10.0.1.11'
   ```

2. Try to establish a *Telnet* session from PC1 to 10.0.1.10. (Note that this address does not exist on this network.)

   ```
   PC1% telnet 10.0.1.10
   ```

   Observe the time interval and the frequency with which PC1 transmits ARP Request packets. Repeat the experiment a number of times to discover the pattern.

3. Save the captured output.

Lab Report

- Using the saved output, describe the time interval between each ARP Request issued by PC1. Describe the method used by ARP to determine the time between retransmissions of an unsuccessful ARP Request. Include relevant data to support your answer.

- Why are ARP Request packets not transmitted (i.e., not encapsulated) like IP packets? Explain your answer.

PART 4.   THE NETSTAT COMMAND

The Linux command `netstat` displays information on the network configuration and activity of a Linux system, including network connections, routing tables, interface statistics, and multicast memberships. The following exercise explores how to use the `netstat` command to extract different types of information about the network configuration of a host.

The list opposite shows four important uses of the `netstat` command.

EXERCISE 4.

On PC1, try the different variations of the `netstat` command (listed later in this exercise) and save the output to a file.

1. Display information on the network interfaces by typing

   ```
   PC1% netstat -in
   ```

2. Display the content of the IP routing table by typing

   ```
   PC1% netstat -rn
   ```

```
netstat -i
```
   Displays a table with statistics of the currently configured network interfaces.
```
netstat -rn
```
   Displays the kernel routing table. The -n option forces netstat to print the IP addresses. Without this option, netstat attempts to display the host names.
```
netstat -an
netstat -tan
netstat -uan
```
   Display the active network connections. The -a option displays all active network connections, the -ta option displays only information on TCP connections, and the -tu option displays only information on UDP traffic. Omitting the -n option prints host names, instead of IP addresses.
```
netstat -s
```
   Displays summary statistics for each protocol that is currently running on the host.

3. Display information on TCP and UDP ports that are currently in use by typing

```
PC1% netstat -a
```

4. Display the statistics of various networking protocols by typing

```
PC1% netstat -s
```

NOTE:

The values of the statistics displayed by some of the netstat commands are reset each time a host is rebooted.

Lab Report Attach the saved output to your report. Using the saved output, answer the following questions.

- What are the network interfaces of PC1 and what are the MTU (maximum transmission unit) values of the interfaces?

- How many IP datagrams, ICMP messages, UDP datagrams, and TCP segments has PC1 transmitted and received since it was last rebooted?

Explain the role of interface lo, the loopback interface. In the output of netstat -in, why are the values of RX-OK (packets received) and TX-OK (packets transmitted) different for interface eth0 but identical for interface lo?

PART 5.   CONFIGURING IP INTERFACES IN LINUX

The ifconfig command is used to configure parameters of network interfaces on a Linux system, such as enabling and disabling of interfaces and setting the IP address. The ifconfig command is usually run when a system boots up. In this case, the parameters of the commands are read from a file. Once the Linux system is running, the `ifconfig` command can be used to modify the network configuration parameters.

The list shows how `ifconfig` is used to query the status of network interfaces.

`ifconfig`

Displays the configuration parameters of all active interfaces.

`ifconfig -a`

Displays the configuration parameters of all network interfaces, including the inactive interfaces.

`ifconfig interface`

Displays the configuration parameters of a single interface. For example, `ifconfig eth0` displays information on interface *eth0*.

There are numerous options for configuring a network interface with `ifconfig`. The example in the list shows how to enable and disable an interface and how to change the IP configuration.

`ifconfig eth0 down`

Disables the *eth0* interface. No traffic is sent or received on a disabled interface.

`ifconfig eth0 up`

Enables the *eth0* interface.

`ifconfig eth0 10.0.1.8 netmask 255.255.255.0 broadcast 10.0.1.255`

Assigns interface *eth0* the IP address `10.0.1.8/24` and a broadcast address of `10.0.1.255`.

EXERCISE 5.
Changing the IP address of an interface.

Use the `ifconfig` command to modify the IP address of the *eth0* interface of PC4.

1. On PC4, run `ifconfig -a` and save the output.

2. Change the IP address of interface *eth0* of PC4 to 10.0.1.11/24.

3. Run `ifconfig -a` again and save the output.

Lab Report Attach the saved files to your report and explain the fields of the `ifconfig` output.

PART 6. DUPLICATE IP ADDRESSES

In this part of the lab, you observe what happens when two hosts have identical IP addresses.

EXERCISE 6.

After completing Exercise 5, the IP addresses of the Ethernet interfaces on the four PCs are as shown in Table 2.3. Note that PC1 and PC4 are assigned the same IP address.

TABLE 2.3. IP addresses for Part 6.

Linux PC	IP Addresses of Ethernet Interface *eth0*
PC1	10.0.1.11/24
PC2	10.0.1.12/24
PC3	10.0.1.13/24
PC4	10.0.1.11/24

1. Delete all entries in the ARP cache on all PCs.

2. Run *ethereal* on PC3 and capture the network traffic to and from the duplicate IP address 10.0.1.11.

3. From PC3, start a *Telnet* session to the duplicate IP address, 10.0.1.11, by typing

   `PC3% telnet 10.0.1.11`

   and log in as root user.

4. Once you have logged in, determine the name of the host to which you are connected. The name of the host can be determined in several ways: (a) issue the command `hostname`, (b) inspect the ARP cache on PC3, or (c) interpret the captured *ethereal* packets.

5. Stop the traffic capture in *ethereal*.

6. Save all ARP packets and the first few TCP packets captured by *ethereal*. Also save the ARP cache of PC3 using the `arp -a` command.

7. When you are done with the exercise, reset the IP address of PC4 to its original value as given in Table 2.1.

Lab Report Explain why the *Telnet* session was established to one of the hosts with the duplicate address and not the other. Explain why the *Telnet* session was established at all and did not result in an error message. Use the ARP cache and the captured packets to support your explanation.

PART 7. CHANGING NETMASKS

In this part of the lab you test the effects of changing the netmask of a network configuration. In Table 2.4, two hosts (PC2 and PC4) have been assigned different network prefixes.

EXERCISE 7.

1. Set up the interfaces of the hosts as shown in Table 2.4. Note that the netmasks of the hosts are different.

TABLE 2.4. IP addresses for Part 7.

Linux PC	IP Address of Ethernet Interface *eth0*	Network Mask
PC1	10.0.1.100/24	255.255.255.0
PC2	10.0.1.101/28	255.255.255.240
PC3	10.0.1.120/24	255.255.255.0
PC4	10.0.1.121/28	255.255.255.240

2. Run *ethereal* on PC1 and capture the packets for the following `ping` commands:

   a. From PC1 to PC3: `PC1% ping -c 1 10.0.1.120`

   b. From PC1 to PC2: `PC1% ping -c 1 10.0.1.101`

   c. From PC1 to PC4: `PC1% ping -c 1 10.0.1.121`

   d. From PC4 to PC1: `PC4% ping -c 1 10.0.1.100`

   e. From PC2 to PC4: `PC2% ping -c 1 10.0.1.121`

   f. From PC2 to PC3: `PC2% ping -c 1 10.0.1.120`

   Explain how PC1 sees the traffic between PC2 and PC4 and PC2 and PC3.

3. Save the *ethereal* output to a text file (setting the *Print summary* option), and save the output of the `ping` commands. Note that not all of the previous scenarios are successful. Save all output, including any error messages.

4. When you are done with the exercise, reset the interfaces to their original values as given in Table 2.1. (Recall that the /24 corresponds to netmask 255.255.255.0.)

Lab Report Use your output data and `ping` results to explain what happened in each of the `ping` commands. Which `ping` operations were successful and which were unsuccessful? Why?

PART 8. STATIC MAPPING OF IP ADDRESSES AND HOST NAMES

Since it is easier to memorize names than IP addresses, there are mechanisms to associate a symbolic name, called *host name*, with an IP address. On the Internet, the resolution between host names and IP addresses is generally done by the Domain Name System (DNS), which is the topic of Lab 8. This experiment illustrates another, simpler method to map IP addresses and domain names using the host file */etc/hosts*.

Before DNS became available, the */etc/hosts* file was the only method to resolve host names in the Internet. All hosts on the Internet had to occasionally synchronize with the content of other */etc/hosts* files.

EXERCISE 8.
Associating names with IP addresses.

In this exercise you manipulate the static mapping of host names and IP addresses using the */etc/hosts* file.

1. On PC1, inspect the content of file */etc/hosts* with *gedit*.

2. On PC1, issue a `ping` command to PC2.

   ```
   PC1% ping 10.0.1.12
   ```

3. Repeat Step 2, but use symbolic names instead of IP addresses (e.g., PC2 instead of 10.0.1.12). You should see that the symbolic name is unreachable at this point.

4. On PC1, edit the file */etc/hosts* and associate host names with the IP addresses and save the changes. Use the names PC1, PC2, and so on, as used throughout this lab to refer to the PCs.

5. Repeat Step 3. You should now be able to `ping` directly using `PC2`, `PC3`, `PC4`, as in

   ```
   PC1% ping PC2
   PC1% ping PC3
   PC1% ping PC4
   ```

6. Reset the */etc/hosts* file to its original state. That is, remove the changes you have made in this exercise, and save the file.

Lab Report

- Explain why a static mapping of names and IP addresses is impractical when the number of hosts is large.

- What will be the result of the host name resolution when multiple IP addresses are associated with the same host name in the */etc/hosts* file?

PART 9. EXPERIMENTS WITH FTP AND TELNET

A severe security problem with the file transfer protocol (FTP) is that the login and password information are transmitted as plain text (not encrypted). Sometimes malicious users exploit this by snooping passwords on the network.

Here you learn how easy it is to crack passwords by snooping traffic from *FTP* and *Telnet* sessions.

> **NOTE:**
>
> The use of applications that do not encrypt passwords, such as *FTP* and *Telnet*, is strongly discouraged. On the Internet, you should use protocols such as Secure Shell (*ssh*) tools for file transfers and remote login.

EXERCISE 9(A).
Snoop Passwords from an *FTP* session.

Capture traffic from an *FTP* session between two hosts.

1. On PC1, run the `ethereal` command with capture filters set to capture traffic between PC1 and PC2. The capture filter is

    `host 10.0.1.11 and host 10.0.1.12`

2. On PC1, initiate an *FTP* session to PC2 by typing

    `PC1% ftp 10.0.1.12`

3. Log in as root.

4. Inspect the payload of packets with FTP payload that are sent from PC1 to PC2. *FTP* sessions use TCP connections for data transfer.

    In *ethereal*, there is a simple method to view the payload sent in a TCP connection. Simply select a packet that contains a TCP segment in the main window of *ethereal*, and then click on *Follow TCP Stream* in the *Tools* menu of the *ethereal* window. This will create a new window that displays only the payload of the selected TCP connection.

5. Save the details of the packets (i.e., select *Print details* in the *Print* window of *ethereal*), which transmit the login name and password. As a hint, you can set the display filter in *ethereal* to show only the desired packet(s).

Lab Report

*   Using the saved output, identify the port numbers of the FTP client and the FTP server.

*   Identify the login name and the password, shown in plain text in the payload of the packets that you captured.

EXERCISE 9(B).
Snoop passwords from a *Telnet* session.

Repeat the previous exercise with the `telnet` command instead of `ftp`. On PC1, establish a *Telnet* session to PC2, and save the *ethereal* output of packets used to transmit the login name and password.

Lab Report Does *Telnet* have the same security flaws as *FTP*? Support your answer using the saved output.

EXERCISE 9(C).
Observing traffic from a *Telnet* session.

This exercise uses the *Telnet* session established in the previous exercise.

1. Run *ethereal* on PC1 and start to capture traffic. If the *ethereal* window from the previous exercise is still open, make sure that *ethereal* is capturing traffic.

2. If the *Telnet* session from the previous exercise is still in place, skip to the next step. Otherwise, follow the steps from the previous exercise and log in from PC1 to PC2 with the `telnet` command.

3. Once you are logged in, type a few characters. Observe the number of packets captured by *ethereal* for each character typed. Observe that for each key you type, three packets are transmitted. Determine why this occurs.

4. Save the *ethereal* output to a text file (using the *Print summary* option).

Lab Report Attach the saved output to your report. Explain why three packets are sent in a *Telnet* session for each character typed on the terminal.

CHECKLIST FORM FOR LAB 2

Complete this checklist as you work through the laboratory exercises and attach the form to your lab report.

Name (please print):_____

☐ Prelab 2 question sheet

☐ Checkoff for Part 1

☐ Checkoff for Part 2

☐ Checkoff for Part 3

☐ Checkoff for Part 4

☐ Checkoff for Part 5

☐ Checkoff for Part 6

☐ Checkoff for Part 7

☐ Checkoff for Part 8

☐ Checkoff for Part 9

☐ Feedback sheet

☐ Lab report

FEEDBACK FORM FOR LAB 2

- Complete this feedback form at the completion of the lab exercises and submit the form when submitting your lab report.

- The feedback is anonymous. *Do not put your name on this form* and keep it separate from your lab report.

- For each exercise, please record the following:

	Difficulty (–2, –1, 0, 1, 2)	**Interest Level** (–2, –1, 0, 1, 2)	**Time to Complete** (minutes)
	–2 = too easy	–2 = low interest	
	0 = just right	0 = just right	
	2 = too hard	2 = high interest	

Part 1.
Using filters in *tcpdump*

Part 2.
Using filters in *ethereal*

Part 3.
ARP—Address
Resolution Protocol

Part 4.
The `netstat` command

Part 5.
Configuring IP interfaces
in Linux

Part 6.
Duplicate IP addresses

Part 7.
Changing netmasks

Part 8.
Static mapping of IP
addresses and host names

Part 9.
Experiments with *FTP*
and *Telnet*

Please answer the following questions:

- What did you like about this lab?

- What did you dislike about this lab?

- Make a suggestion to improve the lab.

Static Routing

OBJECTIVES

- How to turn a computer with multiple interfaces into a router

- How to set up static routing on Linux PC routers and Cisco routers

- How ICMP messages update routing table entries

- How Proxy ARP helps to connect different networks without reconfiguring the hosts

- How to work with different network masks

CONTENTS

PRELAB 3

1. **Network commands in Linux:** Go to the online hypertext man pages at

   `http://www.tcpip-lab.net/links/manual.html`

   and select the OS version Red Hat Linux/i386 7.3. Read the manual pages of the following commands:

   • route
   • traceroute

2. **Proxy ARP:** Go to the website of Cisco at

   `http://www.tcpip-lab.net/links/proxyarp.html`

   and read about Proxy ARP.

3. **Cisco routers:** In this lab you will work with Cisco routers. Go to Cisco's web page (`http://www.cisco.com`) to find out more about the Cisco routers used in your lab (Cisco 2500, 2600, 3600, or 7000).

4. **Cisco IOS:** The Cisco routers in the lab are running a recent version of the Cisco Internet Operating System (IOS). Read about the IOS at

   `http://www.tcpip-lab.net/links/cisco_ios.html`

5. **Navigating IOS:** Read Section 4 in the Introduction for information on how to navigate and work with Cisco IOS.

6. *kermit:* This lab uses the *kermit* utility program to establish a serial connection between a Linux PC and a Cisco router. For more detail refer to

   `http://www.tcpip-lab.net/links/kermit.html`

QUESTION SHEET FOR PRELAB 3

Answer the questions in the space provided below each one. Use extra sheets of paper if needed and attach them to this document. Submit the answers to the question sheet with your lab report.

Name (please print):_____

1. What is the IOS command to change the MTU (Maximum Transmission Unit) for an interface on a Cisco router?

2. How does a router determine whether datagrams to a particular host can be directly delivered through one of its interfaces?

3. Which systems generate ICMP route redirect messages—routers, hosts, or both?

4. What is the default maximum TTL value used by `traceroute` when sending UDP datagrams?

5. Describe the role of a *default gateway* in a routing table.

6. What is the network prefix of IP address 192.110.50.3/24?

7. Explain the difference between a network IP address and a network prefix.

8. An organization has been assigned the network number 140.25.0.0/16 and it needs to create networks that support up to 60 hosts on each IP network. What is the maximum number of networks that can be set up? Explain your answer.

LAB 3

In this lab you work with four different network topologies. The topology for Parts 1–4 is shown in Figure 3.1. These parts address router configuration on a Linux PC and a Cisco router. The topology for Part 5 is shown in Figure 3.2. This topology is used to study the role of *ICMP route redirect* message. For Part 6 we add one more router to the topology of Part 5 and examine the effect of routing loops. The topology for Part 7 is shown in Figure 3.4. There, you explore the relationship between network prefixes and IP forwarding.

RECALL:

- Before you get started, please reboot the Linux PCs.
- During the lab, you need to save data to files. Save all files in the directory /labdata.
- Save your files to a floppy disk before the end of the lab. You will need the files when you prepare your lab report.

PART 1. CONFIGURING A LINUX PC AS AN IP ROUTER

Every Linux PC with at least two network interfaces can be set up as an IP router. Configuring a Linux PC as an IP router involves two steps: (1) modifying the configuration of Linux, so that IP forwarding is enabled, and (2) configuring the routing table. Figure 3.1 shows the network topology used in Parts 1–4 of this lab. PC1 and PC4 are used as hosts, and PC2 and Router1 are set up as IP routers. The PCs and the Cisco router are connected by three Ethernet hubs. In Lab 3, all routing table entries are manually configured, which is known as static routing.

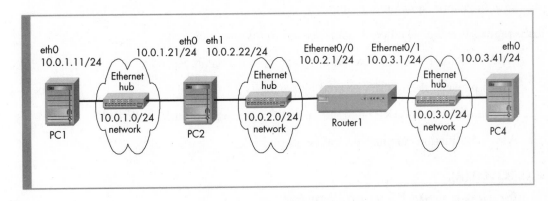

FIGURE 3.1.

Network topology for Parts 1–4.

TABLE 3.1. IP addresses for Parts 1–4.

Linux PC	Ethernet Interface *eth0*	Ethernet Interface *eth1*
PC1	10.0.1.11/24	Disabled
PC2	10.0.1.21/24	10.0.2.22/24
PC4	10.0.3.41/24	Disabled
Cisco Router	**Ethernet Interface Ethernet0/0**	**Ethernet Interface Ethernet0/1**
Router1	10.0.2.1/24	10.0.3.1/24

Note: Table 3.1 assumes that there is an Ethernet interface card in slot 0 of the Cisco router. If the Ethernet is in a different slot, say slot 1, the name has to be changed (e.g., *Ethernet1/0* and *Ethernet1/1*). If the Ethernet interface card, assumed to be in slot 1, is a 100 Mbps interface card, the names are *FastEthernet1/0* and *FastEthernet1/1*. On a router that does not have slotted interfaces (e.g., Cisco 2500 class routers), the names of the Ethernet interfaces are *Ethernet0* and *Ethernet1*.

EXERCISE 1(A).
Network setup.

1. Connect the Ethernet interfaces of the Linux PCs and the Cisco router as shown in Figure 3.1. Configure the IP addresses of the interfaces as given in Table 3.1.

2. Start to capture traffic on PC1 with *ethereal*.

3. Issue a `ping` command from PC1 to PC2, Router1, and PC4. Save the output of each `ping` command.

```
PC1% ping -c 5 10.0.1.21
PC1% ping -c 5 10.0.2.1
PC1% ping -c 5 10.0.3.41
```

4. Save the captured *ethereal* output.

Lab Report Use the saved data to answer the following questions:

• What is the output on PC1 when the `ping` commands are issued?

• Which packets, if any, are captured by *ethereal*?

• Do you observe any ARP or ICMP packets? If so, what do they indicate?

• Which destinations are not reachable? Explain.

EXERCISE 1(B).
Configuring a Linux PC as an IP router.

On a Linux system, IP forwarding is enabled when the file */proc/sys/net/ipv4/ip_forward* contains a 1 and disabled when it contains a 0. You can enable IP forwarding by writing a 1 in the file, with the command

```
PC1% echo "1" > /proc/sys/net/ipv4/ip_forward
```

The command echo writes the given argument, here, the string "1", to the standard output. Using the redirect operator (>) and a filename, the output of the command is written to a file. IP forwarding is disabled with the command

```
PC1% echo "0" > /proc/sys/net/ipv4/ip_forward
```

The command has an immediate effect; however, changes are not permanent and are lost when the system is rebooted. Modifying the IP forwarding state permanently requires changes to the configuration file */etc/sysctl.conf*. IP forwarding is enabled if the file contains a line *net.ipv4.ip_forward = 1*, and IP forwarding is disabled when the line does not exist or the file contains the line *net.ipv4.ip_forward = 0*.[1] Changes to the configuration file */etc/sysctl.conf* take effect the next time Linux is rebooted.

- Enable PC2 as an IP router using the command

```
PC2% echo "1" > /proc/sys/net/ipv4/ip_forward
```

EXERCISE 1(C).
Setting static routing table entries for a Linux PC.

Next, you must set up the routing tables of the Linux PCs. PC1 and PC4 are hosts, and PC2 is an IP router. The routing tables are configured so that they conform to the network topology shown in Figure 3.1 and Table 3.1. The routes are configured manually, which is also referred to as *static routing*.

Configuring static routes in Linux is done with the command route, which has numerous options for viewing, adding, deleting or modifying routing entries. The various uses of the route command are summarized in the list.

```
route add –net netaddress netmask mask gw gw_address
route add –net netaddress netmask mask dev iface
```
   Adds a routing table entry for the network prefix identified by IP address
   netaddress and netmask *mask*. The next-hop is identified by IP address
   gw_address or by interface *iface*.

```
route add –host hostaddress gw gw_address
route add –host hostaddress dev iface
```
   Adds a host route entry for IP address *hostaddress* with the next-hop identified
   by IP address *gw_address* or by interface *iface*.

```
route add default gw gw_address
```
   Sets the default route to IP address *gw_address*.

```
route del –net netaddress netmask mask gw gw_address
route del –host hostaddress gw gw_address
route del default gw gw_address
```
   Deletes an existing route from the routing table. It is not necessary to type all arguments. If enough arguments are provided that it can be matched with an existing routing entry, the first entry that matches the given arguments is deleted.

---

[1]Yet another method to configure a Linux as a router is to add a line *FORWARD_IPV4=true* to the file */etc/sysconfig/ network*. IP forwarding is disabled by setting *FORWARD_IPV4=false*.

```
route —e
    Displays the current routing table with extended fields. The command is identical to
    the netstat —r command.
route —C
    Displays the routing table cache.
```

The command for adding a route for the network prefix 10.21.0.0/16 with next-hop address 10.11.1.4 is

`PC1%route add -net 10.21.0.0 netmask 255.255.0.0 gw 10.11.1.4`

The command to add a host route to IP address 10.0.2.31 with the next-hop set to 10.0.1.21 is

`PC1%route add -host 10.0.2.31 gw 10.0.1.21`

The command to add the IP address 10.0.4.4 as the default gateway is done with the command

`PC1%route add default gw 10.0.4.4`

The commands to delete the entries created with the previous commands are

```
PC1%route del -net 10.21.0.0 netmask 255.255.0.0
PC1%route del -host 10.0.2.31
PC1%route del default
```

In Linux, there is no simple way to delete all entries in the routing table. When the commands are issued interactively in a Linux shell, the added entries are valid until Linux is rebooted. To make static routes permanent, the routes need to be entered in the configuration file */etc/sysconfig/static-routes*, which is read each time Linux is started.

The listed commands are helpful to get information on routing and to find mistakes in the routing setup.

```
ping IPaddress
    Tests whether IPaddress can be reached
traceroute IPaddress
    Displays the route to the interface IPaddress
```

1. Configure the routing table entries of PC1 and PC4. You can either specify a default route or insert separate routing entries for each remote network. For this exercise, add a route for each individual remote network. As a hint, here is the configuration information for PC4:

   ```
   PC4%route add -net 10.0.2.0 netmask 255.255.255.0 gw 10.0.3.1
   PC4%route add -net 10.0.1.0 netmask 255.255.255.0 gw 10.0.3.1
   ```

2. Configure the routing table entries of the IP router PC2. (The correctness of the routing entries will be tested after Router1 has been set up.)

3. Display the routing table of PC1, PC2, and PC4 with `netstat -rn` and save the output.

Lab Report Include the saved output of the routing table. Explain the entries in the routing table and discuss the values of the fields for each entry.

PART 2. CONFIGURING A CISCO ROUTER

The setup of a Cisco router is more involved. The first step is to establish a physical connection to the router, so that configuration commands can be entered. There are different ways to connect to a Cisco router. In the Internet Lab, you establish a serial connection to the router. This is done with a serial cable that connects the serial port of a Linux PC to the console port of a Cisco router. The next step is to run a terminal emulation program on the Linux PC. In the Internet Lab, you use the *kermit* communication software to access the router. Lastly, you have to type IOS commands to configure the Cisco router. Refer to Section 4 in the Introduction for a detailed discussion on how to navigate and work with the IOS.

The network setup for this part is as shown in Figure 3.1 and Table 3.1.

EXERCISE 2(A).
Accessing a Cisco router via the console port with *kermit*.

To access a Cisco router from one of the Linux PCs, connect one of the serial ports of the PC to the console port of the Cisco router via a serial cable. Then, you can use the `kermit` command to establish a remote terminal connection to the router. You will use Router1 as the IP router and PC1 as the console.

The following steps access the console port of Router1 from PC1:

1. Use a serial cable to connect the serial port of PC1 to the console port of Router1. The serial port is labeled *ttyS0* or *ttyS1*.

2. Start *kermit* by typing

```
PC1% kermit
```

This brings up the prompt:

```
[/root]C-kermit>
```

3. Use the `set line` command to select the `ttyS0` serial port.

```
[/root]C-kermit> set line /dev/ttyS0 (or /dev/ttyS1)
```

4. Use the `set carrier-watch` command to disable the requirement for a carrier detect signal

```
[/root]C-kermit> set carrier-watch off
```

5. Connect to the router by issuing the following command:

```
[/root]C-kermit> connect
```

If the connection is successful, you see a command prompt (user EXEC prompt) from Router1:

```
Router1>
```

When you see this prompt, you can type Cisco IOS commands. If the prompt does not appear, then press the Enter key several times.

> **NOTE:**
>
> To terminate a *kermit* session, type Ctrl-\ (control-backslash) and then press the C key or type C. *kermit* takes a few seconds (maybe 10) to exit.

EXERCISE 2(B).
Switching Cisco IOS command modes.

This exercise demonstrates how to log into a router and how to navigate the different Cisco IOS command modes. It is important to understand the different modes so you know where you are and what commands are accepted at any time.

1. Make sure that PC1 is connected to Router1 via a serial cable and that a *kermit* session is started.

2. When PC1 is connected to the router, you see the prompt of the User EXEC mode (`Router>`). To see which commands are available in this mode, type a question mark (`?`):

```
Router1> ?
```

3. To view and change system parameters of a Cisco router, you must enter the Privileged EXEC mode, by typing

```
Router1> enable
Password : <enable secret>
Router1#
```

You need a password, the `enable secret`, to enter the Privileged EXEC mode.

4. To modify systemwide configuration parameters, you must enter the global configuration mode. This mode is entered by typing

```
Router1# configure terminal
Router1(config)#
```

5. To make changes to a network interface, enter the interface configuration mode, with the command

```
Router1(config)# interface Ethernet0/0
Router1(config-if)#
```

The name of the interface is provided as an argument. Here, the network interface that is configured is *Ethernet0/0*.

6. To return from the interface configuration to the global configuration mode or from the global configuration mode to the Privileged EXEC mode, use the exit command:

```
Router1(config-if)# exit
Router1(config)# exit
Router1#
```

The exit command takes you one step up in the command hierarchy. To directly return to the Privileged EXEC mode from any *configuration* mode, use the end command:

```
Router1(config-if)# end
Router1#
```

7. To return from the Privileged EXEC mode to the User EXEC mode, type

```
Router1# disable
Router1>
```

8. To terminate the console session from the User EXEC mode, type

```
Router1> logout
Router1 con0 is now available
Press RETURN to get started.
```

Or type logout or exit from the Privileged EXEC mode.

EXERCISE 2(C).
Configuring IP interfaces on a Cisco router.

The following exercises use basic commands from IOS that are needed to configure a Cisco router. Refer to Section 4 of the Introduction for detailed explanations.

1. Connect PC1 to Router1 via the serial cable and start a *kermit* session.

2. Configure Router1 with the IP addresses given in Table 3.1.

```
Router1> enable
Password: <enable secret>
Router1# configure terminal
Router1(config)# no ip routing
Router1(config)# ip routing
Router1(config)# interface Ethernet0/0
Router1(config-if)# ip address 10.0.2.1 255.255.255.0
Router1(config-if)# no shutdown
Router1(config-if)# interface Ethernet0/1
Router1(config-if)# ip address 10.0.3.1 255.255.255.0
Router1(config-if)# no shutdown
Router1(config-if)# end
```

3. When you are done, use the following command to check the changes you made to the router configuration and save the output:

```
Router1# show interfaces
Router1# show running-config
```

4. Analyze the output to ensure that you have configured the router correctly.

Lab Report Include the output from Step 3 in your lab report.

EXERCISE 2(D).
Setting static routing table entries on a Cisco router.

Next you must add static routes to the routing table of Router1. The routing table must be configured so that it conforms to the network topology shown in Figure 3.1 and Table 3.1.

The IOS command to configure static routing is `ip route`. The command can be used to show, clear, add, or delete entries in the routing table. The commands are summarized in the list.

IOS MODE: PRIVILEGED EXEC

```
show ip route
```
   Displays the contents of the routing table
```
clear ip route *
```
   Deletes all routing table entries
```
show ip cache
```
   Displays the routing cache

IOS MODE: GLOBAL CONFIGURATION

```
ip route-cache
```
   Enables route caching. By default, route caching is enabled on a router.
```
no ip route-cache
```
   Disables route caching.
```
ip route destination mask gw_address
```
   Adds a static routing table entry to `destination` with netmask `mask`. The argument `gw_address` is the IP address of the next-hop router.
```
ip route destination mask Iface
```
   Adds a static routing table entry to `destination` with netmask `mask`. Here, the next-hop information is the name of a network interface (e.g., *FastEthernet0/0*).
```
no ip route destination mask gw_address
no ip route destination mask Iface
```
   Deletes the route table entry with `destination`, `mask`, and `gw_address` or `Iface` from the routing table.

We next show some examples for adding and deleting routing table entries in IOS. Compare these commands to the corresponding Linux commands in Part 1, Exercise

1(C). As in Linux, whenever an IP address is configured for a network interface, routing table entries for the directly connected network are added automatically.

The command for adding a route for the network prefix 10.21.0.0/16 with 10.11.1.4 as the next-hop address is

```
Router1(config)#ip route 10.21.0.0 255.255.0.0 10.11.1.4
```

The command to add a host route to IP address 10.0.2.31 with the next-hop set to 10.0.1.21 is

```
Router1(config)#ip route 10.0.2.31 255.255.255.255 10.0.1.21
```

In IOS, a host route is identified by a 32 bit prefix.

The command to add the IP address 10.0.4.4 as the default gateway is done with the command

```
Router1(config) #ip route 0.0.0.0 0.0.0.0 10.0.4.4
```

Finally, commands to delete the previous entries use the `no ip route` command.

```
Router1(config)# no ip route 10.21.0.0 255.255.0.0 10.11.1.4
Router1(config)# no ip route 10.0.2.31 255.255.255.255 10.0.1.21
Router1(config)# no ip route 0.0.0.0 0.0.0.0 10.0.4.4
```

1. Display the content of the routing table with `show ip route`. Note the routing entries that are already present. Save the output.

2. Add routing entries to Router1 so that the router forwards datagrams for the configuration shown in Figure 3.1. Routing entries should exist for the following networks:

    - 10.0.1.0/24

    - 10.0.2.0/24

    - 10.0.3.0/24

3. Display the routing table again with `show ip route` and save the output.

Lab Report Include the saved output of the routing table from Steps 1 and 2. Explain the fields of the routing table entries of the Cisco router. Explain how the routing table has changed from Step 1 to Step 3.

PART 3. FINALIZING AND EXPLORING THE ROUTER CONFIGURATION

If the configuration of PC2 and Router1 was done correctly, it is now possible to send IP datagrams between any two machines in the network shown in Figure 3.1. However, if the network is not configured properly, you need to debug and test your setup. Table 3.2 illustrates several common problems that may arise. Since it is impossible to cover all scenarios, network debugging is a crucial skill that you need to obtain for your lab experiments to work well.

The network setup for this part is as shown in Figure 3.1 and Table 3.1.

TABLE 3.2. Troubleshooting network configurations.

Problem	Possible Causes	Debugging
Traffic does not reach destinations on local network.	Network interface not configured correctly.	Verify the interface configuration with `show protocols` (in IOS) or `ifconfig` (in Linux).
	Incorrectly connected, faulty or loose cables.	Most interface cards and Ethernet hubs have green LED status lights. Check whether the status lights are on. Verify the connection of the cables. Verify that no crossover cables are used.
Traffic reaches router but is not forwarded to remote networks.	IP forwarding is not enabled.	Use `show protocols` (in IOS) or look into */proc/sys/net/ipv4/ip_forward* (in Linux) to display the forwarding status.
	Routing tables are not configured correctly.	Display routing tables with `show ip route` (in IOS) or `netstat -rn` (in Linux). Run `traceroute` between all hosts and routers.
ICMP Request message reaches destination, but ICMP Reply does not reach source.	Routing tables are not correctly configured for the reverse path.	Display routing tables with `show ip route` (in IOS) or `netstat -rn` (in Linux). Run `ping` and `traceroute` in both directions.
A change in the routing table has no effect on the flow of traffic.	The ARP cache has old entries.	Delete the ARP cache with `clear arp` (in IOS) or delete entries with `arp -d` (in Linux).

EXERCISE 3(A).
Finalizing the network setup.

Continue with the network configuration from Part 2.

Test the network configuration by issuing `ping` commands from each host and router to every other host and router. If some `ping` commands do not work, you need to modify the configuration of routers and hosts. If all `ping` commands are successful, the network configuration is correct, and you can proceed to the next step.

EXERCISE 3(B).
Testing routes with traceroute.

1. Start an *ethereal* session on PC1.

2. Execute a `traceroute` command from PC1 to PC4 and save the output.

    `PC1% traceroute 10.0.3.41`

    Observe how `traceroute` gathers information on the route.

3. Stop the traffic capture of *ethereal* and save the traffic generated by the `traceroute` command.

4. Save the routing table of PC1, PC4, PC2, and Router1.

Lab Report Use the *ethereal* output and the previously saved routing table to explain the operation of `traceroute`.

EXERCISE 3(C).
Observe MAC addresses at a router.

When a router forwards an IP datagram from one Ethernet segment to another, it does not modify the IP destination address. However, the destination Ethernet address in the Ethernet header is modified at a router.

This exercise requires manipulations to the ARP cache. The `arp` command in Linux was covered in Lab 2. The list shows corresponding IOS commands for Cisco routers.

IOS MODE: PRIVILEGED EXEC

`show ip arp`
  Displays the contents of the ARP cache
`clear arp`
  Deletes the entire ARP cache

IOS MODE: GLOBAL CONFIGURATION

`arp IPaddress`
  Adds an entry for `IPaddress` to the ARP cache
`no arp IPaddress`
  Deletes the ARP entry for `IPaddress` from the ARP cache

1. Erase all ARP entries on PC1, PC2, PC4, and Router1.

2. Run *ethereal* on both PC1 (interface *eth0*) and PC4 (interface *eth0*).

3. Issue a `ping` command on PC1 to PC4.

   ```
   PC1% ping -c 5 10.0.3.41
   ```

4. Save the packet transmissions triggered by the `ping` command, including ARP requests, ARP Reply, ICMP Echo Request, and ICMP Echo Reply on both PC1 and PC4.

Lab Report

• Determine the source and destination addresses in the Ethernet and IP headers for the ICMP Echo Request messages that were captured at PC1.

• Determine the source and destination addresses in the Ethernet and IP headers for the ICMP Echo Request messages that were captured at PC4.

• Use your previous answers to explain how the source and destination Ethernet and IP addresses are changed when a datagram is forwarded by a router.

EXERCISE 3(D).
Multiple matches in the routing table.

A router or host uses a routing table to determine the next hop of the path of an IP datagram. In Linux, routing table entries are sorted in the order of decreasing prefix length and are read from top to bottom. In this exercise, you determine how an IP router or Linux PC resolves multiple matching entries in a routing table.

1. Add the following routes to the routing table of PC1:

   ```
   PC1% route add -net 10.0.0.0 netmask 255.255.0.0 gw 10.0.1.71
   PC1% route add -host 10.0.3.9 gw 10.0.1.81
   ```

   From Exercise 1(C) there should be a network route for the network prefix 10.0.3.0/24. If there is no such route, then add the following entry:

   ```
   PC1% route add -net 10.0.3.0 netmask 255.255.255.0
   gw 10.0.1.61
   ```

2. Referring to the routing table, determine how many matches exist for the following IP addresses:

   ```
   10.0.3.9
   10.0.3.14
   10.0.4.1
   ```

3. Start an *ethereal* session on PC1 and issue the following `ping` commands from PC1:

   ```
   PC1% ping -c 1 10.0.3.9
   PC1% ping -c 1 10.0.3.14
   PC1% ping -c 1 10.0.4.1
   ```

Note that gateways with IP addresses 10.0.1.61, 10.0.1.71, and 10.0.1.81 do not exist. However, PC1 still sends ARP Request packets for these IP addresses.

4. Save the output of *ethereal* and PC1's routing table.

Lab Report Use the saved output to indicate the number of matches for each of the preceding IP addresses. Explain how PC1 resolves multiple matches in the routing table. Include only relevant output data in your report to support your analysis of the data.

EXERCISE 3(E).
Default Routes.

1. Delete the routing table entries added in Step 1 of Exercise 3(D). (Otherwise, the entries interfere with the remaining exercises in this lab.)

2. Add default routes on PC1 and PC2.

a. On PC1, add a default route with interface *eth0* of PC2 as the default gateway.

b. On PC2, add a default route with interface *Ethernet0/0* of Router1 as the default gateway.

3. Start to capture traffic on PC1 (on *eth0*) and PC2 (on both *eth0* and *eth1*) with *ethereal*.

4. Issue a `ping` command from PC1 to a host on a network that does not exist.

```
PC1% ping -c 5 10.0.10.110
```

5. Save the *ethereal* output.

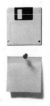

Lab Report Use your saved data to answer the following questions:

*   What is the output on PC1 when the `ping` command is issued?

*   Determine how far the ICMP Echo Request message travels?

*   Which, if any, ICMP Echo Reply message returns to PC1?

PART 4. PROXY ARP

Proxy Address Resolution Protocol (Proxy ARP) is a method by which a router can forward traffic without using its routing table. Proxy ARP is a configuration option when an IP router responds to ARP Requests that arrive from one of its connected networks for a host that is on another of its connected networks. Without Proxy ARP enabled, an ARP Request for a host on a different network would be unsuccessful, since routers do not forward ARP packets to another network.

In this part you explore how Proxy ARP enables routers to forward an IP datagram even though the sender of the datagram is not aware that the IP datagram should be forwarded to a router. Continue with the network configuration from Figure 3.1, and with IP addresses as shown in Table 3.1.

The commands to enable and disable Proxy ARP in IOS are listed.

> **IOS MODE: INTERFACE CONFIGURATION**
>
> ```
> ip proxy-arp
> no ip proxy-arp
> ```
>
> Proxy ARP is enabled and disabled separately on each interface. In IOS, Proxy ARP is enabled by default.

EXERCISE 4.
Observing Proxy ARP.

1. Erase both the ARP table and the routing table of PC4.

2. Set the netmask of PC4 to 255.0.0.0, so that PC4 assumes it belongs to network 10.0.0.0/8, instead of to network 10.0.3.0/24.

3. Run *ethereal* on PC4 (*eth0*), PC2 (*eth1*), and PC1 (*eth0*). Set a display or capture filter to display only ICMP and ARP packets.

4. Issue a `ping` from PC4 to PC1:

```
PC4% ping -c 2 10.0.1.11
```

Explore the captured data and interpret the outcome.

Even though PC4 had no default routing entry in its table for Router1, it was still able to connect to PC1 (i.e., you should not observe a "network unreachable" error message).

5. Save the ARP table of PC4 and the packets captured by *ethereal* on the hosts.

6. Explore the captured data and interpret the outcome.

7. Now disable Proxy ARP on both interfaces of Router1. Is it still feasible to issue a `ping` from PC4 to PC1?

8. Reset the network mask of PC4 to its original value of 255.255.255.0. Then, reenable Proxy ARP on Router1.

 Lab Report Use the captured data to explain the outcome of the exercise. Use the data to explain how Proxy ARP allowed PC4 to communicate with PC1. Include only relevant data from your saved output.

PART 5. ICMP ROUTE REDIRECT

ICMP Route Redirect messages are sent from a router to a host when a datagram should have been forwarded to a different router or interface. In Linux, an ICMP route redirect message updates the *routing cache*, but not the *routing table*.

Both the routing cache and the routing table contain information for forwarding traffic. Before a Linux system performs a routing table lookup, it first inspects the routing cache. If no matching entry is found in the cache, Linux performs a lookup in the routing table. After each routing table lookup, an entry is added to the routing cache. The routing cache does not aggregate table entries, and there is a separate entry for each destination IP address. As a consequence, a lookup in the routing cache does not require a longest-prefix match. An entry in the routing cache is deleted if it has not been used for some time, usually after 10 minutes. When an ICMP Redirect message arrives, an entry is added to the routing cache, but no update is performed to the routing table.

> **NOTE:**
>
> The following are the commands to display the contents of the routing cache:
> - In Linux, use the command `route -C`.
> - In IOS, use the command `show ip cache`.

In this part of the lab, you use three Cisco routers. Figure 3.2 and Table 3.3 describe the network configuration for the later exercises.

> **NOTE:**
>
> When Ethernet interfaces of the Linux PCs (*eth0*, *eth1*) run at 100 Mbps and the Ethernet interfaces of the Cisco routers (*Ethernet0/0*, *Ethernet0/1*) run at 10 Mbps, you should avoid using dual-speed hubs if you connect two or more Cisco routers and one or more Linux PC to the same hub.
>
> If you use dual-speed hubs in such a situation, the Linux PCs cannot observe the traffic between Cisco routers with *ethereal*.

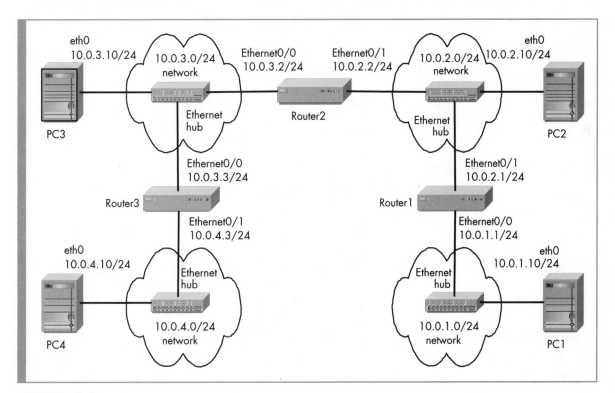

FIGURE 3.2.

Network topology for Part 5.

TABLE 3.3. IP addresses for Part 5.

Cisco Router	Interface *Ethernet0/0*	Interface *Ethernet0/1*
Router1	10.0.1.1/24	10.0.2.1/24
Router2	10.0.3.2/24	10.0.2.2/24
Router3	10.0.3.3/24	10.0.4.3/24
Linux PC	**Interface *eth0***	**Interface *eth1***
PC1	10.0.1.10/24	Disabled
PC2	10.0.2.10/24	Disabled
PC3	10.0.3.10/24	Disabled
PC4	10.0.4.10/24	Disabled

EXERCISE 5.

In the network shown in Figure 3.2, when PC2 sends datagrams with destination 10.0.3.10 (PC3) to 10.0.2.1 (Router1), as opposed to 10.0.2.2 (Router2), then Router1 sends an ICMP route redirect message to PC2. The ICMP route redirect informs PC2 that it should send datagrams with destination 10.0.3.10 to Router2 instead.

In this exercise you create the preceding scenario. First, you will trigger the transmission of an ICMP route redirect message and subsequently observe a change to the routing cache.

1. Connect the Ethernet interfaces of the routers and the hosts to the hubs as shown in Figure 3.2.

2. Delete all routing table entries and all ARP cache entries on all PCs and on Router 1.

    a. Delete the routing cache on PC1 with the command

        `PC1% echo "1" > /proc/sys/net/ipv4/route/flush`

    b. Delete all static routes on Router 1 with the following commands:

        `Router1(config)# no ip routing`
        `Router1(config)# ip routing`

    c. Build a new static routing entry on Router1 for network prefix *10.0.3.0/24* as follows:

        `Router1(config)# ip route 10.0.3.0 255.255.255.0 10.0.2.2`

3. Set up the routing table of PC2 in such a way that it provokes the transmission of an ICMP route redirect message as discussed earlier.

4. Save the contents of the routing table and the routing cache of Router1, Router2, and PC2.

5. Use *ethereal* to capture the ICMP messages being sent, and issue a `ping` from PC2 to PC3:

   ```
   PC2% ping -c 5 10.0.3.10
   ```

6. Save the network traffic and the contents of the routing table and the routing cache after the ICMP route redirect messages.

7. Wait a few minutes and check the contents of the routing cache again. Save the output.

Lab Report

- Is there a difference between the contents of the routing table and the routing cache immediately after the ICMP route redirect message?

- When you viewed the cache a few minutes later, what did you observe?

- Describe how the ICMP route redirect works using the output you saved. Include only relevant data from your saved output to support your explanations.

- Explain how Router1, in the previous example, knows that datagrams destined to network 10.0.3.10 should be forwarded to 10.0.2.2?

PART 6. ROUTING LOOPS

A potential problem when setting routing tables manually is that routing loops may occur. In this part of the lab you intentionally configure a routing loop in the configuration of the routing table and observe what happens to network traffic in such a situation.

EXERCISE 6.

1. Add Router4 to the network topology of Part 5 and configure the interfaces as shown in Figure 3.3 and Table 3.4.

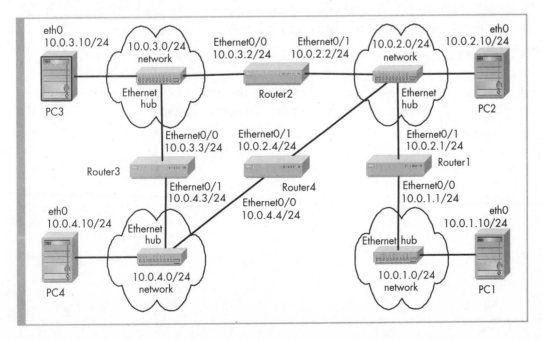

FIGURE 3.3.

Network topology for Part 6.

TABLE 3.4. IP addresses for Part 6.

Cisco Router	Interface *Ethernet0/0*	Interface *Ethernet0/1*
Router4	10.0.4.4/24	10.0.2.4/24

2. Configure the routing tables of Router2, Router3, and Router4 so that an ICMP Echo Request message generated by a `ping` from PC4 to PC1 creates an infinite loop. Issue a `traceroute` to verify that a loop exists:

`PC4% traceroute 10.0.1.10`

You should observe that the traced path is a loop.

3. Start *ethereal* sessions on PC2, PC3, and PC4.

4. Issue a `ping` from PC4 to PC1 by typing

`PC4% ping -c 1 10.0.1.10`

Observe in *ethereal* that the same ICMP Echo Request message is looping.

5. Save the routing tables of Router2, Router3, and Router4. Count the number of times you see the ICMP Echo Request message, as captured by *ethereal* on PC4. Save at least two of these ICMP Echo Request messages for the lab report.

Lab Report

• Are the two ICMP packets that you saved identical? If not, what is different? Include the packet data in your lab report to substantiate your claims.

• Why does the ICMP Echo Request packet not loop forever in the network?

PART 7. NETMASKS AND ROUTING

In this exercise you study the role of *netmasks* when hosts determine whether a datagram can be directly delivered or if it must be sent to a router.

This part uses the network setup shown in Figure 3.4. The network includes one router, four hosts, and two hubs. The IP addresses of all devices are given in Table 3.5. Here, each host has only a default route. In other words, the routing table at a host knows about only the directly connected networks and the default gateway.

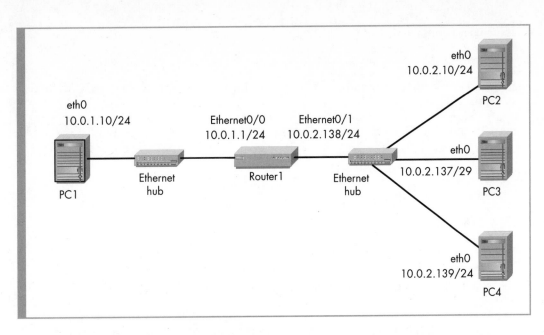

eth0
10.0.2.10/24
PC2

eth0
10.0.1.10/24   Ethernet0/0   Ethernet0/1
                      10.0.1.1/24   10.0.2.138/24

eth0
10.0.2.137/29
PC3

PC1   Ethernet   Router1   Ethernet
             hub   hub

eth0
10.0.2.139/24
PC4

FIGURE 3.4.
Network topology for Part 7.

TABLE 3.5. IP addresses for Part 7.

Linux PC	Interface *eth0*	Interface *eth1*
PC1	10.0.1.10/24	Disabled
PC2	10.0.2.10/24	Disabled
PC3	10.0.2.137/29	Disabled
PC4	10.0.2.139/24	Disabled
Cisco Router	**Interface *Ethernet0/0***	**Interface *Ethernet0/1***
Router1	10.0.1.1/24	10.0.2.138/24

EXERCISE 7.
Exploring the role of netmasks at hosts.

In this exercise, you explore how hosts that are connected to the same local area network, but that have different netmasks, communicate or fail to communicate.

1. Configure the hosts and the router to conform to the topology shown in Figure 3.4 using the IP addresses as given in Table 3.5.

   Note that PC2, PC3, and PC4 have different netmasks.

2. Add Router1 as the default gateway on all hosts. For example, for PC1, the command is

   ```
   PC1% route add default gw 10.0.1.1
   ```

3. Issue `ping` commands from PC1:

a. Clear the ARP table on all hosts.

b. Start *ethereal* on PC1 and on PC4, and set the capture filter to capture ICMP and ARP packets only.

c. Check the ARP table, routing table, and routing cache of each host. Save the output. (Make a note that these are the table entries from Step 2 *before* the `ping` is issued.)

d. Issue a `ping` command from PC1 to PC2 and PC3:

```
PC1% ping -c 2 10.0.2.10
PC1% ping -c 2 10.0.2.137
```

Save the ARP tables, routing tables, and routing caches of each host. (Make a note that these are the table entries from Step 2 *after* the `ping` commands are issued.)

e. Save the output of the `ping` command at PC1 and the output of *ethereal* on PC1 and PC4.

4. Issue a ping command from PC3 to PC4:

a. Clear the ARP table on all hosts.

b. Start *ethereal* on PC3 and set the capture filter to capture ICMP and ARP packets only.

c. Check the ARP table, routing table, and routing cache of each host. Save the output. (Make a note that these are the table entries from Step 3 *before* the `ping` is issued.)

d. Issue a `ping` from PC3 to PC4:

```
PC3% ping -c 3 10.0.2.139
```

e. Save the ARP table, routing table, and routing cache of PC3. (Make a note that these are the table entries from Step 3 *after* the `ping` is issued.)

f. Save the output of the `ping` command and the output of *ethereal* on PC3.

5. Repeat Step 4, but this time issue a `ping` from PC3 to PC2. Note that once an entry is made in the routing cache, you cannot repeat the previous experiment to obtain the same results; you have to wait until the routing cache is reset (which takes some time).

Lab Report

- Explain what you observed in Steps 3, 4, and 5. Use the saved data to support your answers. Provide explanations of the observations. Try to explain each observed phenomenon (e.g., if you observe more ICMP Echo Requests than ICMP Echo Replies, try to explain the reason).

- If PC3 had no default entry in its table, would you have seen the same results? Explain for each of the `ping`s what would have been different.

CHECKLIST FORM FOR LAB 3

Complete this checklist as you work through the laboratory exercises and attach the form to your lab report.

Name (please print):_____

☐ Prelab 3 question sheet

☐ Checkoff for Part 1

☐ Checkoff for Part 2

☐ Checkoff for Part 3

☐ Checkoff for Part 4

☐ Checkoff for Part 5

☐ Checkoff for Part 6

☐ Checkoff for Part 7

☐ Feedback sheet

☐ Lab report

FEEDBACK FORM FOR LAB 3

- Complete this feedback form at the completion of the lab exercises and submit the form when submitting your lab report.

- The feedback is anonymous. *Do not put your name on this form* and keep it separate from your lab report.

- For each exercise, please record the following:

	Difficulty (−2, −1, 0, 1, 2) −2 = too easy 0 = just right 2 = too hard	Interest Level (−2, −1, 0, 1, 2) −2 = low interest 0 = just right 2 = high interest	Time to Complete (minutes)
Part 1. Configuring a Linux PC as a router			
Part 2. Configuring a Cisco router			
Part 3. Finalizing and exploring the router configuration			
Part 4. Proxy ARP			
Part 5. ICMP route redirect			
Part 6. Routing loops			
Part 7. Netmasks and routing			

Please answer the following questions:

- What did you like about this lab?

- What did you dislike about this lab?

- Make a suggestion to improve the lab.

Dynamic Routing Protocols (RIP, OSPF, and BGP)

OBJECTIVES

- How to configure the routing protocols RIP, OSPF, and BGP on a Linux PC and a Cisco router

- How routing protocols converge after a change in the network topology

- How the count-to-infinity problem in RIP can be avoided

- How OSPF can perform hierarchical routing through the use of multiple areas

- How to set up and route traffic between autonomous systems with BGP

CONTENTS

PRELAB 4

1. **Distance vector and link state routing protocols:** Go to the website

   `http://www.tcpip-lab.net/links/routing.html`

   and read the article about dynamic routing protocols. Review your knowledge of interdomain and intradomain routing, distance vector routing, and link state routing.

2. *Zebra:* Go to the website of *Zebra* at

   `http://www.tcpip-lab.net/links/zebra.html`

   and study the information on the *Zebra* routing protocol software for Linux systems. Also read the documents on *zebra*, *ripd*, *ospfd*, and *bgpd* at

   `http://www.tcpip-lab.net/links/zebra_man.html`

3. **RIP:** Read the overview of the Routing Information Protocol (RIP) at

   `http://www.tcpip-lab.net/links/rip.html`

   Study the commands to configure RIP on a Cisco router at

   `http://www.tcpip-lab.net/links/ripconfigure.html`

4. **OSPF:** Read the overview of the Open Shortest Path First (OSPF) routing protocol at
   `http://www.tcpip-lab.net/links/ospf.html`

   Study the commands to configure OSPF on a Cisco router at

   `http://www.tcpip-lab.net/links/osfpconfigure.html`.

5. **BGP:** Read the overview of the Border Gateway Protocol (BGP) at

   `http://www.tcpip-lab.net/links/bgp.html`

   Study the commands to configure BGP on a Cisco router at

   `http://www.tcpip-lab.net/links/bgpconfigure.html`

QUESTION SHEET FOR PRELAB 4

Answer the questions in the space provided. Use extra sheets of paper if needed and attach them to this document. Submit your answers to the prelab with your lab report.

Name (please print):_____

1. Provide the command that configures a Linux PC as an IP router (see Lab 3).

2. What are the main differences between a distance vector routing protocol and a link state routing protocol? Give examples for each type of protocol.

3. What are the differences between an intradomain routing protocol (also called interior gateway protocol, or IGP) and an interdomain routing protocol (also called exterior gateway protocol, or EGP)? Give examples for each type of protocol.

4. Which routing protocols are supported by the software package Zebra?

5. In the *Zebra* software package, the processes *ripd*, *ospfd*, and *bgpd* deal, respectively, with the routing protocols RIP, OSPF, and BGP. Which role does the process *zebra* play?

6. Describe how a Linux user accesses the processes of *Zebra* (*zebra*, *ripd*, *ospfd*, *bgpd*) to configure routing algorithm parameters?

7. What is the main difference between RIP version 1 (RIPv1) and RIP version 2 (RIPv2)?

8. Explain what it means to *run RIP in passive mode*.

9. Explain the meaning of *triggered updates* in RIP.

10. Explain the concept of *split-horizon* in RIP?

11. What is an autonomous system (AS)? Which roles do autonomous systems play in the Internet?

12. What is the AS number of your institution? Which autonomous system has AS number 1?

13. Explain the terms *stub AS*, *multihomed AS*, and *transit AS*?

LAB 4

In the previous lab, you learned how to configure routing table entries manually. This was referred to as *static routing*. The topic of Lab 4 is *dynamic routing*, where *dynamic routing protocols* (from now on, called *routing protocols*) set the routing tables automatically without human intervention. Routers and hosts that run a routing protocol exchange routing protocol messages related to network paths and node conditions and use these messages to compute paths between routers and hosts.

Most routing protocols implement a shortest-path algorithm, which, for a given set of routers, determines the shortest paths between the routers. Some routing protocols allow that each network interface be assigned a *cost metric*. In this case, routing protocols compute paths with least cost. Based on the method used to compute the shortest or least-cost paths, one distinguishes distance vector and link state routing protocols. In a distance vector routing protocol, neighboring routers send the content of their routing tables to each other and update the routing tables based on the received routing tables. In a link state routing protocol, each router advertises the cost of each of its interfaces to all routers in the network. Thus, all routers have complete knowledge of the network topology and can locally run a shortest-path (or least-cost) algorithm to determine their own routing tables.

The notion of an *autonomous system* (AS) is central to the understanding of routing protocols on the Internet. An autonomous system is a group of IP networks under the authority of a single administration. The entire Internet is carved up into a large number of autonomous systems. Examples of autonomous systems are the campus network of a university and the backbone network of a global network service provider. Each autonomous system is assigned a globally unique identifier, called the *AS number*. On the Internet, dynamic routing within an autonomous system and between autonomous systems is handled by different types of routing protocols. A routing protocol that is concerned with routing within an autonomous system is called an *intradomain routing protocol* or *interior gateway protocol* (IGP). A routing protocol that determines routes between autonomous systems is called an *interdomain routing protocol* or *exterior gateway protocol* (EGP).

In this lab, you study the two most common intradomain protocols, namely, the Routing Information Protocol (RIP) and the Open Shortest Path First (OSPF) Protocol. Parts 1–4 of this lab deal with RIP, and Parts 5–6 are about OSPF. In Part 7, you are exposed to a few features of the Border Gateway Protocol (BGP), which is the interdomain routing protocol of the Internet.

SETUP FOR LAB 4

This lab uses three different network configurations. The first network configuration, shown in Figure 4.1, is used in Parts 1–2 and is modified in Part 3 (Figure 4.3) and again in Part 4 (Figure 4.4). The network configuration in Parts 5 and 6 is shown in Figures 4.5 and 4.6. The configuration for BGP in Part 7 is depicted in Figure 4.7.

> **RECALL:**
>
> - Before you get started, please reboot the Linux PCs.
> - During the lab, you need to save data to files. Save all files in the directory /labdata.
> - Save your files to a floppy disk before the end of the lab. You will need the files when you prepare your lab report.

PART 1. CONFIGURING RIP ON A CISCO ROUTER

This lab starts with the same network topology as used in Part 5 of Lab 3. Different from Lab 3, where the routing tables were configured manually, here you run the routing protocol RIP to perform the same task. In Part 1, you configure RIP on the Cisco routers. In Part 2, you configure RIP on the Linux PCs.

RIP is one of the oldest dynamic routing protocols on the Internet that is still in use. This lab uses the latest revision of RIP, RIPv2 (RIP version 2). RIP is an intradomain routing protocol that uses a distance vector approach to determine the paths between routers. RIP minimizes the number of hops of each path, where each point-to-point link or LAN constitutes a *hop*.

Each RIP-enabled router periodically sends the content of its routing table to all its neighboring routers in an update message. For each routing table entry, the router sends the destination (host IP address or network IP address) and the distance to that destination measured in hops. When a router receives an update message from a neighboring router, it updates its own routing table.

Figure 4.1 and Table 4.1 describe the network configuration for this part of the lab.

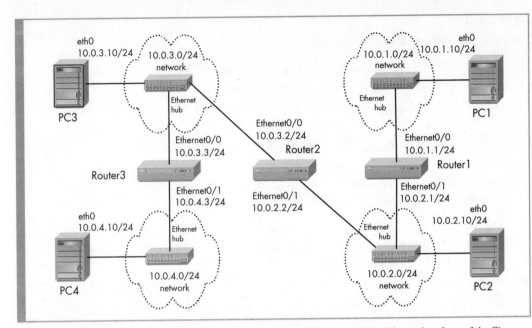

FIGURE 4.1.

Network topology for Parts 1 and 2.

Note: When Ethernet interfaces of the Linux PCs (*eth0, eth1*) run at 100 Mbps and the Ethernet interfaces of the Cisco routers (*Ethernet0/0, Ethernet0/1*) run at 10 Mbps, you should avoid using dual-speed hubs, when you connect two or more Cisco routers and one or more Linux PC to the same hub.

If you use dual-speed hubs in such a situation, the Linux PCs cannot observe the traffic between Cisco routers with *ethereal.*

TABLE 4.1. IP addresses of the Cisco routers and Linux PCs.

Linux PC	Ethernet Interface *eth0*	Ethernet Interface *eth1*
PC1	10.0.1.10/24	Disabled
PC2	10.0.2.10/24	Disabled
PC3	10.0.3.10/24	Disabled
PC4	10.0.4.10/24	Disabled
Cisco Router	**Ethernet Interface** **Ethernet0/0**	**Ethernet Interface** **Ethernet0/1**
Router1	10.0.1.1/24	10.0.2.1/24
Router2	10.0.3.2/24	10.0.2.2/24
Router3	10.0.3.3/24	10.0.4.3/24

EXERCISE 1.

Configuring RIP on Cisco routers.

Configure all three Cisco routers to run the routing protocol RIP. Once the configuration is completed, all Cisco routers can issue `ping` commands to one another. Following is a brief overview of the basic commands used to configure RIP on a Cisco router.

IOS MODE: GLOBAL CONFIGURATION

`router rip`

    Enables the routing protocol RIP on the local router and enters the router configuration mode with the following prompt:

    `Router1(config-router)#`

    You return from the router configuration command to the global configuration command by typing the command `exit`.

`no router rip`

    Disables RIP on the local router.

IOS MODE: PRIVILEGED EXEC

`debug ip rip`

    Enables a debugging mode where the router displays a message for each received RIP packet.

`no debug ip rip`

    Disables the debugging feature.

IOS MODE: ROUTER CONFIGURATION

`network Netaddr`

    Associates the network IP address `Netaddr` with RIP. RIP sends updates only on interfaces on which the network address has been associated with RIP.

`no network Netaddr`

    Disables RIP for the specified network address.

`passive-interface Iface`

    Sets the interface `Iface` in RIP passive mode. On an interface in passive mode, the router processes incoming RIP packets but does not transmit RIP packets.

`no passive-interface Iface`

    Enables active mode on interface `Iface`. This means that RIP packets are transmitted on this interface.

`offset-list 0 in value Iface`

    Increases the metric (hop count) of incoming RIP packets that arrive on interface `Iface` by `value`, where `value` is a number.

`offset-list 0 out value Iface`

    Increases the metric of outgoing RIP packets that are sent on interface `Iface` by `value`.

```
no offset-list 0 in value Iface
```
Disables the specified `offset-list` command for incoming RIP packets.

```
no offset-list 0 out value Iface
```
Disables the specified `offset-list` command for outgoing RIP packets.

```
version 2
```
Sets the RIP version to RIPv2.

```
timers basic update invalid hold-down flush
```
Sets the values of the timers in the RIP protocol. The timers are measured in seconds:

update	The time interval between transmissions of RIP update messages (default: 30 seconds).
invalid	The time interval after which a route, which has not been updated, is declared invalid (default: 180 seconds).
hold-down	Determines how long after a route has been updated as unavailable a router will wait before accepting a new route with a lower metric. This introduces a delay for processing incoming RIP packets with routing updates after a link failure (default: 180 seconds).
flush	The amount of time that must pass before a route that has not been updated is removed from the routing table (default: 240 seconds).

Example: `Router1(config-router)# timers basic 30 180 180 240`

```
flash-update-threshold time
```
Sets the router to not perform triggered updates, when the next transmission of routing updates is due in `time`. If `time` is set to the same value as the update timer, then triggered updates are disabled. In RIP, a triggered update means that a router sends a RIP packet with a routing update, whenever one of its routing table entries changes.

1. Connect the Linux PCs and the Cisco routers as shown in Figure 4.1. The PCs and routers are connected with Ethernet hubs.

2. Verify that the serial interfaces of the PCs are connected to the console port of the routers. PC1 should be connected to Router1, PC2 to Router2, and so on. Once the serial cables are connected, establish a *kermit* session from each PC to the connected router.

3. On Router1, Router2, and Router3, configure the IP addresses as shown in Table 4.1, and enable the routing protocol RIP. The commands to set up Router1 are as follows:

```
Router1> enable
Password: <enable secret>
Router1# configure terminal
Router1(config)# no ip routing
Router1(config)# ip routing
Router1(config)# router rip
Router1(config-router)# version 2
Router1(config-router)# network 10.0.0.0
Router1(config-router)# interface Ethernet0/0
```

```
Router1(config-if)# no shutdown
Router1(config-if)# ip address 10.0.1.1 255.255.255.0
Router1(config-if)# interface Ethernet0/1
Router1(config-if)# no shutdown
Router1(config-if)# ip address 10.0.2.1 255.255.255.0
Router1(config-if)# end
Router1# clear ip route *
```

The command no ip routing is used to reset all previous configurations related to routing (RIP, OSPF, etc.). The command clear ip route * deletes all entries in the routing table. Make sure that all static routing entries are removed, since, by default, RIP does not overwrite static routing entries in IOS.

4. After you have configured the routers, check the routing table at each router by typing

```
Router1# show ip route
```

Each router should have four entries in the routing table: two entries for directly connected networks and two other entries for remote networks that were added by RIP.

5. From each router, issue a ping command to the IP addresses of interfaces *Ethernet0/0* and *Ethernet0/1* on all remote routers. For example, to issue a ping from Router1 to interface *Ethernet0/0* on Router2, type

```
Router1# ping 10.0.3.2
```

Once you can successfully contact the IP addresses of all routers, proceed to the next exercise.

PART 2. CONFIGURING RIP ON A LINUX PC

In this part of the lab, you continue with the network configuration in Figure 4.1 and Table 4.1 and configure RIP on the Linux PCs.

In Figure 4.1, all Linux PCs are set up as hosts. Since hosts do not perform IP forwarding, they need not send routing messages. Therefore, when a routing protocol is configured on a host, the protocol is set to run in *passive mode*, in which a host receives and processes incoming routing messages but does not transmit routing messages. (We note that, normally, routing protocols are not enabled on hosts. Instead, one generally configures a static routing table entry for the *default gateway*. Obviously, when a routing protocol is enabled, there is no need to configure a default gateway.)

The configuration of routing protocols on Linux PCs in Lab 4 is done with the routing software package *Zebra*. Before starting the exercise, we give a brief tutorial on the *Zebra* software package. The tutorial focuses on the features used in the lab exercises and does not mention many interesting features of *Zebra*.

AN INTRODUCTION TO ZEBRA

Zebra is a software package that manages the routing tables of a Linux system and that provides the ability to execute a variety of routing protocols. The *Zebra* architecture, shown in Figure 4.2, consists of a set of processes. The process *zebra*[1] updates the routing tables and exchanges routes between different routing protocols. Each routing protocol has a separate process, and each routing process can be started, stopped, configured, and upgraded independently of the other routing processes. The process *zebra* must be invoked prior to starting and configuring any of the routing protocols. The routing processes used in this lab and the routing protocols they manage follows.

Routing process	Routing protocol
bgpd	BGP-4 (BGP version 4)
ripd	RIPv1 and RIPv2
ospfd	OSPFv2 (version 2)

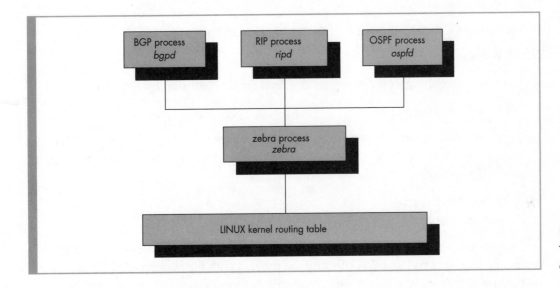

FIGURE 4.2.
The *Zebra* system architecture.

1. **Adding the directory with *Zebra* commands to the search path:** On Linux Red Hat systems, the commands to start, stop, and control the *zebra* process and its routing processes are located in directory */etc/rc.d/init.d*. For example, the command to start the process *zebra* is

```
PC1% /etc/rc.d/init.d/zebra start
```

To facilitate the use of *Zebra* commands, we recommend that you add the directory */etc/rc.d/init.d* to the search path of the shell. The search path contains the set of directories where the shell looks for commands to execute. In the *bash* shell, which

---

[1]We use capitalization to distinguish between the software package *Zebra* and the process *zebra*, which is a component of the *Zebra* software package.

is the default shell program in the Internet Lab, the directory is added to the search path with the command

```
PC1% export PATH=/etc/rc.d/init.d/:$PATH
```

If you are using a different shell, the command may be different. You can view the list of directories currently in the search path by typing

```
PC1% echo $PATH
```

In the following we assume that the directory with the *Zebra* commands has been added to the search path.

2. **Starting and stopping *Zebra* processes:** After you have added the directory to the search path, you can issue *Zebra*-related commands without typing the full pathname. For example, to start the *zebra* process, you simply type

```
PC1% zebra start
```

You can verify whether a *zebra* process is already running by typing

```
PC1% zebra status
```

You terminate the *zebra* process with the command

```
PC1% zebra stop
```

You can stop and restart the *zebra* process in a single command by typing

```
PC1% zebra restart
```

To set up a routing process, you must first start the *zebra* process and then start the routing protocol process. For example, to start the process that runs the RIP routing protocol, you type

```
PC1% zebra start
PC1% ripd start
```

As with the *zebra* process, you can query the status of the RIP process with the command `ripd status` and you can stop the process with the command `ripd stop`. When you type `zebra stop`, then all routing protocol processes are stopped as well.

For the *zebra* process and all other routing processes, a configuration file is read when the process is started. The configuration files are located in the directory */usr/local/etc* or */etc/zebra* and are named *zebra.conf*, *ripd.conf*, and so on. The configuration files look similar to the configuration files of IOS and contain commands that are executed when the process is started.

3. **Configuring the zebra process and the routing protocol processes:** After starting the *zebra* process or any of the routing protocol processes, you can configure each process by establishing a *Telnet* session to that process. Each process listens on a specific port for incoming requests to establish a *Telnet* session. The port numbers of the processes follow.

Routing process	TCP port number
zebra	2601
ripd	2602
ospfd	2604
bgpd	2605

If you establish a *Telnet* session to a routing process, you are asked for a password. If the password is correct, a command prompt is displayed. For example, to access the *ripd* process on the local host, you type

```
PC1% telnet localhost 2602
```

This results in the following output:

```
Trying 127.0.0.1...
Connected to 127.0.0.1 (127.0.0.1).
Escape character is '^]'.
Hello, this is zebra (version 0.93b).
Copyright 1996-2002 Kunihiro Ishiguro.
User Access Verification
Password: <enter password>
ripd>
```

At the prompt, you may type configuration commands. The *Telnet* session is terminated with the command

```
ripd> exit
```

4. **Typing configuration commands:** Once you have established a *Telnet* session to a routing process, you can configure the routing protocol of that process. The command line interface of the routing processes emulates the IOS command line interface; that is, the processes have similar command modes to IOS, and the syntax of commands is generally the same as the corresponding commands in IOS.

For example, the following commands configure the RIP routing protocol for network 10.0.0.0/8 on a Linux PC:

```
ripd> enable
ripd# configure terminal
ripd(config)# router rip
ripd(config-router)# version 2
ripd(config-router)# network 10.0.0.0/8
ripd(config-router)# end
ripd# exit
```

Here, in the default configuration of the *Zebra* processes, an enable password is not required.

After this brief tutorial, you can now complete the configuration of RIP on the Linux PCs.

EXERCISE 2.
Configuring RIP on Linux PCs with *Zebra*.

Enable RIP on all Linux PCs. Since all Linux PCs are running as hosts, RIP is set to passive mode, in which the PCs receive and process incoming RIP packets but do not transmit RIP packets. The following guidelines describe the configuration of PC1. Repeat the steps on each PC.

1. On PC1, add the directory */etc/rc.d/init.d* to the search path of the shell. Assuming that PC1 runs the bash shell, type the command

   ```
   PC1% export PATH=/etc/rc.d/init.d/:$PATH
   ```

   The command is different if you are running a different shell. If you do not change the search path, you need to add the full path name for each Zebra command; that is, instead of typing zebra and ripd, you need to type /etc/rc.d/init.d/zebra and /etc/rc.d/init.d/ripd.

2. On PC1, start the *zebra* and the *ripd* processes by typing

   ```
   PC1% zebra start
   PC1% ripd start
   ```

3. To configure the RIP routing process on PC1, connect to the *ripd* process via *Telnet*:

   ```
   PC1% telnet localhost 2602
   ```

   The system will prompt you for a login password. The password should be the same password as the login password on the Cisco routers.

4. The Linux PCs, which are configured as hosts, will be set to run RIP in *passive mode*. The commands to enable RIP in passive mode are as follows:

   ```
   ripd> enable
   ripd# configure terminal
   ripd(config)# router rip
   ripd(config-router)# version 2
   ripd(config-router)# network 10.0.0.0/8
   ripd(config-router)# passive-interface eth0
   ripd(config-router)# end
   ripd# show ip rip
   ```

   The show ip rip displays the routing database of the RIP protocol. This command does not exist in IOS. It may take a few minutes until RIP has built up its routing database. When the routing table has stabilized—that is, the results of the command show ip rip do not change after subsequent rounds of update messages—save the output of the command and exit the *Telnet* session with the command

   ```
   ripd# exit
   ```

5. On PC1, view the routing table with the command

   ```
   PC1% netstat -rn
   ```

   and save the output to a file.

- Compare the output of `netstat -rn` to the output of `show ip rip`. Note the cost metric for each entry.

6. Repeat Steps 1–5 for the other three Linux PCs.

7. Once you can successfully issue a `ping` from each Linux PC to every other Linux PC, display the route from PC1 to PC4 (10.0.4.10) with the `traceroute` command and save the result to a file.

   ```
   PC1% traceroute 10.0.4.10
   ```

8. Start to capture traffic with *ethereal* on all four Linux PCs. Set a capture filter or display filter to display only RIP packets.

   a. What is the destination IP address of RIP packets?

   b. Do routers forward RIP packets? In other words, does PC1 receive RIP packets sent by Router3?

   c. Which types of routing RIP messages do you observe? The type of a RIP message is indicated by the value of the field *command*. For each packet type that you observed, explain the role that this message type plays in the RIP protocol.

   d. A RIP message may contain multiple routing table entries. How many bytes are consumed in a RIP message for each routing table entry? Which information is transmitted for each message?

9. Stop the traffic *ethereal* capture on the PCs. Save the content of those RIP messages (select the *Print detail* option).

Lab Report

- Use the captured data of a single RIP packet and explain the fields in a RIP message.

- For PC1, include the output of the commands `show ip route` and `netstat -rn` from Steps 4 and 5. Discuss the differences in the output of the commands.

- Include the output of `traceroute` from Step 7.

- Answer the questions posed in Step 8. For each answer, include captured packets to support your answers.

PART 3. RECONFIGURING THE TOPOLOGY IN RIP

In Part 3, you add Router4 to the network topology of Figure 4.1. The configuration of the network with Router4 is illustrated in Figure 4.3. The IP configuration of Router4 is given in Table 4.2. The purpose of this exercise is to explore how RIP detects changes to the network topology and how long it takes until RIP updates the routing tables.

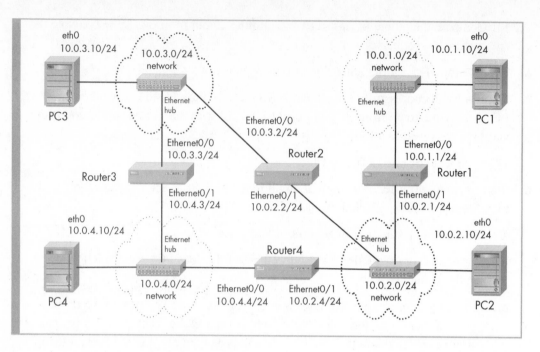

FIGURE 4.3.
Network topology
for Part 3.

TABLE 4.2. IP addresses of Router4.

Cisco Router	Ethernet Interface *Ethernet0/0*	Ethernet Interface *Ethernet0/1*
Router1	10.0.4.4/24	10.0.2.4/24

EXERCISE 3(A).
Updating the routing tables.

Add Router4 to the network and observe the routing table updates made by RIP to reflect the new topology.

1. Continue with the network configuration of Part 2. RIP must be enabled on all routers shown in Figure 4.1, and a RIP process must be running (in passive mode) on all Linux PCs.

 2. Before attaching Router4, save the routing tables on all four Linux PCs with the command `netstat -rn`.

3. Connect Router4 as shown in Figure 4.3 and assign the IP addresses to the interfaces as shown in Table 4.2.

4. Configure Router4 to run RIP, following the same steps as in Part 1.

 5. Use the command `netstat -rn` on the Linux PCs to observe how the routing tables are updated. Once the routing tables on the PCs have converged, save the routing tables on all four Linux PCs.

 Lab Report Include the routing tables of the Linux PCs before the topology was changed (Step 2) and after Router4 has been added and the routing tables have been updated (Step 5). Discuss the time it took to update the routing tables.

EXERCISE 3(B).
Convergence of RIP after a link failure.

Next you disconnect the Ethernet cable of interface *Ethernet0/0* on Router4 and observe how much time RIP takes to update the routing table of the Linux PCs to reflect the new topology.

1. Issue a `ping` command from PC4 to PC1. Do not terminate the `ping` command until this exercise is completed in Step 4.

```
PC4% ping 10.0.1.10
```

2. Disconnect the Ethernet cable connected to interface *Ethernet0/0* on Router4. Now, the output of `ping` on PC4 should show that the destination network is unreachable.

3. Wait until the `ping` command is successful again, that is, ICMP Echo Reply messages arrive at PC4. This occurs once an alternate path has been found between PC4 and PC1 and the routing tables have been updated accordingly. This may take several minutes.

4. Stop the `ping` command with Ctrl-C and save the `ping` statistics output (i.e., the data that appears at the bottom of the terminal screen when you stop the ping process).

- Count the number of lost packets and calculate the time it took RIP to update the routing tables. (The `ping` command issues an ICMP Echo Request message approximately once every second.)

Lab Report Include your answer on the convergence time from Step 4.

PART 4.   COUNT-TO-INFINITY PROBLEM IN RIP

Distance vector routing protocols, such as RIP, are susceptible to a convergence problem known as the *count-to-infinity* problem. This problem is a consequence of the fact that distance vector routing protocols exchange routing information only with their neighbors. Here, it may happen that, after the failure of a link, information about routes that use the failed link are propagated a long time after the failure has occurred. This results in a slow convergence of the routing tables. Each time the routers exchange RIP packets, the cost of a path that uses the failed link increases, but it takes a long time until all routers realize that routes through the failed link are unavailable.

The goal of this part of the lab is to observe the count-to-infinity problem. RIP has a number of protocol features that try to avoid the count-to-infinity problem. These features will be disabled. Still, since the count-to-infinity problem requires that routing updates occur in a certain order, the count-to-infinity problem is not always observable.

The network configuration is shown in Figure 4.4. Different from the network in Figure 4.3, PC3 is reconfigured and set up as an IP router. After the routing tables have converged, you disable the *eth1* interface on PC3. Following the upcoming steps, this may trigger the occurrence of the count-to-infinity problem.

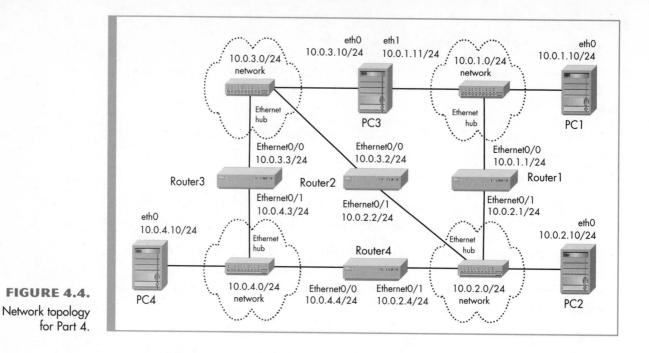

FIGURE 4.4.

Network topology
for Part 4.

EXERCISE 4(A).

Adding PC3 to the network configuration.

Configure PC3 as a RIP router, using the *Zebra* software package. The steps to configure
PC3 are almost the same as those to configure RIP on a Cisco router.

1. Connect the interface *eth1* of PC3 with an Ethernet cable as shown in Figure 4.4.
   Assign an IP address to interface *eth1* of PC3 as indicated in Table 4.3.

TABLE 4.3. IP addresses of the routers and Linux PCs for Part 4.

Linux PC	Ethernet Interface *eth0*	Ethernet Interface *eth1*
PC1	10.0.1.10/24	Disabled
PC2	10.0.2.10/24	Disabled
PC3	10.0.3.10/24	10.0.1.11/24
PC4	10.0.4.10/24	Disabled
Cisco Router	**Ethernet Interface Ethernet0/0**	**Ethernet Interface Ethernet0/1**
Router1	10.0.1.1/24	10.0.2.1/24
Router2	10.0.3.2/24	10.0.2.2/24
Router3	10.0.3.3/24	10.0.4.3/24
Router4	10.0.4.4/24	10.0.2.4/24

2. Restart the processes *zebra* and *ripd* on PC3:

```
PC3% zebra restart
PC3% ripd restart
```

3. On PC3, enable IP forwarding by typing

```
PC3% echo "1" > /proc/sys/net/ipv4/ip_forward
```

4. Establish a *Telnet* session to the *ripd* process using

```
PC3% telnet localhost 2602
```

Log in and issue the following commands, which enable RIP on both interfaces of PC3. Here, since PC3 is set up as an IP router and, therefore, must send RIP packets, the interfaces are enabled in active mode.

```
ripd> enable
ripd# configure terminal
ripd(config)# router rip
ripd(config-router)# version 2
ripd(config-router)# network 10.0.0.0/8
ripd(config-router)# no passive-interface eth0
ripd(config-router)# no passive-interface eth1
ripd(config-router)# redistribute connected
ripd(config-router)# end
ripd# exit
```

The command `redistribute connected` makes sure that the *ripd* process sends updates on its directly connected interfaces. This command is not needed on the Cisco routers.

5. On PC3, start to capture traffic with *ethereal* on both interfaces (*eth0* and *eth1*). Set a capture or display filter to limit the displayed traffic to RIP packets.

6. On PC1 and PC4 use the `netstat -rn` command to observe that the routing tables have been updated accordingly.

```
PC1% netstat -rn
PC4% netstat -rn
```

EXERCISE 4(B).
The count-to-infinity problem.

The goal of this exercise is to observe the effects of the count-to-infinity problem for routes to network 10.0.1.0/24. Note in Figure 4.4 that traffic to network 10.0.1.0/24 passes through either PC3 or Router1. First you ensure that traffic to network 10.0.1.0/24 always prefers the path through PC3. This is done by setting the link metric of the interface of Router1's network 10.0.1.0/24 to a large value. Then you disable the *eth1* interface of PC3. When the interface is disabled, the next update packet from PC3 will list the cost metric for network 10.0.1.0/24 as 16, which, in RIP, is interpreted as *infinity*. If this information is not distributed quickly, then the other routers in the network send RIP packets that assume that PC3 is still connected to network 10.0.1.0/24. For example, Router3 may still believe that it can reach network 10.0.1.0/24 in two hops. When such an update arrives at PC3, then PC3 wrongly assumes that it can reach network 10.0.1.0/24 via Router3 in three hops. In this situation, it may take the hosts and routers a very long time before they realize that the best path to network 10.0.1.0/24 is through Router1. This slow convergence of the routing tables is the count-to-infinity problem.

RIP has several protocol features that try to avoid the count-to-infinity problem. One of them, called *triggered updates*, forces a router to immediately issue a RIP update packet whenever the cost metric of a routing table entry changes. In the previous scenario, the link failure triggers an update message, which ensures that information about the link failure of PC3 is quickly propagated to all systems in the network. This prevents routers from continuing to advertise routes that are based on incorrect information about the network topology. Another feature that avoids count-to-infinity is the *hold-down* mechanisms. When a router receives information that a route is unavailable (i.e., has cost metric 16), it puts the route in a hold-down state. In this state, the router ignores routing updates that advertise a better cost metric for a certain period of time (which is given by the hold-down timer).

To increase the likelihood of the count-to-infinity problem occurring, it is necessary to disable triggered updates and to set the hold-down timer to 0. Still, it may happen that the count-to-infinity problem does not manifest itself, since the problem is dependent on the timing of RIP update messages between the routers. Repeating the exercise several times will eventually exhibit the count-to-infinity problem.

If the *hold-down timer* is set to h, then the RIP process ignores information about an improved route for h seconds, after a RIP update packet has been received that states that this route is not available. Setting the hold-down timer to 0 means that the RIP process immediately accepts updates to a route. The command to set the hold-down timer to 0 seconds is

```
Router1(config-router)# timers basic 30 180 0 240
```

The *triggered update* feature is controlled by setting the value of the flash-update-threshold timer. Suppose the timer is set to h. Then, whenever the metric of a routing table changes, the router sends a RIP update packet only if the next round of (regularly scheduled) update messages is more than h seconds away. Triggered updates are disabled by setting the flash-update-threshold timer to the same value as the update timer. Assuming that the update timer is set to the default value of 30 seconds, the command to disable triggered updates is

```
Router1(config-router) flash-update-threshold 30
```

---

1. On all Cisco routers, set the *hold-down timer* to 0 and disable *triggered updates*. The configuration for Router2 follows.

```
Router2> enable
Password: <enable secret>
Router2# configure terminal
Router2(config)# ip routing
```

```
Router2(config)# router rip
Router2(config-router)# version 2
Router2(config-router)# network 10.0.0.0
Router2(config-router)# timers basic 30 180 0 240
Router2(config-router)# flash-update-threshold 30
Router2(config-router)# end
Router2# clear ip route *
```

2. Next, you make routes to and from network 10.0.1.0/24 through Router1 unattractive by increasing the cost metric of interfaces *Ethernet0/0* and *Ethernet0/1* at Router1 to 10. This simulates a situation in which the hop count from Router1 to network 10.0.1.0/24 is 10 hops.

```
Router1# configure terminal
Router1(config)# router rip
Router1(config-router)# offset-list 0 out 10 Ethernet0/0
Router1(config-router)# offset-list 0 out 10 Ethernet0/1
Router1(config-router)# end
Router1# clear ip route *
```

3. Wait until the routing tables on all routers have converged. Since the cost of the interface on Router1 is set high, you should observe that the traffic from all hosts and routers to network 10.0.1.0/24 passes through PC3. This can be verified by issuing a `traceroute` (in Linux) or `trace` (in IOS) to IP address 10.0.1.10.

4. Start to capture traffic with *ethereal* on interface *eth0* of PC3. Set a display filter to display only RIP packets.

5. Issue a `ping` command from PC2 to PC1:

```
PC2% ping 10.0.1.10
```

6. On Router 3, enable the debugging mode of RIP. In this mode, the router displays all received RIP packets. The mode is enabled by typing

```
Router3# debug ip rip
```

You can disable the command by typing no `debug ip rip`.

7. On PC3, disable interface *eth1* to break the connection between PC3 and network 10.0.1.0. PC3 will send out a RIP packet indicating that the cost metric to network 10.0.1.0/24 is *infinity* (16).

```
PC3% ifconfig eth1 down
```

When the interface is disabled, the `ping`s from PC2 to PC1 will fail. The `ping` commands to PC1 are again successful, once the routing tables have converged.

8. Now you should observe the slow convergence of the routing tables due to the count-to-infinity problem, by observing the content of the RIP messages that are shown by *ethereal* on PC3 and by observing the debugging output on Router3.

> **NOTE:**
>
> If convergence occurs quickly—that is, count-to-infinity has not manifested itself—repeat the experiment. Reenable *eth1* on PC3 (with the command `ifconfig eth1 up`), wait for the routing tables to settle (see Step 3), and then repeat from Step 4. Since the count-to-infinity phenomenon depends on the sequence in which routers send update messages, you may have to repeat these steps a number of times.

9. Save the debug messages on Router3. Then disable RIP debugging on Router3:

```
Router3# no debug ip rip
```

10. Save the RIP packets (selecting the Print detail option) captured by *ethereal* on PC3. You need to save only the packets needed to explain the count-to-infinity problem.

Lab Report Use the saved RIP packets from Router3 and PC3 to describe the count-to-infinity problem in the preceding exercise. Include relevant fields from the saved RIP packets to illustrate your description.

EXERCISE 4(C).
Avoiding the count-to-infinity problem.

This exercise repeats Exercise 4(B), with the difference that triggered updates are enabled and the hold-down timer is set to a nonzero value. As a result, you observe that the count-to-infinity problem does not occur.

1. On Router1, enable triggered updates by setting the flash-update-threshold timer to 0, and by setting the hold-down timer to twice the value of the update timer. You can use the command `show ip protocols` to display the value of the update timer. If the update timer is set to the default value of 30 seconds, set the hold-down timer to 60 seconds. This is done with the following commands:

```
Router1# configure terminal
Router1(config)# router rip
Router1(config-router)# timers basic 30 180 60 240
Router1(config-router)# flash-update-threshold 0
Router1(config-router)# end
```

2. Repeat the previous commands on *all other routers*.

3. Now repeat Steps 3-9 from Exercise 4(B). You should observe that the count-to-infinity problem does not occur. In other words, if the connection between PC3 interface *eth1* and network 10.0.1.0/24 is broken, you should observe that the routing tables converge much faster.

Lab Report Use the output that you saved to show the differences between the outcomes of Exercise 4(B) and 4(C) with regard to the convergence of RIP.

PART 5. CONFIGURING OPEN SHORTEST PATH FIRST (OSPF)

Next, you explore the routing protocol Open Shortest Path First (OSPF). OSPF is a link state routing protocol, in which each router sends information on the cost metric of its network interfaces to all other routers in the network. The information about the interfaces is sent in messages that are called *link state advertisements* (LSAs). LSAs are disseminated using *flooding*; that is, a router sends its LSAs to all its neighbors, which, in turn, forward the LSAs to their neighbors and so on. However, each LSA is forwarded only once. Each router maintains a link state database of all received LSAs, which provides the router with complete information about the topology of the network. Routers use their link state databases to run a shortest-path algorithm that computes the shortest paths in the network.

Unlike distance vector routing protocols, link state routing protocols do not have convergence problems, such as the count-to-infinity problem. This is seen as a significant advantage of link state protocols over distance vector protocols.

OSPF is one of the most important link state routing protocols of the Internet. The functionality of OSPF is rich, and the lab exercises highlight only a small portion of the OSPF protocol. The Internet Lab uses OSPF version 2 (OSPFv2).

The network configuration is shown in Figure 4.5 and Table 4.4. Note that some Linux PCs and routers are connected with *crossover* cables.

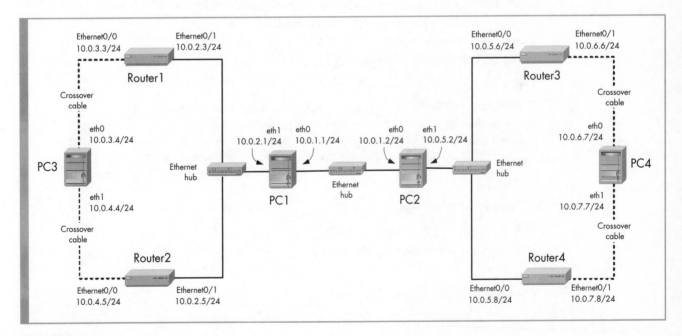

FIGURE 4.5.

Network topology for Part 5.

TABLE 4.4. IP addresses of the routers and Linux PCs for Part 5.

Linux PC	Ethernet Interface *eth0*	Ethernet Interface *eth1*
PC1	10.0.1.1/24	10.0.2.1/24
PC2	10.0.1.2/24	10.0.5.2/24
PC3	10.0.3.4/24	10.0.4.4/24
PC4	10.0.6.7/24	10.0.7.7/24
Cisco Router	**Ethernet Interface Ethernet0/0**	**Ethernet Interface Ethernet0/1**
Router1	10.0.3.3/24	10.0.2.3/24
Router2	10.0.4.5/24	10.0.2.5/24
Router3	10.0.5.6/24	10.0.6.6/24
Router4	10.0.5.8/24	10.0.7.8/24

EXERCISE 5(A).
Configuring OSPF on Cisco routers.

Here, you configure OSPF on the Cisco routers. A brief description of the basic IOS commands used to configure OSPF on a Cisco router follows. As usual, each command must be issued in a particular IOS command mode.

IOS MODE: GLOBAL CONFIGURATION

```
router ospf process-id
```
Enables an OSPF routing process. Each router can execute multiple OSPF processes. `process-id` is a number that identifies the process. In this lab, only one OSPF process is started per router, and the `process-id` value is always set to 1. (The process-id of a router does not need to be the same on all routers). The command enters the router configuration mode, which has the following command prompt:

```
Router1(config-router)#
```
```
no router ospf process-id
```
Disables the specified OSPF process.

IOS MODE: PRIVILEGED EXEC

```
show ip ospf
```
Displays general information about the OSPF configuration.

```
show ip ospf database
```
Displays the link state database.

```
show ip ospf border-routers
```

Displays the Area Border Router (ABR) and Autonomous System Boundary Router (ASBR).

```
clear ip ospf process-id process
```

Resets the specified OSPF process.

IOS MODE: ROUTER CONFIGURATION

```
network Netaddr InvNetmask area AreaID
```

Associates a network prefix with OSPF and associates an OSPF area to the network address. The prefix is specified with an IP address (`Netaddr`) and an inverse netmask (`InvNetmask`). For example, `Netaddr=10.0.0.0` and `InvNetmask=0.255.255.255` specify the network prefix 10.0.0.0/8. `AreaID` is a number that associates an area with the address range. `Area 0` is reserved to specify the *backbone area*.

Example: To run OSPF on Router1 for the address range 10.0.0.0/8 and assign it to Area 1, type

```
Router1(config-router)# network 10.0.0.0 0.255.255.255 area 1
```

```
no network Netaddr InvNetmask area AreaID
```

Disables OSPF for the specified network area.

```
passive-interface Iface
```

Sets interface `Iface` into passive mode. In passive mode, the router only receives and processes OSPF packets and does not transmit OSPF messages.

```
no passive-interface Iface
```

Sets interface `Iface` into active mode. In active mode, the router receives and transmits OSPF messages.

```
router-id IPaddress
```

Assigns the IP address `IPaddress` as the router identifier (`router-id`) of the local OSPF router. In OSPF, the `router-id` is used in LSA messages to identify a router. In IOS, by default, a router selects the highest IP address as the `router-id`. This command can be used to set the value explicitly.

1. Connect the routers as shown in Figure 4.5. Some of the interfaces are connected with crossover cables.

2. Configure the Cisco routers to run OSPF. The following commands are used to configure Router1:

```
Router1> enable
Password: <enable secret>
Router1# configure terminal
Router1(config)# no ip routing
Router1(config)# ip routing
Router1(config)# no router rip
```

```
Router1(config)# router ospf 1
Router1(config-router)# network 10.0.0.0 0.255.255.255 area 1
Router1(config-router)# interface Ethernet0/0
Router1(config-if)# ip address 10.0.3.3 255.255.255.0
Router1(config-if)# interface Ethernet0/1
Router1(config-if)# ip address 10.0.2.3 255.255.255.0
Router1(config-if)# end
Router1# clear ip route *
```

These commands disable RIP, enable OSPF for Area 1 and network 10.0.0.0/8, and configure the IP addresses of the routers. Since no router-id is specified, the highest IP address of Router1, 10.0.3.3, is used as the router-id. The router-id can be verified by issuing the command show ip ospf.

3. Repeat the configuration on the other routers. Refer to Figure 4.5 for the connections and to Table 4.4 for the IP addresses.

EXERCISE 5(B).
Configuring OSPF on Linux PCs.

On the Linux PCs, OSPF is configured using the *Zebra* package. The syntax of the *Zebra* commands is essentially identical to the corresponding IOS commands. All PCs are set up as IP routers. The following describes the configuration of PC1.

1. Connect PC1 as shown in Figure 4.5.

2. Enable IP forwarding on PC1 by typing

```
PC1% echo "1" > /proc/sys/net/ipv4/ip_forward
```

3. Terminate the existing *ripd* process:

```
PC1% ripd stop
PC1% ripd status
```

4. Restart *zebra* and start the *ospfd* process:

```
PC1% zebra restart
PC1% ospfd start
```

5. Set the OSPF configuration on PC1. Note that the commands for configuring OSPF in *Zebra* are very similar to the IOS commands.

```
PC1% telnet localhost 2604
Password: <login password>
ospfd> enable
ospfd# configure terminal
ospfd(config)# router ospf
ospfd(config-router)# network 10.0.0.0/8 area 1
ospfd(config-router)# router-id 10.0.1.1
ospfd(config-router)# no passive-interface eth0
```

```
ospfd(config-router)# no passive-interface eth1
ospfd(config-router)# end
ospfd# exit
```

Note that the command to enable OSPF (`router ospf`) does not use a process-id. Also, there is an explicit command to set the router-id. The latter is necessary since *Zebra* does not assign a default value for the router-id. In *Zebra*, the router-id must be explicitly set. In this exercise, we use the IP address of the Ethernet interface *eth0* as the router-id for the Linux PCs.

6. Repeat the OSPF configuration in Steps 1–5 for *all other* Linux PCs.

7. When the OSPF configuration is complete, all hosts and routers should be able to communicate with one another. You can test the network configuration by running `traceroute` and `ping` commands on a Linux PC (or `trace` and `ping` commands on a Cisco router). When you have verified that the network connection is correct, proceed with the next step.

EXERCISE 5(C).
Observing convergence of OSPF.

In comparison to the distance vector protocol RIP, the link state routing protocol OSPF quickly adapts to changes in the network topology. In this exercise, you observe the interactions of OSPF after a change to the network topology.

1. On PC1, start to capture traffic with *ethereal* on interface *eth0*. Set a filter to display only OSPF packets.

2. From PC3, run a `traceroute` command to PC4:

```
PC3% traceroute 10.0.7.7
```

Confirm from the output and Figure 4.5 whether the path from PC3 to PC4 includes Router3 or Router4.

3. Issue a `ping` command from PC3 to PC4 (10.0.7.7). Do not terminate the `ping` command until this exercise is completed.

```
PC3% ping 10.0.7.7
```

4. If the path from PC3 to IP address 10.0.7.7 from Step 2 included Router3, then disconnect the Ethernet cable of the *Ethernet0/1* interface of Router3. Otherwise, disconnect the Ethernet cable of the *Ethernet0/1* interface of Router4.

When the Ethernet cable is disconnected, the `ping` command on PC3 will show that IP address 10.0.7.7 is not reachable.

5. Now, OSPF updates the routing tables. Use the *ethereal* window on PC1 to observe the transmitted OSPF messages:

- How quickly are OSPF messages sent after the cable is disconnected?

- How many OSPF messages are sent?

- Which type of OSPF packet is used for flooding link state information?

- Describe the flooding of LSAs to all routers.

- Which type of encapsulation is used for OSPF packets (TCP, UDP, or other)?

- What is the destination address of OSPF packets?

6. Wait until the `ping` command is successful again, that is, ICMP Echo Reply messages arrive at PC3. This happens when the routing tables have been updated.

7. Stop the `ping` command with Ctrl-C and save the `ping` statistics output (i.e., the data that appears at the bottom of the terminal screen when you stop the `ping` process).

- Count the number of lost packets and calculate the time it took OSPF to update the routing tables. (The `ping` command issues an ICMP Echo Request message approximately once every second.)

8. Issue another `traceroute` command from PC3 to IP address 10.0.7.7. By now, the output should show the new route to PC4.

9. Save the link state database on all Cisco routers and on all Linux PCs, and verify that all routers indeed have the same link state database. On the Linux PCs, open a *Telnet* session to the *ospfd* process, and then type

```
ospfd# show ip ospf database
```

On the Cisco routers, simply type

```
Router1# show ip ospf database
```

Save the output of the link state databases to a file.

- Can you confirm that the link state databases are identical? Compare the output of the command `show ip ospf database` from the Cisco routers and the Linux PCs.

10. Stop *ethereal* on PC1, and save the different types of OSPF packets captured by *ethereal*. Save one copy of each type of OSPF packet that you observed (selecting the *Print detail* option).

Lab Report

- Include your answer on the convergence time from Step 7.

- From your saved *ethereal* output, include one packet from each of the different OSPF packet types that you have observed. (Include only one packet from each type!)

- Include the output of the link state database of PC2.

- Pick a single link state advertisement packet captured by *ethereal*, and describe how to interpret the information contained in the link state advertisement.

- Answer the questions from Steps 5 and 9.

PART 6. HIERARCHICAL ROUTING IN OSPF

The concept of *areas* in OSPF can be used to construct a hierarchical routing scheme. When the network is partitioned into multiple areas, then routers must have complete topology information only about routers in the same area and only limited information about other areas. All areas must be connected to Area 0, which is a special area called the *backbone area*. This builds a two-level hierarchy: The backbone area is at the top of the hierarchy and the other areas are at the bottom of the hierarchy. Traffic between two areas is routed through the backbone area. Routers that connect to two areas are called *area border routers*.

The configuration in this part is shown in Figure 4.6. Here, the network from Part 5 is partitioned into three areas. The area in the middle is the backbone area (*Area 0*). The IP addresses are the same as in Part 5 and need not be modified. PC1 and PC2 are area border routers.

In the following exercises, you define the areas and then observe how the link state databases are built.

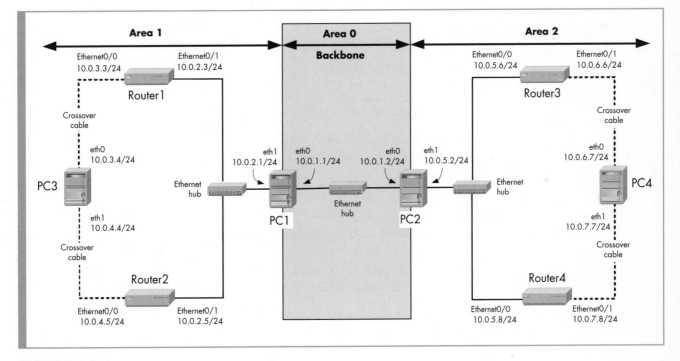

FIGURE 4.6.

Network topology for Part 6.

EXERCISE 6.
Defining multiple areas in OSPF.

1. Restart the *zebra* and *ospfd* processes *on all four* Linux PCs.

```
PC1% zebra restart
PC1% ospfd restart
```

2. Start *ethereal* on PC1 and capture traffic on interface *eth0*.

3. Change the Area IDs of the Cisco routers and the PCs. On each system, the directly connected networks are assigned to an area with a 24 bit prefix. Here are the configurations for PC3, PC1, and Router1. The other configurations are similar.

   PC3, which belongs to only one area, is configured as follows:

```
PC3% telnet localhost 2604
Password: <login password>
ospfd> enable
ospfd# configure terminal
ospfd(config)# router ospf
ospfd(config-router)# router-id 10.0.3.4
ospfd(config-router)# network 10.0.3.0/24 area 1
ospfd(config-router)# network 10.0.4.0/24 area 1
ospfd(config-router)# end
ospfd# exit
```

   PC1 belongs to two areas and is configured as follows:

```
PC1% telnet localhost 2604
Password: <login password>
ospfd> enable
ospfd# configure terminal
ospfd(config)# router ospf
ospfd(config-router)# router-id 10.0.1.1
ospfd(config-router)# network 10.0.2.0/24 area 1
ospfd(config-router)# network 10.0.1.0/24 area 0
ospfd(config-router)# end
ospfd# exit
```

   The configuration of Router1 is as follows:

```
Router1# configure terminal
Router1(config)# no router ospf 1
Router1(config)# router ospf 1
Router1(config-router)# network 10.0.3.0 0.0.0.255 area 1
Router1(config-router)# network 10.0.2.0 0.0.0.255 area 1
Router1(config-router)# end
Router1# clear ip ospf 1 process
```

Once the routing tables have converged, test the network configuration with the commands `traceroute` and `ping` on the Linux PCs and the commands `trace` and `ping` on the Cisco routers. All hosts and routers should be able to communicate with one another.

4. Save the link state database on all Cisco routers and on all Linux PCs. On the Linux PCs, open a *Telnet* session to the *ospfd* process, and then type

```
ospfd# show ip ospf database
```

On the Cisco routers, type

```
Router1# show ip ospf database
```

Save the output of the link state databases to a file.

- Compare the link state databases to those saved in Part 5. Which differences do you note?

- Which information do routers in Area 1 have about Area 2? Which information do they have about the backbone area (Area 0)?

- How much information do the routers in the backbone area (Area 0) have about the topology of Area 1 and Area 2?

- How do the IP routers in Area 1 know how to forward traffic to Area 2?

5. Display the area routers known to Router1 from Area 1, with the command

```
Router1# show ip ospf border-routers
```

Save the output to a file.

6. Save the *ethereal* output of OSPF packet types (selecting the *Print detail* option) that you did not observe in Part 4. Include only one packet of each type.

Lab Report

- Include the *ethereal* output in your report showing, if any, the different types of OSPF packets that you did not observe in Part 5.

- Include the output of the link state databases saved in Step 5.

- Include answers to the questions from Step 5. Refer to the saved link state databases in your answers.

- Explain the output of the command `show ip ospf border-routers` in Step 5.

PART 7. CONFIGURING THE BORDER GATEWAY PROTOCOL (BGP)

The last part of this lab provides some exposure to the interdomain Border Gateway Protocol (BGP), which determines paths between autonomous systems on the Internet. The exercises in this lab cover only the basics of BGP. Essentially, you learn how to set up an autonomous system and observe BGP traffic between autonomous systems. BGP uses a path vector algorithm, where routers exchange full path information of a route. An important feature of BGP is that it can define *routing policies*, which can be used by a network to specify which type of traffic it is willing to process. The current version of BGP, which is also used in the following exercise, is BGP version 4 (BGP-4).

The network configuration for this part is shown in Figure 4.7, and the IP configuration information is given in Table 4.5. The network has three autonomous systems with AS numbers 100, 200, and 300. One Linux PC, PC4, is used to capture the BGP packets transmitted between the ASs.

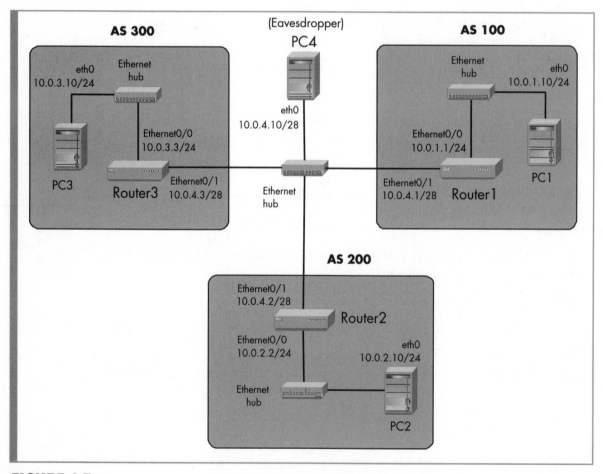

FIGURE 4.7.

Network topology for Part 7.

TABLE 4.5. IP addresses of the routers and Linux PCs for Part 7.

Linux PC	Ethernet Interface *eth0*	Ethernet Interface *eth1*
PC1	10.0.1.10/24	Disabled
PC2	10.0.2.10/24	Disabled
PC3	10.0.3.10/24	Disabled
PC4	10.0.4.10/28	Disabled
Cisco Router	**Ethernet Interface** *Ethernet0/0*	**Ethernet Interface** *Ethernet0/1*
Router1	10.0.1.1/24	10.0.4.1/28
Router2	10.0.2.2/24	10.0.4.2/28
Router3	10.0.3.3/24	10.0.4.3/28

EXERCISE 7(A).
Basic BGP configuration.

Here, you configure the Cisco routers as BGP routers and you assign routers to
autonomous systems. The configuration is completed when you can issue `ping` commands between any two Linux PCs.

Next we summarize the Cisco IOS commands that are used to enable BGP.

IOS MODE: GLOBAL CONFIGURATION

`router bgp ASnumber`

Enables the BGP routing protocol and sets the autonomous system number to
ASnumber. The command enters the router configuration mode with the following
prompt:

`Router1(config-router)#`

`no router bgp ASnumber`

Disables the BGP routing process.

IOS MODE: PRIVILEGED EXEC

`show ip bgp`

Displays the BGP routing table.

`show ip bgp neighbors`

Displays the neighbors, also called *peers*, of this BGP router.

`show ip bgp paths`

Displays the BGP path information in the local database.

`clear ip bgp *`

Deletes BGP routing information.

IOS MODE: ROUTER CONFIGURATION

```
network Netaddr
network Netaddr mask netmask
```

Specifies a network address that will be advertised by the local BGP process. A network mask may be added to denote the length of the network prefix.

```
neighbor IPaddress remote-as ASnumber
```

Adds a neighbor to the BGP neighbor table. *IPaddress* is the IP address and *ASnumber* is the AS number of the neighbor.

```
timers bpg keepalive holdtime
```

Sets the values of the *keepalive* and *holdtime* timers of the BGP process. BGP routers exchange periodic messages to confirm that the connection between the routers is maintained. The interval between these messages is *keepalive* seconds (default: 60 seconds). The number of seconds that a BGP router waits for any BGP message before it decides that a connection is down is specified by the holdtime (default: 180 seconds).

---

1. Disable all RIP or OSPF processes that are running on the Cisco routers and the Linux PCs. On the routers, this is done with the following commands:

   ```
   Router1# no router ospf 1
   Router1# no router rip
   ```

   On the Linux PCs, stopping the *zebra* process terminates all routing protocols:

   ```
   PC1% zebra stop
   ```

2. Assign the IP address to Ethernet interface *eth0* of each Linux PC as indicated in Table 4.5.

3. Add a default gateway to PC1, PC2, and PC3, as follows:

   ```
   PC1% route add default gw 10.0.1.1
   PC2% route add default gw 10.0.2.2
   PC3% route add default gw 10.0.3.3
   ```

4. Start *ethereal* on PC4 and set a display filter to capture only BGP packets.

5. Configure the Cisco routers to run BGP with the autonomous system numbers shown in Figure 4.7. The routers must know the AS number of their neighbors. Following is the configuration for Router2. Router2 is in AS 200 and has neighbors in AS 100 and AS 300.

   ```
   Router2> enable
   Password: <enable secret>
   Router2# configure terminal
   Router2(config)# no ip routing
   Router2(config)# ip routing
   Router2(config)# interface Ethernet0/0
   Router2(config-if)# no shutdown
   Router2(config-if)# ip address 10.0.2.2 255.255.255.0
   ```

```
Router2(config-if)# interface Ethernet0/1
Router2(config-if)# no shutdown
Router2(config-if)# ip address 10.0.4.2 255.255.255.240
Router2(config-if)# router bgp 200
Router2(config-router)# neighbor 10.0.4.1 remote-as 100
Router2(config-router)# neighbor 10.0.4.3 remote-as 300
Router2(config-router)# network 10.0.2.0 mask 255.255.255.0
Router2(config-router)# end
Router2# clear ip bgp *
```

6. On PC1, issue a `ping` command to PC3:

```
PC1% ping 10.0.3.10
```

The command succeeds when BGP has converged.

7. Once the routing tables have converged, you see all the other AS entries in the BGP routing table. On each Cisco router, save the output of the following commands:

```
Router1# show ip route
Router1# show ip bgp
Router1# show ip bgp paths
```

- Describe the different types of BGP messages that you observe in the *ethereal* window on PC4.

- Notice that BGP transmits messages over *TCP* connections. What is a reason that BGP uses *TCP* to transmit its messages?

- What is the IP address of the next-hop attribute for AS 100 on Router2?

- What are the BGP peers in this topology?

8. Stop the *ethereal* traffic capture on PC4 and save the BGP packets captured by *ethereal* (selecting the *Print detail* option).

Lab Report

- Provide answers to the questions in Step 7.

- Which BGP message(s) contain(s) the AS-PATH information? Include a BGP message to illustrate your answer.

- Use the saved output to provide a brief explanation of how the routers find the proper path between the autonomous systems.

EXERCISE 7(B).
BGP convergence.

Disconnect one of the links between two BGP peers and observe how the BGP protocol reconfigures the paths.

1. After completing Exercise 7(A), save the output of the command `show ip bgp neighbors` on Router2. Pay attention to the *neighbor AS* information.

2. On PC4, run *ethereal* and set a display filter for BGP. Observe the flow of BGP packets between the autonomous systems.

3. On all routers, change the keepalive timer to 10 seconds and the holdtime timer to 30 seconds. This speeds up the convergence time by a factor of 6 as compared to the default values. The following are the commands for Router2:

```
Router2# configure terminal
Router2(config)# router bgp 200
Router2(config-router)# timers bgp 10 30
Router2(config-router)# end
Router2# clear ip bgp *
```

4. Disconnect the cable of interface *Ethernet0/1* on Router1.

   - From the output you saved, describe how the BGP routers learn that a link is down. (Hint: Look at the *BGP State* field.)

   - Which BGP messages indicate that there is a link problem? Include a BGP message.

5. Use the command show ip bgp neighbors on Router2 and Router3 to obtain the neighbor information. Save the output.

6. Wait until BGP converges. Save the routing tables on Router2 and Router3.

7. Stop the *ethereal* traffic captured on PC4 and save the *ethereal* BGP packets (selecting the *Print detail* option).

Lab Report Include the answers to the questions in Step 4.

CHECKLIST FORM FOR LAB 4

Complete this checklist as you work through the laboratory exercises and attach the form to your lab report.

Name (please print):_____

- [ ] Prelab 4 question sheet
- [ ] Checkoff for Part 1
- [ ] Checkoff for Part 2
- [ ] Checkoff for Part 3
- [ ] Checkoff for Part 4

- [ ] Checkoff for Part 5
- [ ] Checkoff for Part 6
- [ ] Checkoff for Part 7
- [ ] Feedback sheet
- [ ] Lab report

FEEDBACK FORM FOR LAB 4

- Complete this feedback form at the completion of the lab exercises and submit the form when submitting your lab report.

- The feedback is anonymous. *Do not put your name on this form* and keep it separate from your lab report.

- For each exercise, please record the following:

	Difficulty (–2, –1, 0, 1, 2)	Interest Level (–2, –1, 0, 1, 2)	Time to Complete (minutes)
	–2 = too easy 0 = just right 2 = too hard	–2 = low interest 0 = just right 2 = high interest	
Part 1. Configuring RIP on a Cisco router			
Part 2. Configuring RIP on a Linux PC			
Part 3. Reconfiguring the topology in RIP			
Part 4. Count-to-infinity problem in RIP			
Part 5. Configuring Open Shortest Path First (OSPF)			
Part 6. Hierarchical routing in OSPF			
Part 7. Configuring the Border Gateway Protocol (BGP)			

Please answer the following questions:

- What did you like about this lab?

- What did you dislike about this lab?

- Make a suggestion to improve the lab.

Transport Layer Protocols: UDP and TCP

OBJECTIVES

- The differences between data transfers with UDP and with TCP

- What effect IP fragmentation has on TCP and UDP

- How to analyze measurements of a TCP connection

- The difference between interactive and bulk data transfers in TCP

- How TCP performs retransmissions

- How TCP congestion control works

CONTENTS

PRELAB 5

1. **ttcp:** Go to the online manual pages at

   `http://www.tcpip-lab.net/links/manual.html`

   and select the OS version Red Hat Linux/i386 7.3. Read the manual pages of the following commands:

   - `ttcp`
   - `import`

2. **TCP and UDP:** Read the overview of TCP and UDP available at

   `http://www.tcpip-lab.net/links/tcpudp.html`.

3. **IP fragmentation:** Refer to the website

   `http://www.tcpip-lab.net/links/ipfragment.html`

   for information on IP fragmentation and Path MTU Discovery.

4. **TCP retransmissions:** Refer to RFC 2988, which is available at

   `http://www.tcpip-lab.net/links/rfc2988.html`

   and read about TCP retransmissions.

5. **TCP congestion control:** Refer RFC 2001, which is available at

   `http://www.tcpip-lab.net/links/rfc2001.html`

   and read about TCP congestion control.

QUESTION SHEET FOR PRELAB 5

Answer the questions in the space provided below each one. Use extra sheets of paper if needed and attach them to this document. Submit the answers to the prelab with your lab report.

Name (please print):_____

1. Explain the role of port numbers in TCP and UDP.

2. Provide the syntax of the `ttcp` command for both the sender and receiver, which executes the following scenario:

    A TCP server has IP address 10.0.2.6 and a TCP client has IP address 10.0.2.7. The TCP server is waiting on port number 2222 for a connection request. The client connects to the server and transmits 2000 bytes to the server, which are sent as four write operations of 500 bytes each.

3. Answer the following questions on Path MTU Discovery:

    a. How does TCP decide the maximum size of a TCP segment?

    b. How does UDP decide the maximum size of a UDP datagram?

    c. What is the ICMP error generated by a router when it needs to fragment a datagram with the DF bit set? Is the MTU of the interface that caused the fragmentation also returned?

    d. Explain why a TCP connection over an Ethernet segment never runs into problems with fragmentation.

4. Assume a TCP sender receives an acknowledgment (ACK)—that is, a TCP segment with the ACK flag set—in which the acknowledgment number is set to 34567 and the window size is set to 2048. Which sequence numbers can the sender transmit?

5. Describe the following heuristics used in TCP and explain why they are used:

   a. Nagle's algorithm

   b. Karn's algorithm

6. Answer the following questions about TCP acknowledgments:

   a. What is a *delayed acknowledgment*?

   b. What is a *piggybacked acknowledgment*?

7. Describe how the retransmission timeout (RTO) value is determined in TCP.

8. Answer the following questions on TCP flow control and congestion control:

   a. Describe the sliding window flow control mechanism used in TCP.

   b. Describe the concepts of *slow start* and *congestion avoidance* in TCP.

   c. Explain the concept of *fast retransmit* and *fast recovery* in TCP.

LAB 5

This lab explores the operation of the Transmission Control Protocol (TCP) and the User Datagram Protocol (UDP), the two transport protocols of the Internet protocol architecture.

UDP is a simple protocol for exchanging messages from a sending application to a receiving application. UDP adds a small header to the message, and the resulting data unit is called a *UDP datagram*. When a UDP datagram is transmitted, the datagram is encapsulated in an IP header and delivered to its destination. There is one UDP datagram for each application message.

The operation of TCP is more complex. First, TCP is a connection-oriented protocol, in which a TCP client establishes a logical connection to a TCP server before data transmission can take place. Once a connection is established, data transfer can proceed in both directions. The data unit of TCP, called a *TCP segment*, consists of a TCP header and payload that contains application data. A sending application submits data to TCP as a single stream of bytes without indicating message boundaries in the byte stream. The TCP sender decides how many bytes are put into a segment.

TCP ensures reliable delivery of data, and uses checksums, sequence numbers, acknowledgments, and timers to detect damaged or lost segments. The TCP receiver acknowledges the receipt of data by sending an acknowledgment segment (ACK). Multiple TCP segments can be acknowledged in a single ACK. When a TCP sender does not receive an ACK, the data is assumed lost and is retransmitted.

TCP has two mechanisms that control the amount of data that a TCP sender can transmit. First, the TCP receiver informs the TCP sender how much data the TCP sender can transmit. This is called *flow control*. Second, when the network is overloaded and TCP segments are lost, the TCP sender reduces the rate at which it transmits traffic. This is called *congestion control*.

The lab covers the main features of UDP and TCP. Parts 1 and 2 compare the performance of data transmissions in TCP and UDP. Part 3 explores how TCP and UDP deal with IP fragmentation. The remaining parts address important components of TCP. Part 4 explores connection management, Parts 5 and 6 look at flow control and acknowledgments, Part 7 explores retransmissions, and Part 8 is devoted to congestion control.

SETUP FOR LAB 5

This lab has two different network topologies. The topology for Parts 1–4 is shown in Figure 5.1. In this configuration, PC1 and PC2 are used as hosts, and PC3 is set up as an IP router. The network configuration for Parts 5–8 is shown in Figure 5.2. Here, the four Cisco routers interconnected via Ethernet and serial WAN links are as shown in Figure 5.2.

RECALL:

- Before you get started, please reboot the Linux PCs.
- During the lab, you need to save data to files. Save all files in the directory /labdata.
- Save your files to a floppy disk before the end of the lab. You will need the files when you prepare your lab report.

PART 1. LEARNING HOW TO USE TTCP

The `ttcp` command is a Linux tool used to generate synthetic UDP and TCP traffic loads. Together with `ping` and `traceroute`, `ttcp` is an essential utility program for debugging problems in IP networks. Running the *ttcp* tool consists of setting up a *ttcp* receiver on one host and then a *ttcp* sender on another host. Once the *ttcp* sender is started, it blasts the specified amount of data as fast as possible to the *ttcp* receiver.

A ttcp receiver process is started with the command

`ttcp -rs[-lbuflen][-nnumbufs][-pport][-u]`

A ttcp sender process is started with the command

`ttcp -ts[-lbuflen][-nnumbufs][-pport][-u][-D] IPaddress`

The options of the command are:

`-t`	Specifies the transmit mode.
`-r`	Specifies the receive mode.
`-u`	Specifies to use UDP instead of TCP. By default, *ttcp* uses TCP to send data.
`-s`	Sends a character string as payload of the transmitted packets. Without the `-s` option, the default is to transmit data from the terminal window (*stdin*) of the sender and to print the received data to the terminal window (*stdout*) at the receiver.
`-nnumbufs`	Number of blocks of application data to be transmitted (default value is 2048).
`-lbuflen`	Length of the application data blocks that are passed to UDP or TCP in bytes (default is 8192). When UDP is used, this value is the number of data bytes in UDP datagram.
`-D`	Disables buffering of data in TCP and forces immediate transmission of the data at the *ttcp* sender. Used only in the context of TCP.
`-pport`	Port number to send to or listen on. The port number must be identical at the sender and at the receiver. The default value is 5000.
`IPaddress`	IP address of the *ttcp* receiver.

By default, *ttcp* transmits data over a TCP connection. The *ttcp* sender opens a TCP connection to a *ttcp* receiver, transmits data, and then closes the connection. The *ttcp* receiver must be running when the *ttcp* sender is started. UDP data transfer is specified with the –u option. Since UDP is a connectionless protocol, the *ttcp* sender starts immediately sending UDP datagrams, regardless of whether a *ttcp* receiver is established.

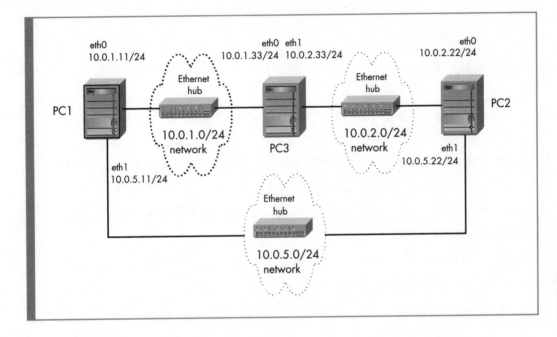

FIGURE 5.1.
Network topology for Parts 1–4.

TABLE 5.1. IP addresses of the Linux PCs.

Linux PC	Ethernet Interface *eth0*	Ethernet Interface *eth1*
PC1	10.0.1.11/24	10.0.5.11/24
PC2	10.0.2.22/24	10.0.5.22/24
PC3	10.0.1.33/24	10.0.2.33/24

EXERCISE 1(A).
Network setup.

1. Connect the Ethernet interfaces of the Linux PCs as shown in Figure 5.1. Configure the IP addresses of the interfaces as given in Table 5.1.

2. PC1 and PC2 are set up as hosts, and IP forwarding should be disabled. On PC1, this is done with the command

   ```
   PC1% echo "0" > /proc/sys/net/ipv4/ip_forward
   ```

3. PC3 is set up as an IP router. Enable IP forwarding on PC3 with the command

   ```
   PC3% echo "1" > /proc/sys/net/ipv4/ip_forward
   ```

4. Add default routes to the routing tables of PC1 and PC2, so that PC3 is the default gateway. For PC1 the command is as follows:

```
PC1% route add default gw 10.0.1.33
```

5. Verify that the setup is correct by issuing a `ping` command from PC1 to PC2 over both paths:

```
PC1% ping 10.0.2.22
PC1% ping 10.0.5.22
```

EXERCISE 1(B).
Transmitting data with UDP.

This exercise consists of setting up a UDP data transfer between two hosts, PC1 and PC2, and observing the UDP traffic.

1. On PC1, start *ethereal* to capture packets on interface *eth1* between PC1 and PC2:

```
PC1% ethereal -i eth1 -f "host 10.0.5.22"
```

This sets a capture filter to packets that include IP address 10.0.5.22 in the IP header. Start to capture traffic.

2. On PC2, start a *ttcp* receiver that receives UDP traffic with the following command:

```
PC2% ttcp -rs -l1024 -n10 -p4444 -u
```

3. On PC1, start a *ttcp* sender that transmits UDP traffic by typing

```
PC1% ttcp -ts -l1024 -n10 -p4444 -u 10.0.5.22
```

Observe the captured traffic captured by *ethereal*.

- How many packets are exchanged in the data transfer? How many packets are transmitted for each UDP datagram? What is the size of the UDP payload of these packets?

- Compare the total number of bytes transmitted, in both directions, including Ethernet, IP, and UDP headers, to the amount of application data transmitted.

- Inspect the fields in the UDP headers. Which fields in the headers do not change in different packets?

- Observe the port numbers in the UDP header. How did the *ttcp* sender select the source port number?

4. Stop the *ethereal* capture on PC1 and save the captured traffic. Go to the Print menu and save both the summary (*Print summary*) and the details (*Print detail*) of the traffic to files.

Lab Report Use the data captured with *ethereal* to answer the questions in Step 3. Support your answers with the saved *ethereal* data.

EXERCISE 1(C).
Transmitting data with TCP.

Here, you repeat the previous exercise, but use TCP for data transfer.

1. On PC1, start *ethereal* and capture packets on interface *eth1* between PC1 and PC2:

```
PC1% ethereal -i eth1 -f "host 10.0.5.22"
```

2. Start a *ttcp* receiver on PC2 that receives packets sent by PC1:

```
PC2% ttcp -rs -l1024 -n10 -p4444
```

3. Start a *ttcp* sender on PC1 that transmits packets from PC1 to PC2:

```
PC1% ttcp -ts -l1024 -n10 -p4444 -D 10.0.5.22
```

- How many packets are exchanged in the data transfer? What are the sizes of the TCP segments?

- What is the range of the sequence numbers?

- How many packets are transmitted by PC1, and how many packets are transmitted by PC2?

- How many packets do not carry a payload, that is, how many packets are control packets?

- Compare the total number of bytes transmitted, in both directions, including Ethernet, IP, and UDP headers, to the amount of application data transmitted.

- Inspect the TCP headers. Which packets contain flags in the TCP header? Which types of flags do you observe?

4. Stop the *ethereal* capture on PC1, and save the captured traffic to files. Save both the summary and detail output in the *Print* menu.

Lab Report

- Use the data captured with *ethereal* to answer the questions in Step 3. Support your answers by including data from the saved *ethereal* data captures.

- Compare the amount of data transmitted in the TCP and the UDP data transfers.

- Take the biggest UDP datagram and the biggest TCP segment that you observed, and compare the amount of application data that is transmitted in the UDP datagram and the TCP segment.

PART 2. FILE TRANSFERS USING TCP AND UDP

Here you compare the throughput of a file transfer with TCP and UDP, using the application programs *FTP* and *TFTP*.

The File Transfer Protocol (*FTP*) for copying files between hosts, as described in the Introduction, employs TCP as its transport protocol, thereby ensuring a reliable transfer of transmitted data. Two TCP connections are established for each *FTP* session: a control connection for exchanging commands and a data connection for the file transfer.

The Trivial File Transfer Protocol (*TFTP*) is a minimal protocol for transferring files without authentication. *TFTP* employs UDP for data transport. A *TFTP* session is initiated when a *TFTP* client sends a request to upload or download a file to UDP port 69 of a *TFTP* server. When the request is received, the *TFTP* server picks a free UDP port and uses this port to communicate with the *TFTP* client. Since UDP does not recover lost or corrupted data, *TFTP* is responsible for maintaining the integrity of the data exchange. *TFTP* transfers data in blocks of 512 bytes. A block must be acknowledged before the next block can be sent. When an acknowledgment is not received before a timer expires, the block is retransmitted.

The purpose of the following exercises is to observe that, despite the overhead of maintaining a TCP connection, file transfers with *FTP* generally outperform those with UDP.

EXERCISE 2.
Comparison of *FTP* and *TFTP*.

Study the performance of *FTP* and *TFTP* file transfers for a large file.

1. **Create a large file:** On PC1, create a file with name *large.d* in directory */tftpboot* by copying a large system file. On Redhat 9.0 systems, use the file */usr/lib/libstdc++.so.2.7.2.8*. If this file does not exist, locate a file on a system that has a size of approximately 1 megabyte. Copy the file and change its access permissions as follows:

```
PC1% cp /usr/lib/libstdc++.so.2.7.2.8 /tftpboot/large.d
PC1% chmod 644 /tftpboot/large.d
```

Use the command ls -l to check the length of the file.

2. **Start *ethereal*:** Invoke *ethereal* on interface *eth1* of PC1 with a capture filter set for PC2, and start to capture traffic:

```
PC1% ethereal -i eth1 -f "host 10.0.5.22"
```

3. ***FTP* file transfer:** On PC2, perform the following steps:

  - Change the current directory to */labdata*.

  - Invoke an *FTP* session to PC1 by typing

    ```
    PC2% ftp 10.0.5.11
    ```

    Log in as the root user.

  - Transfer the file *large.d* from PC1 to directory */labdata* on PC2 by typing

    ```
    ftp> cd /tftpboot
    ftp> get large.d
    ftp> quit
    ```

Observe the output of the *FTP* session and save the output to a file.

4. ***TFTP file transfer:*** On PC2 perform the following tasks:

   *   Start a *TFTP* session to PC1 by typing

       ```
       PC2% tftp 10.0.5.11
       ```

   *   Transfer the file *large.d* from PC1 to PC2:

       ```
       tftp> get large.d
       tftp> quit
       ```

       By default, *TFTP* copies data from the directory */tftpboot*.

   *   Observe the output of the *TFTP* session and save the output to a file.

5. **Analysis of outcome:** On PC1, stop the *ethereal* output. (There is no need to save the captured data if you record the answers to the following questions.)

   *   From the timestamps recorded by *ethereal*, obtain the times it took to transfer the file with *FTP* and with *TFTP*. Use your knowledge of *FTP*, *TFTP*, TCP, and UDP to explain the outcome.

   *   Identify the TCP connections that are created in the *FTP* session, and record the port numbers at the source and at the destination.

Lab Report Include the answers to the questions in Step 5.

PART 3. IP FRAGMENTATION OF UDP AND TCP TRAFFIC

In this part of the lab, you observe the effect of IP fragmentation on UDP and TCP traffic. Fragmentation occurs when the transport layer sends a packet of data to the IP layer that exceeds the Maximum Transmission Unit (MTU) of the underlying data link network. For example, in Ethernet networks, the MTU is 1500 bytes. If an IP datagram exceeds the MTU size, the IP datagram is fragmented into multiple IP datagrams, or, if the *Don't Fragment* (*DF*) flag is set in the IP header, the IP datagram is discarded.

When an IP datagram is fragmented, its payload is split across multiple IP datagrams, each satisfying the limit imposed by the MTU. Each fragment is an independent IP datagram and is routed in the network independently from the other fragments. Fragmentation can occur at the sending host or at intermediate IP routers. Fragments are reassembled only at the destination host.

Even though IP fragmentation provides flexibility that can hide differences of data link technologies to higher layers, it incurs considerable overhead and, therefore, should be avoided. TCP tries to avoid fragmentation with a *Path MTU Discovery* scheme that determines a maximum segment size (MSS), which does not result in fragmentation.

You explore the issues with IP fragmentation of TCP and UDP transmissions in the network configuration shown in Figure 5.1, with PC1 as sending host, PC2 as receiving host, and PC3 as intermediate IP router.

EXERCISE 3(A).
UDP and fragmentation.

In this exercise you observe IP fragmentation of UDP traffic. In the following exercise, use *ttcp* to generate UDP traffic between PC1 and PC2, across IP router PC3, and gradually increase the size of UDP datagrams until fragmentation occurs. You can observe that IP headers do not set the DF bit for UDP payloads.

1. Verify that the network is configured as shown in Figure 5.1 and Table 5.1. The PCs should be configured as described in Exercise 1(A).

2. Start *ethereal* on the *eth0* interfaces of both PC1 and PC2, and start to capture traffic. Do not set any filters.

3. Use *ttcp* to generate UDP traffic between PC1 and PC2. The connection parameters are selected so that IP fragmentation does not occur initially.

    a. On PC2, execute the following command:

        ```
        PC2% ttcp -rs -l1024 -n12 -p4444 -u
        ```

    b. On PC1, execute the command

        ```
        PC1% ttcp -ts -l1024 -n12 -p4444 -u 10.0.2.22
        ```

4. Increment the size of the UDP datagrams, by increasing the argument given with the −l option.

    a. Determine the exact UDP datagram size at which fragmentation occurs.

    b. Determine the maximum size of the UDP datagram that the system can send and receive, regardless of fragmentation (i.e., fragmentation of data segments occurs until a point beyond which the segment size is too large to be handled by IP).

5. Stop the traffic capture on PC1 and PC2, and save the *ethereal* output. Select the *Print detail* option.

Lab Report

*   From the saved *ethereal* data, select one IP datagram that is fragmented. Include the complete datagram before fragmentation and include all fragments after fragmentation. For each fragment of this datagram, determine the values of the fields in the IP header that are used for fragmentation (Identification, Fragment Offset, Don't Fragment Bit, More Fragments Bit).

*   Include the outcome of the experiment in Step 4. Indicate the UDP datagram size at which fragmentation occurs. Also, determine the maximum size of the UDP datagram that the system can send.

EXERCISE 3(B).
TCP and fragmentation.

TCP tries to completely avoid fragmentation with the following two mechanisms:

- When a TCP connection is established, it negotiates the maximum segment size (MSS). Both the TCP client and the TCP server send the MSS in an option that is attached to the TCP header of the first transmitted TCP segment. Each side sets the MSS so that no fragmentation occurs at the outgoing network interface, when it transmits segments. The smaller value is adopted as the MSS value for the connection.

- The exchange of the MSS addresses MTU constraints only at the hosts, not at the intermediate routers. To determine the smallest MTU on the path from the sender to the receiver, TCP employs a method known as *Path MTU Discovery*, which works as follows. The sender always sets the DF bit in all IP datagrams. When a router needs to fragment an IP packet with the DF bit set, it discards the packet and generates an ICMP error message of type "destination unreachable; fragmentation needed". Upon receiving such an ICMP error message, the TCP sender reduces the segment size. This continues until a segment size that does not trigger an ICMP error message is determined.

1. Modify the MTU of the interfaces with the values shown in Table 5.2.

TABLE 5.2. MTU sizes.

Linux PC	MTU Size of Interface *eth0*	MTU Size of Interface *eth1*
PC1	1500	Not used
PC2	500	Not used
PC3	1500	1500

In Linux, you can view the MTU values of all interfaces in the output of the `ifconfig` command. For example, on PC2, you type

```
PC2% ifconfig
```

The same command is used to modify the MTU value. For example, to set the MTU value of interface *eth0* on PC2 to 500 bytes, use the `ifconfig` command as follows:

```
PC2% ifconfig eth0 mtu 500
```

2. Start *ethereal* on the *eth0* interfaces of both PC1 and PC3, and start to capture traffic with no filters set.

3. Start a *ttcp* receiver on PC2 and a *ttcp* sender on PC1 and generate TCP traffic with the following commands:

```
PC2% ttcp -rs -l1024 -n2 -p4444
PC1% ttcp -ts -l1024 -n2 -p4444 -D 10.0.2.22
```

Observe the output of *ethereal*:

- Do you observe fragmentation? If so, where does it occur? Explain your observation.

- Explain why there is no ICMP error message generated in the first part of the experiment (Step 3). Is the DF bit set in the IP datagrams?

4. Now change the MTU size on interface *eth1* of PC3 to 500 bytes. Change the MTU size of interface *eth0* on PC2 to 1500 bytes.

5. Repeat the *ttcp* transmission in Step 3.

- Do you observe fragmentation? If so, where does it occur? Explain your observation.

- If you observe ICMP error messages, describe how they are used for *Path MTU Discovery*.

6. Save all *ethereal* output (select the *Print detail* option).

Lab Report

- Answer the questions in Steps 3 and 5. Include *ethereal* data to support your answer.

- If you observed ICMP error messages, include one such message in the report. Also include the first TCP segment that is sent after PC1 has received the ICMP error message.

PART 4. TCP CONNECTION MANAGEMENT

TCP is a connection-oriented protocol. The establishment of a TCP connection is initiated when a TCP client sends a request for a connection to a TCP server. The TCP server must be running when the connection request is issued.

TCP requires three packets to open a connection. This procedure is called a *three-way handshake*. During the handshake the TCP client and TCP server negotiate essential parameters of the TCP connection, including the initial sequence numbers, the maximum segment size, and the size of the windows for the sliding window flow control. TCP requires three or four packets to close a connection. Each end of the connection is closed separately, and each part of the closing is called a *half-close*.

TCP does not have separate control packets for opening and closing connections. Instead, TCP uses bit flags in the TCP header to indicate that a TCP header carries control information. The flags involved in the opening and the closing of a connection are SYN, ACK, and FIN.

Here, you use *Telnet* to set up a TCP connection and observe the control packets that establish and terminate a TCP connection. The experiments involve PC1 and PC2 in the network shown in Figure 5.1.

EXERCISE 4(A).
Opening and closing a TCP connection.

Set up a TCP connection and observe the packets that open and close the connection.
Determine how the parameters of a TCP connection are negotiated between the TCP
client and the TCP server.

1. This part of the lab uses only PC1 and PC2 in the network configuration in Figure
   5.1. If the network is not set up, follow the instructions of Exercise 1(A).

   Verify that the MTU values of all interfaces of PC1 and PC2 are set to 1500 bytes,
   which is the default MTU for Ethernet networks.

2. Start *ethereal* on the *eth1* interface of PC1 to capture traffic of the *Telnet* connection.
   Do not set any filters.

3. **Establishing a TCP connection:** Establish a *Telnet* session from PC1 to PC2 as
   follows:

   ```
   PC1% telnet 10.0.5.22
   ```

   Observe the TCP segments of the packets that are transmitted:

   - Identify the packets of the three-way handshake. Which flags are set in the TCP
     headers? Explain how these flags are interpreted by the receiving TCP server or
     TCP client.

   - During the connection setup, the TCP client and TCP server tell each other the
     first sequence number they will use for data transmission. What are the initial
     sequence numbers of the TCP client and the TCP server?

   - Identify the first packet that contains application data. What is the sequence
     number used in the first byte of application data sent from the TCP client to the
     TCP server?

   - The TCP client and TCP server exchange window sizes to get the maximum
     amount of data that the other side can send at any time. Determine the values of
     the window sizes for the TCP client and the TCP server.

   - What is the MSS value that is negotiated between the TCP client and the TCP
     server?

   - How long does it take to open a TCP connection?

4. **Closing a TCP connection (initiated by client):** On PC1, type Ctrl-] at the *Telnet*
   prompt and type `quit`, to terminate the connection. (If the *Telnet* session is no
   longer running, first create a new session.)

   In the output of *ethereal*, observe the TCP segments of the packets that are
   transmitted:

   - Identify the packets that are involved in closing the TCP connection. Which flags
     are set in these packets? Explain how these flags are interpreted by the receiving
     TCP server or TCP client.

5. **Closing a TCP connection (initiated by server):** The closing of a connection can also be initiated by the server application, as seen next.

Establish a *Telnet* session on PC1 to PC2 as follows:

```
PC1% telnet 10.0.5.22
```

Do not type anything. After a while, the connection will be closed by the TCP server and a message displayed at the *Telnet* client application.

- Describe how the closing of the connection is different from Step 4.

- How long does the *Telnet* server wait until it closes the TCP connection?

6. Save the *ethereal* output (select the *Print detail* option).

EXERCISE 4(B).
Requesting a connection to a nonexisting host.

Here you observe how often a TCP client tries to establish a connection to a host that does not exist before it gives up.

1. Start a new traffic capture with *ethereal* on interface *eth1* of PC1.

2. Set a static entry in the ARP table for the IP address 10.0.5.100. Note that the IP address does not exist.

```
PC1% arp -s 10.0.5.100 00:01:02:03:04:05
```

3. From PC1, establish a *Telnet* session to the nonexisting host:

```
PC1% telnet 10.0.5.100
```

Observe the TCP segments that are transmitted:

- How often does the TCP client try to establish a connection? How much time elapses between repeated attempts to open a connection?

- Does the TCP client terminate or reset the connection when it gives up trying to establish a connection?

- Why does this experiment require setting a static ARP table entry?

4. Save the *ethereal* output (select the *Print detail* option).

EXERCISE 4(C).
Requesting a connection to a nonexisting port.

When a host tries to establish a TCP connection to a port at a remote server, and no TCP server is listening on that port, the remote host terminates the TCP connection. This is observed in the following exercise.

1. Start a new traffic capture with *ethereal* on interface *eth1* of PC1.

2. Establish a TCP connection to port 80 of PC2:

```
PC1% telnet 10.0.5.22 80
```

There should not be a TCP server running on PC2 that is listening at this port number. Observe the TCP segments of the packets that are transmitted:

- How does TCP at the remote host close this connection? How long does the process of ending the connection take?

3. Save the *ethereal* output (Select the *Print detail* option).

Lab Report Answer the questions in Exercise 4(A) (Steps 3, 4, and 5), Exercise 4(B) (Step 3), and Exercise 4(C) (Step 2). For each answer, include *ethereal* data to support your answer.

PART 5. TCP DATA EXCHANGE—INTERACTIVE APPLICATIONS

In Parts 5 and 6 you study acknowledgments and flow control in TCP. The receiver of TCP data acknowledges the receipt of data in segments that have the ACK flag set. These segments are called *acknowledgments*, or ACKs. In TCP, each transmitted byte of application data has a sequence number. The sender of a segment writes the sequence number of the first byte of transmitted application data in the sequence number field of the TCP header. When a receiver sends an ACK, it writes a sequence number in the acknowledgment number field of the TCP header. The acknowledgment number is larger by 1 than the highest sequence number that the receiver wants to acknowledge. Whenever possible, a TCP receiver sends an ACK in a segment that carries a payload. This is called *piggybacking*. A TCP receiver can acknowledge multiple segments in a single ACK. This is called *cumulative acknowledgments*.

In this lab, you study acknowledgments separately for interactive applications, such as *Telnet*, and for bulk transfer applications, such as file transfers. You will observe that different TCP mechanisms play a role for these different types of applications. In this part, you study the data transfer of interactive applications.

Interactive applications typically generate a small volume of data. Since interactive applications are generally delay sensitive, a TCP sender does not wait until the application data fills a complete TCP segment, and, instead, TCP sends data as soon as it arrives from the application. This, however, results in an inefficient use of bandwidth since small segments mainly consist of protocol headers. Here, TCP has mechanisms that keep the number of segments with a small payload small. One such mechanism, called *delayed acknowledgments*, requires that the receiver of data wait for a certain amount of time before sending an ACK. If, during this delay, the receiver has data for the sender, the ACK can be piggybacked to the data, thereby saving the transmission of a segment. Another such mechanism, called *Nagle's algorithm*, limits the number of small segments that a TCP sender can transmit without waiting for an ACK.

The network configuration is shown in Figure 5.2. The network connects two Linux PCs, PC1 and PC2, such that there are three paths between the PCs. One route goes over three Ethernet links (with either 10 Mbps or 100 Mbps), and one route goes over a serial WAN link (which will be set to 125 kbps), and one route goes over a direct Ethernet link (also with 10 Mbps or 100 Mbps).

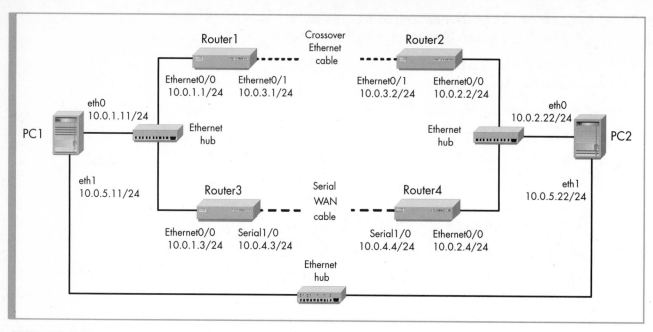

FIGURE 5.2.

Network topology for Parts 5–8.

EXERCISE 5(A).

Network setup.

The following network configuration is used in the remaining parts of the lab.

1. Set up the Ethernet and serial connections as shown in Figure 5.2. On the Cisco routers, we assume that there is an Ethernet interface in slot 0 and that there is a serial WAN interface in slot 1. Router1 and Router2 are connected via an Ethernet crossover cable, and Router3 and Router4 are connected via a serial WAN cable (DB-60-to-DB-60 crossover cable).

   The serial WAN interfaces can operate in full-duplex mode at rates of up to 2 Mbps. The connectors of the interfaces have a Cisco proprietary format and are called DB-60 connectors. Two such interfaces can be directly connected with a DB-60-to-DB-60 crossover cable. Refer to Section 1.4 of the Introduction for additional information.

2. Configure the IP addresses and the routing tables of the PCs as shown in Tables 5.3 and 5.4.

   a. IP forwarding should be disabled on both PC1 and PC2.

   b. Set new default gateways on PC1 and PC2. Remove the default gateway entry that was set in Part 1 of the lab. Changing the default gateway on PC1 is done with the following commands:

   ```
   PC1% route del default gw 10.0.1.33
   PC1% route add default gw 10.0.1.3
   ```

TABLE 5.3. IP addresses of Linux PCs and Cisco routers.

Linux PC	Interface *eth0*	Interface *eth1*
PC1	10.0.1.11/24	10.0.5.11
PC2	10.0.2.22/24	10.0.5.22
Cisco Router	**Interface Ethernet0/0**	**Interface Ethernet0/1**
Router1	10.0.1.1/24	10.0.3.1/24
Router2	10.0.2.2/24	10.0.3.2/24
Cisco Router	**Interface Ethernet0/0**	**Interface Serial1/0**
Router3	10.0.1.3/24	10.0.4.3/24
Router4	10.0.2.4/24	10.0.4.4/24

TABLE 5.4. Routing table entries for Parts 5–8.

Routing Table Entries		
Linux PC	**Destination**	**Next Hop**
PC1	Default gateway	10.0.1.3
PC2	Default gateway	10.0.2.4
Cisco Router	**Destination**	**Next Hop**
Router1	Network 10.0.4.0/24	10.0.1.3
	Default gateway	10.0.3.2
Router2	Network 10.0.4.0/24	10.0.2.4
	Default gateway	10.0.3.1
Router3	Network 10.0.3.0/24	10.0.1.1
	Default gateway	10.0.4.4
Router4	Network 10.0.3.0/24	10.0.2.2
	Default gateway	10.0.4.3

Repeat the steps on PC2. Use the command netstat -rn, to verify that there are no other static routing entries.

3. Verify that the PCs are connected to the console ports of routers. PC1 should be connected to Router1, PC2 to Router 2, and so on. On each PC, establish a *kermit* session to the connected router.

4. Configure the IP addresses and routing table entries of the routers. The commands for Router4 are as follows:

```
Router4> enable
Password: <enable secret>
Router4# configure terminal
Router4(config)# no ip routing
Router4(config)# ip routing
Router4(config)# ip route 0.0.0.0 0.0.0.0 10.0.4.3
Router4(config)# ip route 10.0.3.0 255.255.255.0 10.0.2.2
Router4(config)# interface Ethernet0/0
Router4(config-if)# no shutdown
Router4(config-if)# ip address 10.0.2.4 255.255.255.0
Router4(config-if)# interface Serial1/0
Router4(config-if)# no shutdown
Router4(config-if)# ip address 10.0.4.4 255.255.255.0
Router4(config-if)# end
```

Use the commands `show ip route` and `show interfaces` to verify that the routing table and the interfaces are set correctly.

5. When the serial WAN interfaces of Router3 and Router4 are directly connected by a serial WAN cable as in Figure 5.2, one interface functions as *DCE* (*data circuit-terminating equipment*) and the other as *DTE* (*data terminal equipment*). In IOS, a clock rate must be set on the serial interface that functions as DCE. Whether an interface functions as DCE or DTE is determined by the orientation of the serial WAN cable.

- **Determine the DCE end:** To check whether a DB-60-to-DB-60 crossover cable connected to a serial interface of a router is of type DCE or DTE, type the following command:

  ```
  Router3# show controllers Serial1/0
  ```

  The command displays low-level information on the serial interface, including whether an interface functions as DTE or DCE. Look for statements "V.35 DTE cable" or "V.35 DCE cable" in the output of the command.

- **Set the clock rate at the DCE end:** Once the DCE has been identified, you must set the clock rate. Assuming that the serial interface of Router3 functions as DCE, type the following commands:

  ```
  Router3# configure terminal
  Router3(config)# interface Serial1/0
  Router3(config-if)# clock rate 9600
  ```

  This sets the clock rate of the serial link to 9600 bps.

6. Test the network connectivity by issuing `ping` commands between PC1 and PC2. Verify the route taken by traffic between the PCs by issuing `traceroute` commands:

```
PC1% traceroute 10.0.2.22
PC1% traceroute 10.0.5.22

PC2% traceroute 10.0.1.11
PC2% traceroute 10.0.5.11
```

Also, you should be able to issue `ping` commands between the routers. If the commands are not successful, use the command `traceroute` (on Linux) or `trace` (on IOS) and the content of the routing tables to locate configuration problems.

If all commands are successful, then you are ready to continue.

EXERCISE 5(B).
TCP data transfer—interactive applications over a fast link.

Here you observe interactive data transfer in TCP, by establishing a TCP connection from PC1 to PC2 over the Ethernet link between the PCs. Depending on the type of hub, the Ethernet link has a maximum data rate of 10 Mbps or 100 Mbps.

1. Start *ethereal* on PC1 for interface *eth1*, and start to capture traffic. Do not set any filters.

2. On PC1, establish a *Telnet* session to PC2 by typing

```
PC1% telnet 10.0.5.22
```

Log in as root user.

3. Now start to type a few characters in the window that contains the *Telnet* session. The *Telnet* client sends each typed character in a separate TCP segment to the *Telnet* server, which, in turn, echoes the character back to the client. Including ACKs, one would expect to see four packets for each typed character. However, due to delayed acknowledgments, this is not the case.

Observe the output of *ethereal*:

- Observe the number of packets exchanged between the Linux PCs for each keystroke. Describe the payload of the packets. Use your knowledge of delayed acknowledgments to explain the sequence of segment transmissions. Explain why you do not see four packets per typed character.

- When the TCP client receives the echo of a character, it waits a certain time before sending the ACK. Why does the TCP client delay? How long is this delay? How much does the delay vary?

- What is the time delay associated with the transmission of ACKs from the *Telnet* server on PC2?

- Which flags, if any, are set in the TCP segments that carry typed characters as payload? Explain the meaning of these flags.

- Why do segments that have an empty payload carry a sequence number? Why does this not result in confusion at the TCP receiver?

- What is the window size that is advertised by the *Telnet* client and the *Telnet* server? How does the value of the window size field vary as the connection progresses?

4. Type characters in the *Telnet* client program as fast as you can (e.g., by pressing a key and holding it down).

   - Do you observe a difference in the transmission of segment payloads and ACKs?

5. Terminate the *Telnet* session by typing `exit`.

6. Stop the traffic capture with *ethereal* and save the captured packets (Select the *Print detail* option).

Lab Report

- Include your answers to the questions in Steps 3 and 4. Include examples from the saved *ethereal* data to support your answers.

- For one character typed at the *Telnet* client, include a drawing that shows the transmission of TCP segments between PC1 and PC2 due to this character.

EXERCISE 5(C).
TCP data transfer—interactive applications over a slow link.

This exercise repeats the previous exercise but establishes a data connection over the serial WAN link. The rate of this link has been set to 9600 bps. This low rate introduces significant delays between PC1 and PC2. Due to the long delay, one would expect that the TCP sender transmits multiple segments, each carrying a payload of one typed character. However, this is not the case. A heuristic in TCP, called *Nagle's algorithm*, forces the sender to wait for an ACK after transmitting a small segment, even if the window size would allow the transmission of multiple segments. Therefore, no matter how slow or fast you type, you should observe only one TCP segment in transmission at a time when the TCP segments are small.

1. Start to capture traffic with *ethereal* on interface *eth0* of PC1. Do not set any display filters.

2. On PC1, establish a *Telnet* session to PC2 by typing

   ```
   PC1% telnet 10.0.2.22
   ```

Log in as root user. Note with this IP address the route between PC1 and PC2 passes through the serial WAN link between Router3 and Router4.

3. As in the previous exercise, type a few characters in the window that contains the *Telnet* session. Vary the rate at which you type characters in the *Telnet* client program.

Observe the output of *ethereal*:

* Observe the number of packets that are exchanged between the Linux PCs for each keystroke. Observe how the transmission of packets changes when you type characters more quickly.

* Do you observe delayed acknowledgments? Why is the outcome expected?

* If you type very quickly (i.e., if you hold a key down), you should observe that multiple characters are transmitted in the payload of a segment. Explain this outcome.

4. Terminate the *Telnet* session by typing *exit*.

5. Stop the traffic capture with *ethereal* and save the captured packets (select the *Print detail* option).

Lab Report

* Include your answers to the questions in Step 3. For each answer, include *ethereal* data to support your answer.

* Include an example from the saved *ethereal* data that shows that Nagle's algorithm is used by the TCP sender.

PART 6. TCP DATA EXCHANGE—BULK DATA TRANSFER

The TCP receiver can use acknowledgments to control the transmission rate at the TCP sender. This is called *flow control*. Flow control is not an issue for interactive applications, since the traffic volume of these applications is small, but plays an important role in bulk transfer applications.

Bulk data transfers generally transmit full segments. In TCP, the receiver controls the amount of data that the sender can transmit using a *sliding window flow control* scheme. This prevents the receiver from getting overwhelmed with data. The number of bytes that the receiver is willing to accept is written in the window size field. An ACK that has values (250, 100) for the acknowledgment number and the window size tells the TCP sender that it can transmit data with sequence numbers 250, 251,..., 349. The TCP sender may have already transmitted some data in that range.

In this part of the lab, you observe acknowledgments and flow control for bulk data transfers, with traffic generated with the *ttcp* tool. To observe the bulk data transfer, we introduce a feature of *ethereal* that allows you to view the data of a TCP connection in a graph. This is done in Exercise 6(C). We also show how to save the graphs to a file.

All exercises are done with the network configuration from Figure 5.2.

EXERCISE 6(A).
TCP data transfer—bulk transfer (fast link).

The purpose of this exercise is to observe the operation of the sliding window flow control scheme in a bulk data transfer, with PC1 sending a large number of segments to PC2 using the *ttcp* traffic generation tool.

1. The network configuration is the same as in Part 5. If the network is not set up accordingly, then follow the instructions in Exercise 5(A).

2. Start *ethereal* on PC1 for interface *eth1*, and start to capture traffic. Do not set any display filters.

3. Use *ttcp* to generate TCP traffic between PC1 and PC2:

   a. On PC2, start a *ttcp* receiving process by typing

   ```
   PC2% ttcp -rs -l1000 -n500 -p4444
   ```

   b. On PC1, start a *ttcp* sender process that sends 500 blocks of application data by typing

   ```
   PC1% ttcp -ts -l1000 -n500 -p4444 -D 10.0.5.22
   ```

   By using 10.0.5.22 as destination address, traffic will go over the direct Ethernet link between PC1 and PC2.

4. From the output of *ethereal* on PC1, observe the sliding window flow control scheme. The sender transmits data up to the window size advertised by the receiver and then waits for ACKs.

> **NOTE:**
>
> The outcome of this experiment is dependent on the data rate of the Ethernet link between PC1 and PC2. If PC1 and PC2 are connected directly by an Ethernet crossover cable or by a dual-speed hub, they will most likely exchange traffic at a data rate of 100 Mbps. If the Linux PCs are connected by a 10 Mbps Ethernet hub, the data rate is limited accordingly. The rate of the connection has a big impact on the outcome of the experiment.

- Observe the transmission of TCP segments and ACKs. How frequently does the receiver send ACKs? Is there an ACK sent for each TCP segment or less often? Can you determine the rule used by TCP to send ACKs? Can you explain this rule?

- How much data (measured in bytes) does the receiver acknowledge in a typical ACK? What is the most data that is acknowledged in a single ACK?

- What is the range of the window sizes advertised by the receiver? How does the window size vary during the lifetime of the TCP connection?

- Select an arbitrary ACK packet in *ethereal* sent by PC2 to PC1. Locate the acknowledgment number in the TCP header. Now relate this ACK to a segment sent by PC1. Identify this segment in the *ethereal* output. How long did it take from the transmission of the segment until the ACK arrives at PC1?

- Determine whether or not the TCP sender generally transmits the maximum amount of data allowed by the advertised window. Explain your answer.

- When the *ttcp* sender has transmitted all its data, it closes the connection, but acknowledgments from PC2 still trickle in. What does PC2 do when it has sent all ACKs?

5. Stop the traffic capture with *ethereal* and save the *ethereal* output (select the *Print summary* option.)

Lab Report Include your answers to the questions in Step 4. Include captured traffic to support your answers.

EXERCISE 6(B).
TCP data transfer—bulk transfer (slow link).

This exercise repeats the previous experiment, with the exception that traffic is sent over the serial WAN link.

1. Set the data rate of the serial WAN link to 125 kbps. As in Exercise 5(B), this is done by setting the clock rate at the DCE end of the serial WAN link, which is either Router3 or Router4. Assuming that the serial interface of Router3 functions as DCE, type the following commands:

```
Router3# configure terminal
Router3(config)# interface Serial1/0
Router3(config-if)# clock rate 125000
```

2. Create a new *ethereal* session on PC1 for interface *eth0*, and start to capture traffic. Do not set any display filters.

3. Use *ttcp* to generate TCP traffic between PC1 and PC2:

a. On PC2, start a *ttcp* receiving process by typing

```
PC2% ttcp -rs -11000 -n500 -p4444
```

b. On PC1, start a *ttcp* sender process that sends 500 blocks of application data by typing

```
PC1% ttcp -ts -11000 -n500 -p4444 -D 10.0.2.22
```

With the given destination address, traffic will go through the slow serial WAN link.

4. Observe the differences to the data transmission in the previous exercise.

- How does the pattern of data segments and ACK change, as compared to the fast Ethernet link?

- Does the frequency of ACKs change?

- Is the range of window sizes advertised by the receiver different from those in Exercise 6(A)?

- Does the TCP sender generally transmit the maximum amount of data allowed by the advertised window? Explain your answer.

5. Stop the traffic capture with *ethereal* and save the *ethereal* output (select the *Print summary* option.)

Lab Report Include your answers to the questions in Step 4. Emphasize the differences to the observations made in Exercise 6(A).

EXERCISE 6(C).
View a graph of TCP data transfer.

ethereal can generate graphs that illustrate the transmissions of segments on a PC connection. This exercise familiarizes you with the graphing capabilities of *ethereal* and shows how you can extract information from the graphs.

1. Select a TCP connection: In the *ethereal* main window, select a packet from the TCP connection for which you want to build a graph.

Here, select a TCP packet sent from PC1 to PC2 in Exercise 6(B).

2. Select the type of graph: Select the *Tools* menu from the *ethereal* main window, and then select *TCP Stream Analysis* in the pull-down menu, as shown in Figure 5.3. This displays the plotting functions available in *ethereal*:

- *Time-Sequence Graph (Stevens):* Plots the transmission of sequence numbers as a function of time. There is one data point for each transmission of a TCP segment.

- *Time-Sequence Graph (tcptrace):* Generates a plot as shown in Figure 5.4. The graph is similar to the previous one, but additional information is included on the state of the sliding window.

- *Throughput Graph:* Shows the rate of data transmission as a function of time.

- *RTT Graph:* Shows the round-trip time (RTT) as a function of time.

- Try out each of the graphs for the TCP connection from Exercise 6(B). Make sure that you select a packet with TCP payload from PC1 to PC2 in the *ethereal* main window before you generate a graph.

3. Navigating the graphs: It is possible to navigate the graphs generated by *ethereal*. For example, you can zoom into a graph to display an area of interest at a greater level of detail. The complete set of available options are listed on page 198.

4. Interpreting the Time-Sequence Graph (*tcptrace*): A lot of information can be extracted from the Time-Sequence Graph (*tcptrace*). Refer to the Figure 5.4 graph of a TCP connection. This graph shows the transmission of TCP segments and acknowledgments. The short vertical bars indicate the transmission of TCP segments. Each short bar represents one TCP segment, and the length of a bar corresponds to

FIGURE 5.3.
Selecting the type of graph for a TCP connection.

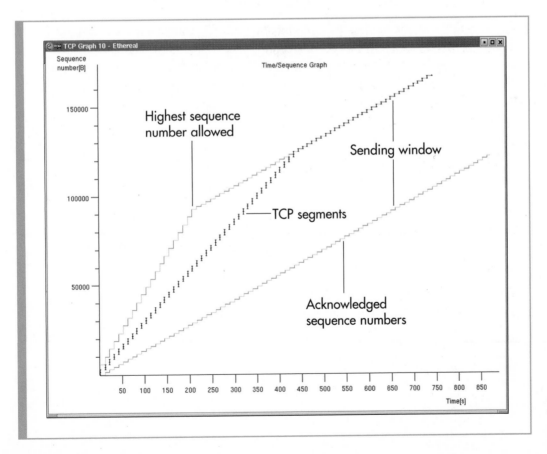

FIGURE 5.4.
Time-Sequence Graph (*tcptrace*).

NAVIGATING GRAPHS OF TCP CONNECTIONS IN ETHEREAL

Left mouse button	Selecting a data point highlights the corresponding segment in the *ethereal* main window.
Middle mouse button	Zooms to a selected part of the graph.
Shift +middle mouse button	Zooms out.
Right mouse button	Holding this button down and moving the mouse moves the displayed section of the graph. This works only if the graph is zoomed in.
Ctrl + right button	Magnifies a small portion of the graph.
Space	Toggles between showing and not showing crosshairs.
S	Toggles between relative and absolute sequence numbers.
T	Toggles the display of the *x*-axis.

the length of a segment. The figure also shows two step curves. The top step curve shows the highest allowed sequence number, and the bottom step curve shows the acknowledged sequence numbers. These functions are determined from the acknowledgment number and the window size fields of received ACKs. The vertical distance between the two step curves shows the open part of the sliding window, that is, the sequence numbers that the TCP sender may transmit.

From Figure 5.4, you can see that, most of the time, TCP segments are transmitted in groups of two segments. An inspection of the vertical plot shows that no segments are retransmitted. The figure shows that the sequence numbers of transmitted segments are close to the upper step curve. This indicates that the TCP sender utilizes the entire sliding window and that the transmissions by the TCP sender are triggered by arrivals of ACKs from the TCP receiver.

- Study the Time-Sequence Graph (*tcptrace*) of the TCP connections in Exercises 6(A) and 6(B). Review the questions in Step 4 of Exercise 6(A) and Step 4 in Exercise 6(B), and try to determine the answers to the questions directly from the graphs.

5. **Saving graphs to a file:** Unfortunately, *ethereal* does not allow you to save the graphs for a TCP connection. However, there is a simple method in Linux to save a window on the desktop to a file.

Suppose you have constructed a TCP graph similar to that in Figure 5.4 on PC1 and want to save it as a TIFF file. This is done by typing

```
PC1% import lab6c.tif
```

and then clicking on the window with the TCP graph. This saves the graph to a TIFF file with name *lab6c.tif*. If you use a different file extension, the file is saved to a different image format. Select a file format that you can use in your lab report and that has sufficient image quality. The `import` command supports numerous file formats, including those in Table 5.5. We recommend that you use the TIFF file format, which offers the highest quality image. The size of the file can be reduced to less than 20 kB if you compress the file according to the following instructions:

TABLE 5.5. File formats for `import` command.

File Extension	Format	Approximate Size of Resulting File
.jpeg	JPEG	30 kB
.eps	Encapsulated Postscript	3.5 MB
.gif	GIF	300 kB
.tif	TIFF	3.5 MB

- Save the Time-Sequence Graph (*tcptrace*) that you created for the TCP connections in Exercises 6(A) and 6(B). Select a file format that you can use in your lab report. If you want to include detailed areas from the graphs, you may want to save multiple files for each graph.

- Verify the file has been correctly saved. This can be done by opening the image file in a web browser or running the command `gimp`.

6. **Compress and save data to floppy disk:** Save the image files to a floppy disk.

   Since the generated files are generally too large to fit on a floppy disk, compress the files with the `zip` command. To compress all files in directory */labdata*, use the command

   ```
   PC1% zip -r lab6 /labdata
   ```

   This command creates a zip archive file with name *lab6.zip* in the current directory. The archive file can be uncompressed by any standard file archiving application (e.g., *WinZip*) on a Windows system or with the `unzip` command on a Linux system. On a Linux system, refer to the man pages of `zip` and `unzip` for additional information.

Lab Report Include the Time-Sequence Graph (*tcptrace*) graphs that you saved in Step 6. You may also use these graphs for your answers to the lab report questions for Exercises 6(A) and 6(B).

PART 7. RETRANSMISSIONS IN TCP

Next you observe retransmissions in TCP. TCP uses ACKs and timers to trigger retransmissions of lost segments. A TCP sender retransmits a segment when it assumes that the segment has been lost. This occurs in two situations:

- **No ACK has been received for a segment:** Each TCP sender maintains one retransmission timer for the connection. When the timer expires, the TCP sender retransmits the earliest segment that has not been acknowledged. The timer is started when a segment with payload is transmitted and the timer is not running, when an ACK arrives that acknowledges new data, and when a segment is retransmitted. The timer is stopped when all outstanding data has been acknowledged.

  The retransmission timer is set to a retransmission timeout (RTO) value, which adapts to the current network delays between the sender and the receiver. A TCP connection performs round-trip measurements by calculating the delay between the transmission of a segment and the receipt of the acknowledgment for that segment. The RTO value is calculated based on these round-trip measurements (see RFC 2988 from the prelab). Following a heuristic called *Karn's algorithm*, measurements are not taken for retransmitted segments. Instead, when a retransmission occurs, the current RTO value is simply doubled.

- **Multiple ACKs have been received for the same segment:** A duplicate acknowledgment for a segment can be caused by an out-of-order delivery of a segment or by a lost packet. A TCP sender takes multiple, in most cases three, duplicates as an indication that a packet has been lost. In this case, the TCP sender does not wait until the timer expires, but immediately retransmits the segment that is presumed lost. This mechanism is known as *fast retransmit*. The TCP receiver expedites a fast retransmit by sending an ACK for each packet that is received out of order.

A disadvantage of cumulative acknowledgments in TCP is that a TCP receiver cannot request the retransmission of specific segments. For example, if the receiver has obtained segments 1, 2, 3, 5, 6, 7 with cumulative acknowledgments the receiver can send ACKs only for segments 1, 2, 3 but not for the other correctly received segments. This may result in an unnecessary retransmission of segments 5, 6, and 7. The problem can be remedied with an optional feature of TCP, which is known as *selective acknowledgments* (*SACK*s). Here, in addition to acknowledging the highest sequence number of contiguous data that has been received correctly, a receiver can acknowledge additional blocks of sequence numbers. The range of these blocks is included in TCP headers as an option. Whether SACKs are used is negotiated in TCP header options when the TCP connection is created.

The exercises in this part explore aspects of TCP retransmissions that do not require access to internal timers. Unfortunately, the round-trip time measurements and the RTO values are difficult to observe and are, therefore, not included in this lab.

The network configuration for this part is the network shown in Figure 5.2.

EXERCISE 7(A).
TCP retransmissions.

The purpose of this exercise is to observe when TCP retransmissions occur. As before, you transmit data from PC1 to PC2. Here, data is sent over the serial link, which is set to 125 kbps. When you disconnect one of the cables of the network, ACKs cannot reach the sending host. As a result, a timeout occurs and the sender performs retransmissions.

The network configuration is the same as in Part 5. If the network is not set up accordingly, then follow the instructions in Exercise 5(A).

1. Set the data rate of the serial WAN link to 125 kbps. If you continue from Part 6, this is the current value of the data rate of the link. If not, you proceed as in Exercise 5(A) by setting the clock rate at the DCE end of the serial WAN link, which is either Router3 or Router4. Assuming that the serial interface of Router3 functions as DCE, type the following commands:

```
Router3# configure terminal
Router3(config)# interface Serial1/0
Router3(config-if)# clock rate 125000
```

2. Start *ethereal* on PC1 and capture traffic on interface *eth0*. Set a display filter to TCP traffic. This is done by typing tcp in the window at the bottom of the main window of *ethereal*, next to the label *Filter*.

3. Start a *ttcp* receiving process on PC2:

```
PC2% ttcp -rs -l1000 -n500 -p4444
```

4. Start a *ttcp* sending process on PC1:

```
PC1% ttcp -ts -l1000 -n500 -p4444 -D 10.0.2.22
```

   • When the connection is created, do the TCP sender and TCP receiver negotiate to permit SACKs? Describe the process of the negotiation.

5. Once *ethereal* has transmitted at least 100 packets, disconnect the cable that connects *Ethernet0/0* of Router3 to the Ethernet hub. Disconnect the cable at the hub. Wait at least 5 minutes before you reconnect the cable.

   Observe TCP retransmissions from PC1 in the output of *ethereal*:

   • Observe the time instants when retransmissions take place. How many packets are retransmitted at one time?

   • Try to derive the algorithm that sets the time when a packet is retransmitted. (Repeat the experiment, if necessary). Is there a maximum time interval between retransmissions?

   • After how many retransmissions, if at all, does the TCP sender stop to retransmit the segment? Describe your observations.

6. Now reconnect the cable, and wait until the transmission resumes (this may take some time). Now quickly disconnect and reconnect the cable that connects the interface *Ethernet0/0* of Router3 to the Ethernet hub. Repeat this procedure a number of times, by varying the length of time that the cable is disconnected.

   Now observe the retransmissions from PC1:

   - Are the retransmissions different from those in Step 5? Specifically, do you observe fast retransmits and/or SACKs?

7. Use the instructions from Exercise 6(C) to build a Time-Sequence Graph (*tcptrace*) in *ethereal* for the TCP connection.

   - Study the output of the graph and use the graph to provide answers to the previous questions. Use the navigating features to zoom in to parts of the graph that are of interest.

8. Follow the instructions from Exercise 6(C) to generate image files for the Time-Sequence Graph (*tcptrace*). Save enough images so that you can use the graphs to answer the preceding questions in your lab report. Generate images that show clearly the retransmission attempts in Steps 5 and 6. Compress the files and copy the files to a floppy disk.

Lab Report Include the answers to the questions from Steps 4, 5, and 6. Include the image files saved in Step 8, and use them to support your answers. Annotate the graphs as necessary.

EXERCISE 7(B).
TCP performance at an overloaded link.

Next you perform an experiment in which you overload the serial WAN link between Router3 and Router4 and cause losses and retransmissions due to buffer overflows at Router3.

As in Exercise 7(A), you set up a TCP connection from PC1 to PC2. Here, however, you flood Router3 with ICMP Echo Request messages. The purpose of this exercise is to observe how a TCP connection performs when a router is overloaded.

1. Set the data rate of the serial WAN link to 64 kbps. Assuming that the serial interface of Router3 functions as DCE, type the following commands on Router3:

   ```
   Router3# configure terminal
   Router3(config)# interface Serial1/0
   Router3(config-if)# clock rate 64000
   ```

2. Start *ethereal* on PC1 for interface *eth0*, and start to capture traffic. Set a display filter to TCP traffic.

3. Start a *ttcp* receiving process on PC2:

   ```
   PC2% ttcp -rs -l1000 -n500 -p4444
   ```

4. Start a *ttcp* sending process on PC1:

```
PC1% ttcp -ts -l1000 -n500 -p4444 -D 10.0.2.22
```

5. Once *ethereal* has transmitted at least 100 TCP packets, start to flood ICMP Echo Request messages by typing on PC1

```
PC1% ping -f 10.0.2.22
```

Recall that with the **-f** option, PC2 sends ICMP Echo Request packets as fast as possible. The ICMP traffic sent from PC1 to PC2 will overflow the buffers of Router3 at the serial WAN link.

6. Follow the instructions from Exercise 6(C) to build a Time-Sequence Graph (*tcp-trace*) in *ethereal* for the TCP connection.

If you do not observe any retransmissions, reduce the data rate of the serial link. You can obtain a list of valid rates by typing on Router3 (assuming it is the DCE of the serial WAN link)

```
Router3# configure terminal
Router3(config)# interface Serial1/0
Router3(config-if)# clock rate ?
```

As long as the *ttcp* sender is transmitting packets, rerun the construction of the graph to observe how the graph changes as time progresses. In the graph, observe the progress of the TCP connection:

- Describe the losses that occur in the graph when the `ping` command is started. Do losses occur in regular intervals or irregularly?

- From the graph, describe the size of the advertised window changes when the flooding `ping` is started.

- Try to determine if retransmissions occur due to fast retransmit or due to time-outs of the retransmission timers. How can you determine which type of retransmissions you observe?

- Generate a Throughput Graph to view the data rate of the TCP connection. How does the throughput change after the flood of `pings` is started?

7. Follow the instructions from Exercise 6(C) to generate image files for the Time-Sequence Graph (*tcptrace*) and Throughput Graph. Save enough images so that you can use the graphs to answer the preceding questions in your lab report. Generate an image that shows in detail the loss events that occur right after the `ping` command is started. Compress the files and copy the files to a floppy disk.

Lab Report Include your answers to the questions in Step 6. Include the saved image files. Annotate and describe the plots to support your answers.

PART 8. TCP CONGESTION CONTROL

TCP congestion control consists of a set of algorithms that adapt the sending rate of a TCP sender to the load conditions in the network. When the network is not congested, the TCP sender is allowed to increase its sending rate, and when the network is congested, the TCP sender reduces its rate. The TCP sender maintains a *congestion window* that limits the number of segments that can be sent without waiting for an acknowledgment. The actual number of segments that can be sent is the minimum of the congestion window and the window size sent by the receiver.

For congestion control, each TCP sender keeps two variables, the congestion window (cwnd) and the slow-start threshold (ssthresh). The initial values are set to one segment for cwnd and 65535 bytes for ssthresh. TCP congestion control operates in two phases, called *slow start* and *congestion avoidance*. The sender is in the slow-start phase when cwnd ≤ ssthresh. Here, cwnd is increased by 1 for each arrived ACK. This results in a doubling of cwnd for each round-trip time. When cwnd > ssthresh, the TCP sender is in the congestion-avoidance phase. Here, the cwnd is incremented by 2 only after cwnd ACKs. This is done by incrementing cwnd by a fraction of a segment when an ACK arrives.

The TCP sender assumes that the network is congested when a segment is lost, that is, when the retransmission timer has a timeout or when three duplicate ACKs arrive. When a timeout occurs, the TCP sender sets ssthresh to half the current value of cwnd and then sets cwnd to 1. This puts the TCP sender in slow-start mode. When a third duplicate ACK arrives, the TCP sender performs what is called a *fast recovery*. Here, ssthresh is set to half the current value of cwnd, and cwnd is set to the new value of ssthresh.

The goal of this part of the lab is to observe the development of the congestion window. Since the number of the segments that can be transmitted by a TCP sender is the result of the congestion window as well as the advertised window and since data segments and returning ACKs interleave, the size of the congestion window is not derived by observing traffic.

EXERCISE 8(A).
Network setup.

The network configuration used is that in Figure 5.2. To observe the slow-start features, change the routing table entries so that traffic from PC1 to PC2 traverses the path PC1→R1→R2→PC2, and the reverse path is PC2→R4→R3→PC1. When PC1 sends data to PC2, data segments can be transmitted quickly to PC2, but ACKs only slowly return to PC1. The sender will therefore transmit a full window of packets up to the threshold of the congestion window and then be forced to wait to receive the ACKs before transmitting the next batch of packets.

1. The network configuration is similar to that in Parts 5–7. If the network is not set up accordingly, then follow the instructions in Exercise 5(A). The following two steps are modifications to the setup of Exercise 5(A).

2. Set a new default gateway of PC1 to Router1. If the default gateway from Table 5.4 is still set, you must first delete the existing entry. Use the command `netstat -rn` to see if a default gateway is configured. Assuming that the configuration from Table 5.4 is still set, you must enter the following commands:

```
PC1% route del default gw 10.0.1.3
PC1% route add default gw 10.0.1.1
```

The default gateway of PC2 remains unchanged and should be as shown in Table 5.4.

With this modification, traffic from PC1 to PC2 passes through Router1 and Router2, and traffic from PC2 to PC1 passes through Router4 and Router3. Verify that this is the case.

3. Set the data rate of the serial WAN link to 1 Mbps. Assuming that the serial interface of Router3 functions as DCE, type the following commands:

```
Router3# configure terminal
Router3(config)# interface Serial1/0
Router3(config-if)# clock rate 1000000
```

> **NOTE:**
>
> The outcome of this experiment is dependent on the data rate of the link between Router1 and Router2 and between Router3 and Router4, respectively. The outcome of the experiment is different when the Ethernet link between Router1 and Router2 is running at 10 Mbps or at 100 Mbps. The preceding settings are optimized for a 10 Mbps Ethernet link between Router1 and Router2.

EXERCISE 8(B).
Observing TCP congestion control.

This exercise is similar to Exercise 6(A), that is, PC1 transmits TCP segments to PC2.

1. Start *ethereal* for interface *eth0* on PC1, and start to capture traffic. Set a display filter to TCP traffic.

2. Start a *ttcp* receiving process on PC2:

```
PC2% ttcp -rs -l1000 -n5000 -p4444
```

3. Start a *ttcp* sending process on PC1 that transmits 5000 blocks of data, each with 1000 bytes:

```
PC1% ttcp -ts -l1000 -n5000 -p4444 -D 10.0.2.22
```

4. Once *ethereal* has transmitted at least 100 TCP packets, disconnect the cable that connects *Ethernet0/0* of Router1 to the Ethernet hub. Disconnect the cable at the hub. Now reconnect the cable, and wait until the transmission resumes. Repeat this for a few times, varying the durations when the cable is disconnected.

5. Use the instructions from Exercise 6(C) to build a Time-Sequence Graph (*tcptrace*) in *ethereal* for the TCP connection. Study the graph at the time instants when the cable is reconnected and the TCP sender resumes transmission. Use the navigating features to zoom in to parts of the graph that are of interest.

    • Try to observe periods when the TCP sender is in a slow-start phase and when the sender switches to congestion avoidance. Verify that the congestion window follows the rules of the slow-start phase.

    • Can you deduct the size of the `ssthresh` parameter during the times when the congestion window is small?

    • Can you find occurrences of fast recovery?

6. Follow the instructions from Exercise 6(C) to generate image files for the Time-Sequence Graph (*tcptrace*). Save enough images so that you can use the graphs to answer the previous questions in your lab report. Make sure you include an image that shows a portion of the graph that illustrates the slow-start phase. Compress the files and copy the files to a floppy disk.

Lab Report Include the answers to the questions from Step 5. Use the saved image files to support your answers. Annotate the events in this graph, and explain the events that you observe (e.g., segments dropped, retransmission, congestion window, slow start, congestion avoidance, fast recovery, etc.).

CHECKLIST FORM FOR LAB 5

Complete this checklist as you work through the laboratory exercises and attach the form to your lab report.

Name (please print):_____

☐ Prelab 5 question sheet

☐ Checkoff for Part 1   ☐ Checkoff for Part 6

☐ Checkoff for Part 2   ☐ Checkoff for Part 7

☐ Checkoff for Part 3   ☐ Checkoff for Part 8

☐ Checkoff for Part 4   ☐ Feedback sheet

☐ Checkoff for Part 5   ☐ Lab report

FEEDBACK FORM FOR LAB 5

- Complete this feedback form at the completion of the lab exercises and submit the form when submitting your lab report.

- The feedback is anonymous. *Do not put your name on this form* and keep it separate from your lab report.

- For each exercise, please record the following:

	Difficulty (–2, –1, 0, 1, 2) −2 = too easy 0 = just right 2 = too hard	**Interest Level** (–2, –1, 0, 1, 2) −2 = low interest 0 = just right 2 = high interest	**Time to Complete** (minutes)
Part 1. Learning how to use ttcp			
Part 2. File transfers using TCP and UDP			
Part 3. IP fragmentation of UDP and TCP traffic			
Part 4. TCP connection management			
Part 5. TCP data exchange— interactive applications			
Part 6. TCP data exchange— Bulk data transfer			
Part 7. Retransmissions in TCP			
Part 8. TCP congestion control			

Please answer the following questions:

- What did you like about this lab?

- What did you dislike about this lab?

- Make a suggestion to improve the lab.

LAN Switching

OBJECTIVES

- How to configure a Cisco router and a Linux PC as a LAN switch

- How LAN switches update their forwarding tables

- How LAN switches run a spanning tree protocol for loop-free routing

CONTENTS

PRELAB 6

1. **Bridging:** Read about LAN switching and bridging at

   `http://www.tcpip-lab.net/links/bridging.html`

2. **Transparent bridges and spanning tree protocol:** Read about transparent bridges and the spanning tree protocol at

   `http://www.tcpip-lab.net/links/transbdg.html`

3. **Bridge protocol data unit (BPDU):** Familiarize yourself with the format of bridge protocol data units (BPDUs) by reading the information at

   `http://www.tcpip-lab.net/links/bpdu.html`

4. **Configuring a PC as a bridge:** Explore the website

   `http://www.tcpip-lab.net/links/linuxbridge.html`

   which describes the *bridge-utils* software package for configuring a Linux PC as a bridge.

QUESTION SHEET FOR PRELAB 6

Answer the questions in the space provided below each one. Use extra sheets of paper if needed and attach them to this document. Submit the answers to the prelab with your lab report.

Name (please print):_____

1. Describe the difference between a LAN switch/bridge and a router.

2. What is the difference between an Ethernet switch and an Ethernet hub? Which is more suitable for a network with a high traffic load, a switch or a hub? Explain.

3. What motivates the use of the term *transparent* in transparent bridges?

4. Which role does the spanning tree protocol play when interconnecting LAN switches/bridges?

5. In the context of the IEEE 802.1d specification of the spanning tree protocol, define the following terms:

   (a) Root bridge

   (b) Root port

(c) Designated bridge

(d) Designated port

(e) Blocked port

6. In the spanning tree protocol, how does a LAN switch/bridge decide which ports are in a blocking state?

LAB 6

A *bridge* or *LAN switch* is a device that interconnects two or more local area networks (LANs) and forwards packets between these networks. Different from IP routers, bridges and LAN switches operate at the data link layer. For example, bridges and LAN switches forward packets based on MAC addresses, whereas IP routers forward packets based on IP addresses.

LAN switches are widely deployed in enterprise networks, including university campus networks. Many enterprise networks primarily use LAN switches to interconnect LANs, using IP routers only to connect the enterprise network to the public Internet.

The term *bridge* was coined in the early 1980s. Today, when referring to data link layer interconnection devices, the terms *LAN switch* or *Ethernet switch* (in the context of Ethernet) are much more common. Since many of the concepts, configuration commands, and protocols for LAN switches in Lab 6 use the old term *bridge*, we will, with few exceptions, refer to LAN switches as *bridges*.

This lab covers the main concepts of LAN switching in Ethernet networks: how packets are forwarded between LANs and how the routes of packets are determined. In the first and second parts of Lab 6, you learn how to configure a Linux PC and a Cisco router as a bridge. The third part illustrates the difference between an Ethernet hub and an Ethernet switch. Parts 4, 5, and 6 explore how forwarding tables of bridges are set up. You learn about the concepts of *learning bridges* and *transparent bridges*, as well as the operation of the spanning tree protocol that enables loop-free routing between interconnected LANs. The last part of the lab explores issues that arise when IP routers and bridges operate in the same network.

SETUP FOR LAB 6

The configuration of the equipment in Lab 6 is changed several times during the course of the lab. With the exception of the last part, the IP address configuration of the Linux PCs is as shown in Table 6.1. Note that all IP addresses have the same netmask.

TABLE 6.1. IP addresses of the PCs.

Linux PC	Interface *eth0*	Interface *eth1*
PC1	10.0.1.11/24	10.0.1.12/24
PC2	10.0.1.21/24	10.0.1.22/24
PC3	10.0.1.31/24	10.0.1.32/24
PC4	10.0.1.41/24	10.0.1.42/24

PART 1. CONFIGURING A LINUX PC AS A BRIDGE

The exercises in this lab show how to configure a Linux PC as a bridge. Ethernet bridging functionality is integrated in all recent versions of Linux. The configuration of bridging functions in Linux is done with configuration commands and tools. In this lab, we provide the bridge configuration tool *gbrctl*.

The network configuration for Part 1 is shown in Figure 6.1. Here, PC1 and PC3 act as hosts, and PC2 is set up as a bridge.

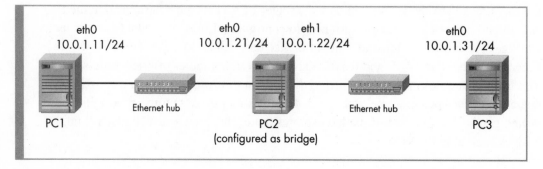

FIGURE 6.1.

Network topology for Part 1.

EXERCISE 1(A).
IP configuration of Linux PCs.

1. Set up the network configuration as shown in Figure 6.1.

2. Configure the interfaces of PC1, PC2, and PC3, with the IP addresses given in Table 6.1. Disable the interfaces that are not used in the configuration, that is, disable interface *eth1* on both PC1 and PC3.

3. Since, throughout Lab 6, you frequently work with MAC addresses, you should record the MAC addresses of the Linux PCs. Log in to each of the PCs and obtain the MAC addresses of both Ethernet interfaces with the command `ifconfig -a`. Enter the MAC addresses in Table 6.2. (In Part 2, you will repeat the same exercise on the Cisco routers.)

TABLE 6.2. MAC addresses of the Linux PCs.

Linux PC	MAC Address of Interface *eth0*	MAC Address of Interface *eth1*
PC1		
PC2		
PC3		
PC4		

EXERCISE 1(B).

Configure a Linux PC as a bridge.

In this exercise, you configure PC2 as a bridge that forwards packets between the two Ethernet segments shown in Figure 6.1. The bridge configuration on the Linux PCs is done with the tool *gbrctl*. The *gbrctl* tool has a graphical user interface to configure bridging functions on a Linux PC.

1. **Starting *gbrctl*:** Start *gbrctl* by typing the following command in a terminal window:

    ```
    PC2% gbrctl
    ```

    The command displays the main *gbrctl* window as shown in Figure 6.2, which is used to configure the bridging functions. The *gbrctl* tool is terminated by selecting *File* and then *Exit*.

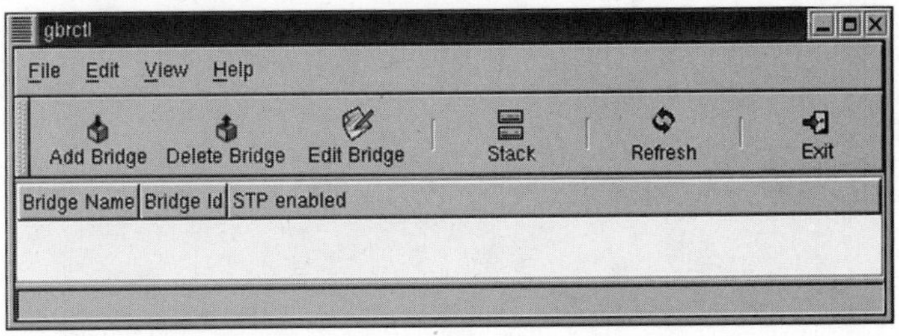

FIGURE 6.2.
Main *gbrctl* window.

2. **Creating a bridge with *gbrctl*:** It is possible to configure multiple independently operating bridges on the same PC. Each bridge is assigned a name and is associated with a set of interfaces. Here, you configure one bridge on PC2 and assign the bridge the name *Bridge1*.

    To start the configuration of PC2, select *Add Bridge* in the *gbrctl* main window in Figure 6.2. A window pops up as shown Figure 6.3, which asks for a name for the new bridge. Enter the name *Bridge1*. When you click *OK*, the newly created bridge is displayed in the *gbrctl* main window.

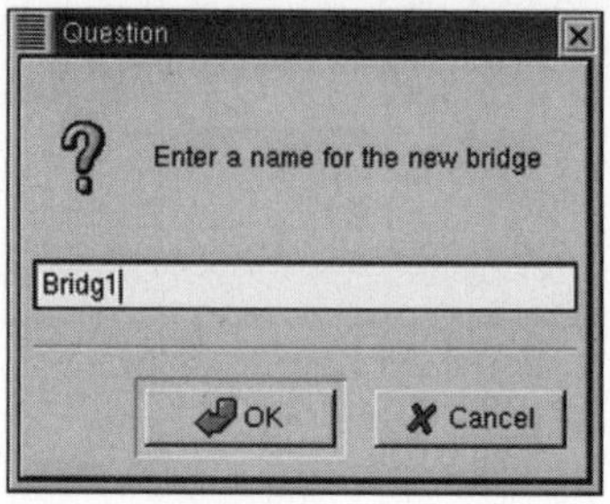

FIGURE 6.3.

Prompt to add
new bridge.

3. **Configuring a bridge with *gbrctl*:** After the bridge is created, the bridge is configured in the following steps:

   a. From the *gbrctl* main window, select the bridge name *Bridge1*, and then select
       Edit Bridge. This displays the *Bridge Configuration* window, which is shown in
       Figure 6.4.

   b. The first part of the configuration is the assignment of network interfaces to the
       bridge. Interfaces are assigned by clicking on the *Interfaces* tab and selecting
       Add Interface. Then, type the name of the interface to be added. For PC2, add
       the interfaces *eth0* and *eth1*.

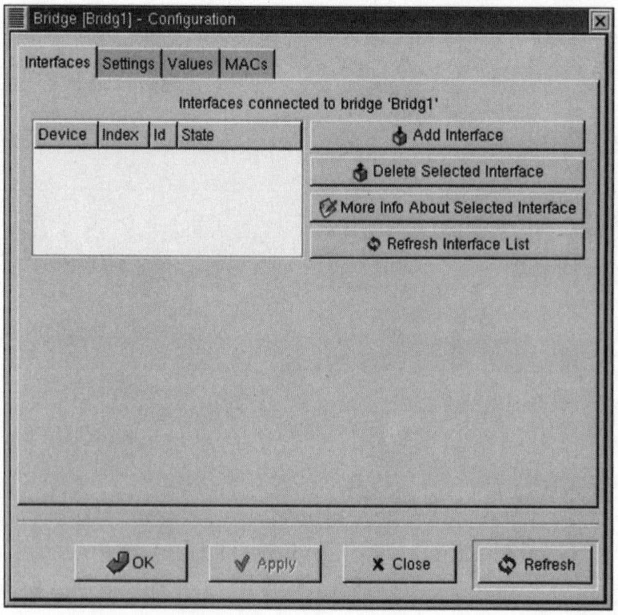

FIGURE 6.4.

*Bridge configuration
window (Interfaces).*

   c. The next part of the configuration sets the parameters of the spanning tree protocol (STP). Select the *Settings* tab in the *Bridge Configuration* window (see
       Figure 6.4). In Part 1, the spanning tree protocol is not used. Therefore, you need
       to disable the spanning tree protocol by toggling the button next to the STP
       label, so that it shows the label *Disabled*.

d. When the interfaces and the spanning tree protocol parameters are configured, terminate the *gbrctl* application by selecting *File* and then *Exit* in the *gbrctl* main window.

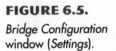

FIGURE 6.5.

Bridge Configuration window (Settings).

e. In the last part of the bridge configuration, you activate the bridge *Bridge1* from a terminal window. On a Linux PC, each created bridge is represented as a network interface. Therefore, if you type the command `ifconfig -a` on PC2, the command shows an interface *Bridge1*, in addition to the other interfaces *eth0*, *eth1*, and *lo*. The bridge is activated by enabling the interface associated with the bridge. This is done with the following command:

```
PC1% ifconfig Bridge1 up
```

NOTE:

Activating the bridge command disables the IP configuration of the interfaces assigned to a bridge. Hence, it is no longer possible to issue `ping` commands to these interfaces.

EXERCISE 1(C).
Observing a bridge in operation.

When the bridge configuration of PC2 is complete, PC2 forwards packets between PC1 and PC3. This exercise asks you to observe the forwarding of packets.

1. Start *ethereal* on PC1 and PC3, and capture traffic on interface *eth0* on both systems.

2. When bridging is activated on PC2, the configured IP addresses on PC2 should be disabled. To verify this, issue a `ping` command to interfaces *eth0* and *eth1* of PC2 from PC1 and PC3:

```
PC1% ping 10.0.1.21
PC3% ping 10.0.1.22
```

If PC2 is configured as a bridge, these `ping` commands should fail.

3. Clear the ARP caches on PC1 and PC3. Note that, in Linux, each ARP entry has to be deleted separately with the command `arp -d IPaddress`.

4. Issue a `ping` command from PC1 to PC3 and save the output:

```
PC1% ping -c 1 10.0.1.31
```

   • Observe that PC2 actually forwards the packets between PC1 and PC3.

   • Does PC2 modify the source and destination MAC and IP addresses? What would be different if PC2 was configured as an IP router?

   • Does the bridge manipulate any of the fields in the MAC and IP headers?

5. Run `traceroute` from PC1 to PC3 and save the output:

```
PC1% traceroute 10.0.1.31
```

Here, you should observe that PC2 does not appear in the output of `traceroute`.

   • Why is PC2 not visible from PC1?

   • If PC2 was configured as an IP router, how would the output differ?

6. Next, change the IP address of PC3 to 10.0.2.12/24. Note that PC1 and PC3 now have different IP network prefixes. Repeat Step 4.

   • Does the `ping` command from PC1 to PC3 still work? Explain the outcome.

7. Save the ICMP Echo Request packet(s) captured by *ethereal* on PC1 and PC3.

Lab Report

• Do the source and destination MAC/IP addresses change when a packet traverses a bridge? Provide an explanation and include an example from the captured data. Suppose that PC2 was configured as an IP router, which differences would you observe in the Ethernet and IP headers?

• Include the output of the `traceroute` command from Step 5. Provide an explanation why PC2 does not appear in the output of the `traceroute` command in Step 5. Include the answers to the questions in Step 5.

EXERCISE 1(D).
Manipulating a PC bridge.

This exercise familiarizes you with a few tasks related to running *gbrctl* on a Linux PC. You learn how to display the MAC forwarding table, how to delete the contents of the MAC forwarding table, and, finally, how to turn off the bridging functions. All of the tasks are performed on PC2.

1. First, reset the IP address of the *eth0* interface of PC3 to 10.0.1.31/24.

2. **Displaying the MAC forwarding table:** The MAC forwarding table of a bridge plays the same role as the routing table of an IP router. To view the contents of the MAC forwarding table of *Bridge1* on PC2, perform the following steps:

   a. Start *gbrctl*.

   b. Select *Bridge1* in the *gbrctl* main window and then select *Edit Bridge*.

   c. Select the *MACs* tab. This displays a window as shown in Figure 6.6.

   d. Click the *Refresh MAC list* button as shown at the bottom of Figure 6.6. This displays the current state of the MAC forwarding table.

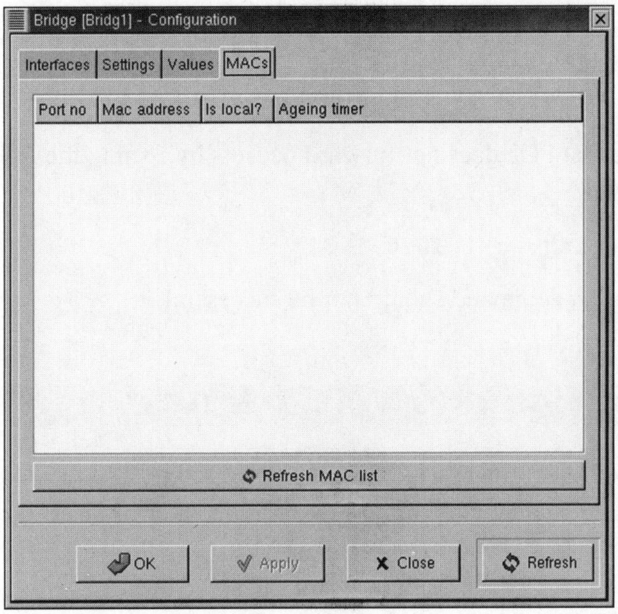

FIGURE 6.6.
Bridge configuration window (MACs).

3. **Clearing the MAC forwarding table of a bridge:** The *gbrctl* tool does not have a convenient way to delete the contents of the MAC forwarding table. Instead you must exploit that a bridge automatically deletes an entry in the forwarding table if it has not been looked up for a certain time, which is determined by the *Ageing* parameter in *gbrctl*. To delete the entries in the forwarding table, you must set the *Ageing* parameter to 0 seconds. Here are the steps to delete the entries on PC2:

   a. In the *gbrctl* main window, select the *Settings* tab and obtain a window as shown in Figure 6.5.

   b. Set the *Ageing* field to *0* and click *Apply*. All entries in the MAC forwarding tables are immediately removed.

   c. Select the *MACs* tab and click *Refresh MAC list*. You should now see only the MAC addresses of the local interfaces at PC2.

d. Once the entries are deleted, set the *Ageing* entry back to the original value (the default value is 300 seconds).

4. **Disabling a bridge:** Disabling a bridge on a Linux PC is done in two steps. To disable *Bridge1* on PC2:

a. First, deactivate the interface associated with *Bridge1*. This is done by typing

```
PC2% ifconfig Bridge1 down
```

b. Second, in the *gbrctl* main window (Figure 6.2), select *Bridge1*, and select *Delete Bridge*.

You can verify that the bridge is disabled as follows:

(1) Verify that PC2 is operating as a normal host. To do this, issue a `ping` command to interfaces *eth0* and *eth1* of PC2 from PC1 and PC3:

```
PC1% ping –c 1 10.0.1.21
PC3% ping –c 1 10.0.1.22
```

(2) Verify that PC2 does not forward packets by issuing the following `ping` command:

```
PC1% ping –c 1 10.0.1.31
```

The `ping` command should not be successful.

PART 2. CONFIGURING A CISCO ROUTER AS A BRIDGE

Next you learn how to configure a Cisco router as a bridge. The topology for this part is shown in Figure 6.7. Router1 is configured as a bridge that connects the two Ethernet segments.

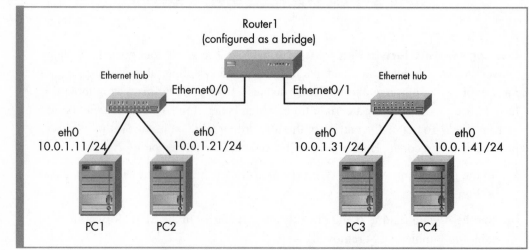

FIGURE 6.7.

Network topology for Parts 2 and 3(B).

EXERCISE 2(A).
Setup of network configuration.

After the network is configured as in Exercise 1(A) for the Linux PCs, you are asked to record the MAC addresses of the Cisco routers.

1. Connect the PCs and Router1 with Ethernet hubs as shown in Figure 6.7.

2. Configure the *eth0* interfaces of the Linux PCs with the IP addresses given in Table 6.1. (The IP addresses of PC1, PC2, and PC3 are the same as in Part 1.) Disable the *eth1* interfaces of all Linux PCs.

3. Establish a *kermit* session to each Cisco router. From PC1 establish a *kermit* session to Router1, from PC2 establish a *kermit* session to Router2, and so on.

4. On each router, type `enable` and then use the command `show interfaces` to display the MAC addresses of the Ethernet interfaces. Record the MAC addresses in Table 6.3.

TABLE 6.3. MAC addresses of the Ethernet interfaces on the Cisco routers.

Router	MAC Address of Interface *Ethernet0/0*	MAC Address of Interface *Ethernet0/1*
Router1		
Router2		
Router3		
Router4		

EXERCISE 2(B).
Configuring a Cisco router as a bridge.

Next you configure Router1 as a bridge. A Cisco router is configured as a bridge by disabling IP forwarding functions (with the command `no ip routing`) and by enabling bridging functions.

Similarly to the Linux PCs, a Cisco router can be configured to perform the functions of multiple independently operating bridges. This is done by defining a bridge group, which is identified by a number, and associating two or more network interfaces with each bridge group. Packets are forwarded only between interfaces that are assigned to the same bridge group. Since the exercises in Lab 6 use only one bridge group, we always use 1 to identify the group.

IOS MODE: GLOBAL CONFIGURATION

```
bridge 1 protocol ieee
```

Defines a bridge group and assigns the spanning tree protocol as defined in the IEEE 802.1d Standard to bridge group 1. After the command is issued, the Cisco router forwards packets between all interfaces that are assigned to bridge group 1. A bridge group can be any number between 1 and 63. After defining a bridge group, one can assign network interfaces to the bridge group. It is possible to define multiple bridge groups. In Lab 6, only one bridge group (with identifier 1) is used.

```
bridge 1 priority 128
```

Assigns the priority 128 to bridge group 1. The priority of a bridge group plays a role in the spanning tree protocol, which is covered in Part 5.

Each interface is individually configured to participate in a bridge group. This is done with the commands listed next.

IOS MODE: INTERFACE CONFIGURATION

```
bridge-group 1
```

Assigns this network interface to bridge group 1

```
no bridge-group 1
```

Removes this network interface from bridge group 1

```
bridge-group 1 spanning-disabled
```

Disables the spanning tree protocol on this interface for bridge group 1

```
no bridge-group 1 spanning-disabled
```

Enables the spanning tree protocol on this interface for bridge group 1

Once a Cisco router is configured as a bridge, the commands in the next list can be used to display the status of the bridge.

IOS MODE: PRIVILEGED EXEC

```
show bridge
```

Displays the entries of the MAC forwarding table

```
show spanning-tree
```

Displays the spanning tree topology information known to this bridge

```
show interfaces
```

Displays statistics of all interfaces, including the MAC addresses of all interfaces

---

The commands in the next list disable bridging functions on a Cisco router.

IOS MODE: PRIVILEGED EXEC

```
no bridge 1
```
Deletes the defined bridge group. After the command is issued, the Cisco router stops forwarding packets between interfaces that are assigned to bridge group 1.

```
clear bridge
```
Removes all entries from the MAC forwarding table.

```
clear arp-cache
```
Clears the ARP table.

1. **Configure a Cisco router as a bridge:** Use the preceding commands to configure Router1 as a bridge. On Router1, type the following commands:

```
Router1> enable
Password: <enable secret>
Router1# configure terminal
Router1(config)# no ip routing
Router1(config)# bridge 1 protocol ieee
Router1(config)# bridge 1 priority 128
Router1(config)# interface Ethernet0/0
Router1(config-if)# bridge-group 1
Router1(config-if)# bridge-group 1 spanning-disabled
Router1(config-if)# no shutdown
Router1(config-if)# interface Ethernet0/1
Router1(config-if)# bridge-group 1
Router1(config-if)# bridge-group 1 spanning-disabled
Router1(config-if)# no shutdown
Router1(config-if)# end
Router1# clear bridge
Router1# clear arp-cache
```

The commands disable IP forwarding and set up Router1 as a bridge that runs with priority 128. Both Ethernet interfaces are assigned to the bridge, but the spanning tree protocol is disabled.

2. Once Router1 has been configured as a bridge, configure the Linux PCs as shown in Figure 6.7 with the IP addresses of Table 6.1.

3. Delete all entries in the ARP caches of PC1 and PC3.

4. Issue a `ping` command from PC1 to PC3:

```
PC1% ping -c 1 10.0.1.31
```

5. Run *traceroute* from PC1 to PC3 and save the output:

```
PC1% traceroute 10.0.1.31
```

- Compare the results to the outcome of the `traceroute` command in Exercise 1(C).

- Why is it not possible to issue a `ping` command to Router1?

Lab Report

- Include the output of the `traceroute` command.

- Provide the answers to the questions in Step 5.

PART 3. THE DIFFERENCE BETWEEN AN ETHERNET HUB AND AN ETHERNET SWITCH

In this part of the lab, you try to observe the difference between the operation of an Ethernet hub and an Ethernet switch. The main observation to be made is that traffic going over an Ethernet hub may experience collisions, whereas an Ethernet switch does not have collisions.

An Ethernet hub is a relatively simple device that merely repeats a signal received on one network interface (port) to all other ports. When multiple devices connected to the same hub transmit a packet at the same time, the transmissions are corrupted. This is referred to as a *collision*.

An Ethernet switch, which performs the functions of a bridge for Ethernet segments, is a store-and-forward device. When a packet is received, the Ethernet switch looks up the destination MAC address in its MAC forwarding table and then forwards the packet to one of its ports. Transmissions on an outgoing link are done one packet at a time, and packets are buffered if multiple packets must be forwarded on the same output port at the same time.

In this context, dual-speed Ethernet hubs, which connect both 10 Mbps (10BaseT) and 100 Mbps (100BaseTX) Ethernet devices, are a special case. A dual-speed hub operates as two Ethernet hubs—one running at 10 Mbps and one running at 100 Mbps—that are connected by a bridge. Thus, there can be collisions between devices that operate at the same speed, but there are no collisions between devices at different speeds.

We point out that it is not always possible to observe collisions on an Ethernet hub. Not only does the rate of collision depend on the traffic load and pattern, but also hubs increasingly use internal buffering and avoid collisions in many cases.

EXERCISE 3(A).
Observe collisions on an Ethernet hub.

Try to generate collisions by flooding an Ethernet hub with traffic. The network configuration is as shown in Figure 6.8. You intentionally flood the hub that connects PC1 and PC2 with traffic and hopefully force collisions to occur.

NOTE:

The Ethernet hubs used in Figure 6.8 should not be dual-speed hubs, otherwise collisions may not occur.

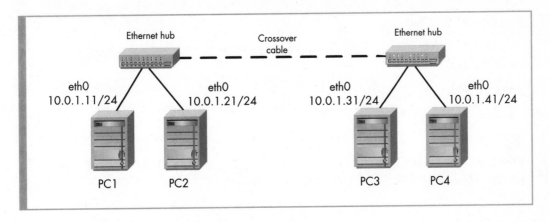

FIGURE 6.8.
Network Topology for Part 3(A).

1. Configure the network as shown in Figure 6.8. Starting from the network configuration from Part 2 (in Figure 6.7), disconnect Router1 and connect the two hubs directly with a crossover Ethernet cable.

2. Determine the number of collisions on interface *eth0* of PC1 and PC3 that have occurred since the PCs have been rebooted the last time, by typing

   ```
   PC1% ifconfig -a
   PC3% ifconfig -a
   ```

   Save the output.

3. Flood the network by generating a large number of ICMP Echo Request and Reply packets between PC1 and PC2, by typing

   ```
   PC1% ping -f 10.0.1.21
   ```

4. While the preceding `ping` command is running, start sending 100 ICMP Echo Request packets from PC3 to PC4:

   ```
   PC3% ping -c 100 10.0.1.41
   ```

   Hopefully, these `ping` messages cause some collisions at the Ethernet hub.

5. On PC1 and PC3, save the output of `ifconfig -a` again. Observe the number of new collisions that the previous experiment has generated.

Lab Report Calculate the number of new collisions as seen by PC1 and PC3, in the preceding exercise. Briefly explain what causes the collisions.

EXERCISE 3(B).
No collisions when using an Ethernet switch.

Repeat the steps of the previous exercise, but place an Ethernet switch (Router1, which has been configured as a bridge) between the two Ethernet hubs.

1. Reconstitute the network configuration shown in Figure 6.7, by connecting Router1 between the two hubs.

2. Obtain the number of collisions that have been observed on interface *eth0* of PC1 and PC3 by typing

```
PC1% ifconfig -a
PC3% ifconfig -a
```

Save the output.

3. Flood the network with traffic by generating a large number of ICMP Echo Request and Reply packets between PC1 to PC2, by typing

```
PC1% ping -f 10.0.1.21
```

4. Now issue 100 ICMP Echo Request packets from PC3 to PC4:

```
PC3% ping -c 100 10.0.1.41
```

5. Once again, save the output of the command `ifconfig -a` on PC1 and PC3, and record the number of collisions on interface *eth0*.

6. Access Router1 and run the `show bridge` command to display the bridge forwarding table. Save the data.

 Lab Report Use the `ifconfig -a` output to calculate the new collisions seen at the interfaces of PC1 and PC3. Explain the differences between the outcomes in Exercises 3(A) and 3(B).

PART 4.   LEARNING BRIDGES

Each bridge has a MAC forwarding table that determines the outgoing port for a packet. When a packet arrives, the bridge looks up the destination MAC address of the packet in its MAC forwarding table and retrieves the outgoing port for this packet. If the destination MAC address is not found in the MAC forwarding table, the bridge floods the packet on all ports, with the exception of the port where the packet arrived.

Bridges update their MAC forwarding table using what is called a *learning algorithm*, which works as follows. A bridge examines the source MAC address of each packet that arrives on a particular port and memorizes that the source address is reachable via that port. This is done by adding the source MAC address and the port to the MAC forwarding table. The next time the bridge receives a packet that has this MAC address as destination, the bridge finds the outgoing port in its forwarding table. Bridges that run this algorithm are referred to as *learning bridges*. All currently deployed Ethernet switches execute the learning algorithm.

An entry in the MAC forwarding table is deleted if is not used (looked up) for a certain amount of time. The maximum time that a MAC address can stay in the forwarding table without a lookup is determined by the *ageing* value, which is a configuration parameter.

Here you investigate the learning algorithm of bridges. The network configuration is as shown in Figure 6.9.

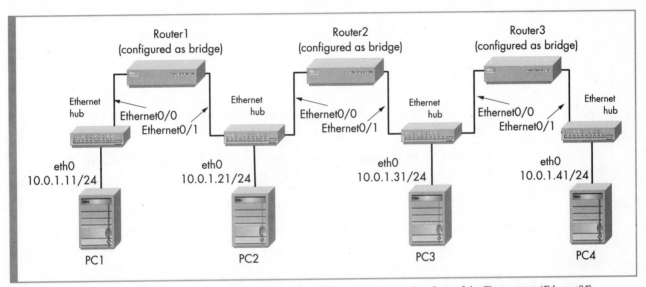

Note: When Ethernet interfaces of the Linux PCs (*eth0, eth1*) run at 100 Mbps and the Ethernet interfaces of the Cisco routers (*Ethernet0/0, Ethernet0/1*) run at 10 Mbps, you should avoid using dual-speed hubs when you connect two or more Cisco routers and one or more Linux PCs to the same hub.

 If you use dual-speed hubs in such a situation, the Linux PCs cannot observe the traffic between Cisco routers with *ethereal*.

FIGURE 6.9.

Network topology for Part 4.

EXERCISE 4(A).
Exploring the learning algorithm of bridges.

In this exercise you study how bridges set up their MAC forwarding tables from the network traffic.

1. Set up the network configuration as shown in Figure 6.9.

2. Establish a *kermit* session to Router1, Router2, and Router3.

    a. Configure Router1, Router2, and Router3 as bridges (disable the spanning tree protocol).

    b. On each of the bridges, delete the contents of the MAC forwarding table with the *clear bridge* command

3. Verify that PC2 is not running as a bridge. If necessary, follow the instructions in Exercise 1(D) to disable the bridging functions on PC2.

    Also, verify that on each PC only interface *eth0* is enabled.

4. Start to capture traffic with *ethereal* on the *eth0* interfaces of PC1, PC2, PC3, and PC4.

5. Clear the ARP cache on PC1, PC2, and PC3.

6. Now, issue a set of `ping` commands. After each command, save the MAC forwarding table on all bridges with the command `show bridge`, and observe how far the ICMP Echo Request and Reply packets travel.

```
PC1% ping -c 1 10.0.1.21
PC2% ping -c 1 10.0.1.11
PC2% ping -c 1 10.0.1.41
PC3% ping -c 1 10.0.1.21
```

- Use the captured data to illustrate the algorithm used by bridges to forward packets.

- For each of the transmitted packets, explain if the learning algorithm results in changes to the MAC forwarding table. Describe the changes.

7. Stop the traffic capture on the PCs, and save the *ethereal* output.

Lab Report Provide the answers to the problems in Step 6. Use the captured data to support your answers.

EXERCISE 4(B).
Learning about new locations of hosts.

Learning bridges adapt their MAC forwarding tables automatically when the location of a host changes. Due to the learning algorithm, the time it takes to adapt to a change depends on the network traffic and on the value of the *ageing* parameter. This is illustrated in the following exercise.

1. Continue with the configuration of the previous exercise. First, create or refresh entries in the MAC forwarding table at the bridges by issuing the following commands from PC1:

```
PC1% ping -c 3 10.0.1.31
PC1% ping -c 3 10.0.1.41
```

Now, connect PC2 to the same hub that PC4 is connected to.

2. Issue a `ping` command from PC1 that continuously sends ICMP Echo Request packets to PC2:

```
PC1% ping 10.0.1.21
```

Since Router2 does not know that PC2 has moved, it does not forward the ICMP Echo Request packet, and the packet does not reach PC2. As a result, the ARP requests and the `ping` are unsuccessful. Eventually, since the MAC forwarding entry for PC2 is not refreshed at Router2 and Router3, the entry is deleted. When the entry is removed, the next ICMP Echo Request from PC1 is flooded on all ports, thus reaching PC2. When PC2 responds, all bridges update their MAC forwarding table using the source MAC address of PC2.

- Record the amount of time that the `ping` from PC1 to PC2 is not successful after PC2 has been moved to a different hub.

3. Now connect PC3 to the same hub as PC4.

4. Issue a `ping` command from PC1 to PC3 that continuously sends ICMP Echo Request packets to PC3:

```
PC1% ping 10.0.1.31
```

5. Then, generate a single ICMP Echo Request packet from PC3 to PC1 with the command

```
PC3% ping -c 1 10.0.1.11
```

- Now, if you look on PC1, you notice that the `ping` command is successful again. Explain this outcome and compare it to the outcome of Step 2.

Lab Report

- Include the times that you recorded in Step 2.

- Explain the outcome of Step 5. That is, explain why the `ping` issued by PC3 has the effect that the `ping` commands from PC1 to PC3 (in Step 4) are successful. Compare the outcome with the outcome in Step 2.

PART 5. SPANNING TREE PROTOCOL

The learning algorithm from Part 4 builds the MAC forwarding tables of bridges, without the need for a routing protocol. However, since learning bridges flood a packet on all ports when a destination is not known, it may happen that packets are forwarded in a cycle and loop indefinitely. The spanning tree protocol for bridges, standardized in the IEEE 802.1d specification, prevents such forwarding loops from occurring. This is done by organizing the bridges in a spanning tree topology. Learning bridges that run the spanning tree protocol are called *transparent bridges*.

The spanning tree protocol, which is used by virtually all Ethernet switches, works as follows. One bridge, called the *root bridge*, is elected to be the root of the tree. Each bridge determines which of its ports has the best path to the root bridge. This is the *root port* of the bridge. On each LAN, the bridges elect one bridge, called the *designated bridge*, which, among all bridges on the same LAN, has the best path to the root bridge. The port that connects a bridge to the LAN where it is a designated bridge is called the *designated port*. Then, all bridges disable all ports that are not root ports or designated ports. What results is a spanning tree of bridges. Since a tree topology does not have a loop, forwarding packets along the edges of the tree guarantees that forwarding loops are entirely avoided.

This part of the lab has three components: (1) You set up a new network configuration. (2) You verify that bridges without the spanning tree result in forwarding loops. (3) You configure the spanning tree protocol and observe how it prevents loops from occurring.

EXERCISE 5(A).

Configuring a topology that results in forwarding loops.

1. Set up the network topology as shown in Figure 6.10. Router1, Router2, Router3, Router4, and PC2 are configured as bridges. PC1, PC3, and PC4 are configured as hosts.

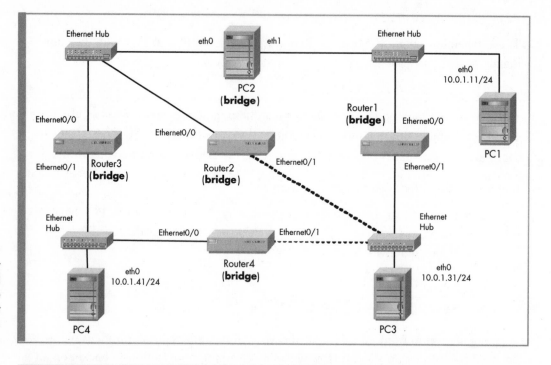

FIGURE 6.10.

Network topology for Part 5; the dotted lines indicate Ethernet cables that are added in Exercise 5(B).

> **NOTE:**
>
> For the time being, do not connect the cables to *Ethernet0/1* of Router2 and Router4, shown as dotted lines in Figure 6.10. Making these two connections will result in a forwarding loop. We delay the completion of the loop until you have set up the tools that allow you to observe the forwarding loop.

2. Verify that the MAC addresses of the Linux PCs and the Cisco routers are recorded in Tables 6.2 and 6.3. You need to refer to these tables frequently in the following exercises and in the lab report.

3. Since ARP traffic interferes with the forwarding and bridge learning operations that you need to observe, preconfigure the ARP tables with static entries so that no ARP Request packets need to be sent.

    First clear the ARP tables of PC1, PC3, and PC4; then enter static entries for interface *eth0* of PC1, PC3, and PC4, with the following commands:

    ```
    PC1% arp -s 10.0.1.31 MACaddress
    PC1% arp -s 10.0.1.41 MACaddress

    PC3% arp -s 10.0.1.11 MACaddress
    PC3% arp -s 10.0.1.41 MACaddress
    ```

```
PC4% arp -s 10.0.1.11 MACaddress
PC4% arp -s 10.0.1.31 MACaddress
```

In the preceding commands, *MACaddress* is the 48-bit MAC address of the corresponding interface from Table 6.2. The MAC addresses are entered in hexadecimal notation, with each byte separated by a colon (e.g., 00:a0:24:71:e4:44).

EXERCISE 5(B).
Observing forwarding loops.

The problem with learning bridges that do not run the spanning tree algorithm is that bridges flood a packet on all outgoing links when a destination MAC address is not found in the MAC forwarding table. If this results in a forwarding loop, the packet will be flooded over and over again, with each reception of the packet at a bridge generating a new round of copies. Thus, not only are packets forwarded in an infinite loop, but also, the number of packets that are forwarded increases due to the repeated flooding of the same packet in each round of the loop.

In this exercise you observe that the bridges in the topology of Figure 6.10 forward packets in a loop.

1. Once the network topology of Figure 6.10 is set up, verify that the spanning tree protocol (STP) is disabled on all bridges as follows:

   a. On the Cisco routers, type `show running-config` and verify that the line `bridge-group 1 spanning-disabled` is displayed for both Ethernet interfaces.

   b. On PC2, run *gbrctl* and verify that STP is set to *Disabled* in the *Settings* tab.

2. Clear the contents of the forwarding tables on all bridges with the following commands:

   a. On the Cisco routers, execute the command `clear bridge`.

   b. On PC2, follow the instructions for "Clearing the MAC forwarding table of a bridge" in Exercise 1(D).

3. Start *ethereal* on PC1, PC3, and PC4, and capture all traffic on interface *eth0*.

4. Now complete the topology in Figure 6.10 by connecting interface *Ethernet0/1* of Router2 and Router4 to the hubs.

5. Issue a `ping` command from PC1 to PC4:

   ```
   PC1% ping -c 1 10.0.1.41
   ```

   Use the *ethereal* output to observe the route of the ICMP Echo Request and Reply packets. You should be able to observe that the ICMP packet is looping.

6. Wait for several seconds and break the loop by disconnecting the cables at the *Ethernet0/1* interface of Router2 and Router4. Otherwise, the packets will loop forever and cause the bridges to become overloaded and stop forwarding packets.

> **NOTE:**
>
> Should the routers freeze up, disconnect the cables of both Ethernet interfaces on all routers and then wait for a few minutes. When you reconnect the interfaces, the routers should have returned to normal operation. There is no need to reboot the Cisco routers.

7. Stop the traffic capture with *ethereal* on all PCs. On each PC, save a few ICMP packets so that you can document that packets are actually looping.

8. On all bridges, that is, on Router1, Router2, Router3, Router4, and PC2, save the output of the MAC forwarding tables. On PC2, you need to cut and paste the MAC forwarding table from the *gbrctl* window.

Lab Report:

- Use the data saved in Step 7 to document for a single packet, that the packet is forwarded in a loop.

- Use the output from *ethereal* and the MAC forwarding tables to explain why some packets are looping indefinitely.

- The network topology of Figure 6.10 has more than one cycle. Explain why the ICMP packets continue looping in the same cycle.

EXERCISE 5(C).
Enabling the spanning tree protocol.

Next, you enable the spanning tree protocol on the bridges in Figure 6.10 and in this way complete forwarding loops. Before starting the exercise, we provide a brief description of the spanning tree protocol.

> **AN OVERVIEW OF THE SPANNING TREE PROTOCOL**
>
> The IEEE 802.1d spanning tree protocol (STP) organizes bridges in a tree topology without any central coordination. Every bridge has only a limited view of the spanning tree, and no bridge has complete knowledge of the spanning tree.
>
> **Bridge ID:** In the spanning tree protocol, each bridge has a unique identifier, called the *bridge ID*. The bridge ID has a length of 8 bytes. The first 2 bytes are the bridge priority, and the remaining 6 bytes are the bridge MAC address. The bridge priority is a configuration parameter. The bridge MAC address is set to the lowest MAC address of any of the ports of the bridge. In the spanning tree protocol, the bridge with the lowest bridge ID is elected as the root bridge.
>
> **BPDUs:** Bridges build the spanning tree by exchanging bridge protocol data units (BPDU). Bridges send BPDUs approximately once every 4 seconds. BPDUs are exchanged only between bridges that are connected to the same LAN.
>
> In Table 6.4, we illustrate the four fields of a BPDU that are relevant to the spanning tree protocol. The BPDU of a bridge advertises the best path from this bridge to the root bridge. Specifically, a BPDU—(R, C, B, P), where R is the value of the root ID, C is the

value of the root path cost, *B* is the bridge ID, and *P* is the port ID—is interpreted as follows: "I am bridge *B* and I am sending from my port *P*. I believe *R* to be the root bridge, and the cost of my path to the root bridge is *C*."

TABLE 6.4. Fields of a BPDU relevant to the spanning tree construction.

Length (in Bytes)	Field Name	Content
8	Root ID	Identifies the root bridge (as seen by the sender of this BPDU)
4	Root path cost	Cost of the path from the sender of this BPDU to the root bridge
8	Bridge ID	Identifies the sender of this BPDU
2	Port ID	Identifies the network interface (port) where this BPDU is sent

Operations of the spanning tree protocol: Each bridge listens on all its ports to BPDUs sent by other bridges. If a bridge receives a BPDU that advertises a "better" path than advertised in its own BPDU, the bridge updates its BPDU. To determine if a received BPDU advertises a better path, the bridge compares the received BPDU to its own BPDU. If the root ID in the received BPDU is smaller than the root ID of the bridge, the received BPDU is seen as advertising a better path. If the root IDs are identical, the BPDU with the lower root path cost advertises a better path. If both the root ID and root path cost are identical, then the BPDU with the lower bridge ID is seen as advertising a better path. Finally, if root ID, root path cost, and bridge ID are all identical, then the BPDU with the lowest port ID is interpreted as advertising a better BPDU.

When a bridge with BPDU (*R1, C1, B1, P1*) receives a BPDU (*R2, C2, B2, P2*) and the received BPDU advertises a better path, the bridge updates its own BPDU to (*R2, C2+increment, B1, P1*). The *increment* value is a configuration parameter that accounts for the cost increase of the path due to bridge *B1*. When the increment value is set to 1 on all bridges, then the bridges establish a minimum hop route to the root bridge. The *increment* can also be set to account for the data rate of a LAN. For example, to make a path on a 100 Mbps LAN more desirable than on a 10 Mbps LAN, the 10 Mbps LAN can be assigned a larger increment value.

A bridge transmits its BPDU on a port only if its BPDU advertises a better route than any of the BPDUs received on that port. In this case, the bridge assumes that it is the *designated bridge* for the LAN to which the port connects, and the port that connects the bridge to the LAN is called the *designated port* of the LAN. A bridge that is not the designated bridge for a LAN does not send BPDUs on that LAN.

On each bridge, the port where the bridge receives the BPDU that advertises the best route is called the *root port*.

Constructing the spanning tree: Each bridge locally decides which of its ports are part of the spanning tree. Only the root port and the designated ports of a bridge are part of the spanning tree; the other ports are not part of the spanning tree. One can reconstruct the complete tree by connecting, for each LAN, the root ports that connect to this LAN with the designated port of the LAN.

Each bridge forwards packets only on ports that are part of the spanning tree, that is, if they are received on the root port or sent on its designated ports. These ports are said to be in a *Forwarding* state. All other ports are said to be in a *Blocking* state. In this way, packets are forwarded only along the edges of the spanning tree. As a result, since a tree topology does not have a loop, the forwarding of packets does not result in loops.

Initializing the spanning tree protocol: When a bridge, say, with bridge ID B, is started, it assumes that it is the root bridge. It sends a BPDU (*B, 0, B, p*) on all its ports *p*. The root path cost is set to 0, since B believes itself to be root. Within a short amount of time, the bridge learns about better paths, and the protocol quickly converges to a new spanning tree.

Your task in this exercise is to capture the BPDUs in the network of Figure 6.10 and trace how the spanning tree is constructed.

1. Delete all entries in the MAC forwarding tables on all bridges (Router1, Router2, Router3, Router4, and PC2) as done in Step 2 of Exercise 5(B).

2. Next, enable the spanning tree protocol on all bridges:

   a. On the Cisco routers, the following commands, shown here for Router1, must be executed:

```
Router1# configure terminal
Router1(config)# interface Ethernet0/0
Router1(config-if)# bridge-group 1
Router1(config-if)# no bridge-group 1 spanning-disabled
Router1(config-if)# interface Ethernet0/1
Router1(config-if)# bridge-group 1
Router1(config-if)# no bridge-group 1 spanning-disabled
Router1(config-if)# exit
```

   b. On PC2, the spanning tree protocol is enabled with *gbrctl*, following the instructions given in Exercise 1(D): Start *gbrctl*, go to *Edit Bridge*, select the *Settings* tab, and toggle the STP field to *Enabled*.

3. Set the bridge priority to 128 on all bridges:

   a. On the Cisco routers, you can view the bridge priority by typing

```
Router1# show spanning-tree
```

   The output should include a line that states: "Bridge Identifier has priority 128 ...." If the priority is different from 128, use the following IOS global configuration command to change the priority:

```
Router1(config)# bridge 1 priority 128
```

   b. On PC2, setting the priority of a bridge in *gbrctl* is not very intuitive. The priority value is displayed under the *Settings* tab of the *Bridge Configuration* window as shown in Figure 6.5. The value is displayed as hexadecimal numbers. When a bridge is created, *gbrctl* initially sets the priority to 0x8000. (When the SPT toggle is used to disable and then enable the spanning tree protocol, somehow the priority value is changed to 0x0001.)

To set the bridge priority to 128, go to *Edit Bridge* in *gbrctl*, select the *Settings* tab, and enter the value *512* in the *Bridge Priority* field. When you click the *Apply* button, the *Bridge Priority* value will change to 0x0080, which corresponds to the decimal value 128.

Table 6.5 shows the input values that need to be typed to set a certain bridge priority value. For other input values, the priority is set to 0.

TABLE 6.5. Valid bridge priority values for *gbrctl*.

Input Value in Bridge Priority Field of *gbrctl*	Bridge Priority Value Displayed by *gbrctl* (hexadecimal)	Bridge Priority Value (decimal)
16	0008	8
32	0010	16
64	0020	32
256	0040	64
512	0080	128
1024	0100	256

4. Wait until the spanning tree stabilizes. The spanning tree has stabilized when all interfaces of the bridges are either in state *Blocking* or *Forwarding*. You can obtain the state of the interfaces of a bridge by typing:

   - On the Cisco routers, execute the command `show spanning-tree`.

   - On PC2, start *gbrctl*, select *Bridge1*, go to *Edit Bridge*, select the *Values* tab.

5. Clear the ARP cache on all Linux PCs, including the static entries that you included in Exercise 5(A).

6. Run *ethereal* on the *eth0* interfaces of all PCs, and capture all packets.

7. Issue a `ping` command from PC1 to PC4 by typing

   ```
   PC1% ping -c 1 10.0.1.41
   ```

8. Access each Cisco router, and save the output of the following commands:

   ```
   Router1# show spanning-tree
   Router1# show bridge
   ```

9. Study the output of the commands in Step 8 and the BPDUs captured by *ethereal* to derive the spanning tree configuration.

   • Obtain information on the root bridge, the root ports of each bridge, the designated ports, the forwarding ports, and the blocked ports.

   • By how much is the path cost incremented at each bridge?

   • Since *gbrctl* does not display all information on the state of the ports, on PC2, you need to infer some information from the BPDUs transmitted by PC2, as well as from the topology of the network in Figure 6.10.

10. On each PC, save a small number of BPDUs, and save all ICMP and ARP packets that have been captured by *ethereal*. You may want to set a display filter `arp || icmp || stp` to limit the packets shown by *ethereal*.

Lab Report

• Use the saved data to draw the spanning tree for the network in Figure 6.10 as seen by the bridges. For each bridge, include information on the root bridge, the root port, the designated ports, and the blocked ports.

• Identify the bridges that transmit BPDUs after the spanning tree protocol has converged. For each Ethernet segment, determine the following fields for the BPDU sent on that segment: root ID, root path cost, and bridge ID. Explain how these messages are interpreted. Show how the entire spanning tree can be constructed from these messages.

• Use Figure 6.10 to trace the path of the packets that are sent as a result of the `ping` command (e.g., ARP Request and Reply, ICMP Echo Request and Reply). Justify your answer with the saved data from Step 10.

PART 6.   RECONFIGURATIONS OF THE SPANNING TREE

The spanning tree protocol adapts to changes in the network topology. Here you observe how the spanning tree topology adapts when a link fails.

EXERCISE 6(A).
Reconfiguration of the spanning tree.

You simulate a failed link in the network shown in Figure 6.10 by disconnecting an Ethernet cable. Then you observe how the bridges adjust to a change in the network topology.

1. Continue with the network configuration from Figure 6.10 as it was at the end of Exercise 5(C). If the network is not configured, you need to follow the instructions in Part 5.

   Make sure that the spanning tree protocol is enabled on Router1, Router2, Router3, Router4, and PC2 and that the priorities of all bridges are set to 128.

2. Start to capture traffic with *ethereal* on the *eth0* interfaces of PC1, PC3, and PC4.

3. Issue a `ping` command from PC1 to PC4 that sends one ICMP Echo Request every second:

```
PC1% ping -i 1 10.0.1.41
```

4. Disconnect one of the cables connected to the root bridge. (If you did not *just* complete Part 5, you need to determine the root bridge in the current network configuration.)

   • From the display of *ethereal* on the PCs, observe the BPDUs of the bridges that build a new spanning tree.

   • Observe that the `ping` command at PC1 fails for a certain period of time, but is successful again when the new spanning tree is built.

   • Terminate the `ping` command with Ctrl-C. Use the statistics that are displayed when the `ping` command is terminated to estimate the amount of time it took to build the new spanning tree.

5. Save the information that describes the new spanning tree, by repeating Steps 8 and 10 in Exercise 5(C).

Lab Report Use the saved output to draw the spanning tree as seen by the bridges after the spanning tree has been rebuilt. For each bridge, indicate the root port, the designated ports, and the blocked ports. Briefly explain the changes of the spanning tree.

EXERCISE 6(B).
Fixing a bridge to become the root bridge.

Here you force a certain bridge to become the root bridge. Recall that the priority of a bridge is used in the first 2 bytes of the bridge ID. Thus, the bridge with the lowest priority value has the lowest bridge ID. Since the spanning tree protocol elects the bridge with the lowest bridge ID as the root bridge, the root bridge can be fixed by modifying the priority field.

Being able to fix a certain bridge as the root bridge provides some control over the spanning tree topology. For example, one can select the device with the highest capacity to become the root bridge.

1. Continue with the topology at the end of Exercise 6(A). (Do not reconnect the Ethernet cable that was disconnected in Exercise 6(A).)

2. Select one of the bridges from Figure 6.10, other than the root bridge in Exercise 6(A). Change the priority of this bridge to 64. Since all other bridges in the network have a bridge priority of 128, this bridge becomes the root bridge.

   a. If you selected Router1, then the commands to set the bridge priority are as follows:

```
Router1# configure terminal
Router1(config)# bridge 1 priority 64
Router1(config)# end
```

b. If you selected PC2, select *Edit Bridge* in *gbrctl*, select the *Settings* tab, and enter the value *256* in the *Bridge Priority* field. This changes the bridge priority to 64.

3. Verify that a new root bridge has been selected, and save the information that describes the new spanning tree (as in Steps 8 and 10 in Exercise 5(C)).

Lab Report Draw the spanning tree as seen by the bridges after a new root bridge has been configured.

PART 7. MIXED ROUTER AND BRIDGE CONFIGURATION

In this part of the lab, you set up a network topology that contains bridges as well as IP routers. Both bridges and routers are devices that connect networks and forward packets between networks. Bridges make forwarding decisions based on destination MAC addresses. IP routers make forwarding decisions based on destination IP. In a properly configured network, bridges and IP routers coexist without causing network problems. Sometimes, however, the forwarding of packets in a network with bridges and IP routers can be difficult to trace. The following exercises explore such a scenario.

EXERCISE 7(A).
Setting up the network configuration.

1. Connect the Linux PCs and Cisco routers as shown in Figure 6.11.

2. If you continue from Part 6, disable bridging on PC2, Router2, and Router3:

a. On Router2 and Router3, you disable the bridging functions by typing

```
Router2# no bridge 1
```

b. On PC2, follow the steps in Exercise 1(D) for disabling the bridge functions on a Linux PC.

3. Complete the IP configuration of all Linux PCs and of Cisco routers Router2 and Router3 as given in Tables 6.6 and 6.7.

a. All routing table entries are statically configured.

b. You must enable IP forwarding on Router2 and Router3.

c. The netmask of PC4 is 16 bits long. All other IP network interfaces have 24 bit long netmasks.

Here are the configuration commands for Router2:

```
Router2# configure terminal
Router2(config)# ip routing
Router2(config)# ip route 0.0.0.0 0.0.0.0 10.0.3.3
Router2(config)# interface ethernet0/0
```

```
Router2(config-if)# ip address 10.0.3.2 255.555.255.0
Router2(config-if)# interface ethernet0/1
Router2(config-if)# ip address 10.0.1.2 255.555.255.0
Router2(config-if)# end
```

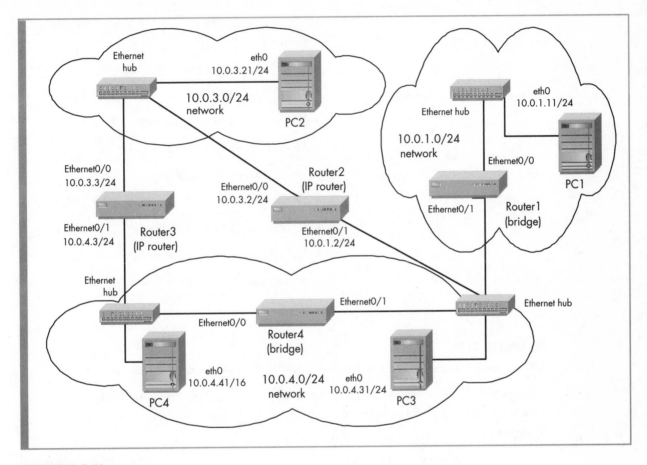

FIGURE 6.11.

Network topology for Part 7.

TABLE 6.6. PC configurations for Part 7.

Linux PC	Ethernet Interface *eth0*	Ethernet Interface *eth1*	Default Gateway
PC1	10.0.1.11/24	Disabled	10.0.1.2
PC2	10.0.3.21/24	Disabled	10.0.3.2
PC3	10.0.4.31/24	Disabled	10.0.4.3
PC4	10.0.4.41/16	Disabled	10.0.4.3

TABLE 6.7. Configuration of Cisco routers for Part 7.

Cisco Router	Configured As	Configuration Information
Router1	Bridge	• Enable bridging on both interfaces *Ethernet0/0* and *Ethernet0/1*.
Router4		• The spanning tree protocol can be enabled or disabled. • IP addresses need not be configured.
Router2	IP router	• IP configuration on *Ethernet0/0*: 10.0.3.2/24. • IP configuration on *Ethernet0/1*: 10.0.1.2/24. • Default gateway set to 10.0.3.3. • IP forwarding is enabled.
Router3	IP router	• IP configuration on *Ethernet0/0*: 10.0.3.3/24. • IP configuration on *Ethernet0/1*: 10.0.4.3/24. • Default gateway set to 10.0.3.2. • IP forwarding is enabled.

EXERCISE 7(B).
Observing traffic flow in a network with IP routers and bridges.

Here you observe the paths of packets between the Linux PCs. You will see that in a mixed IP router and bridge environment, tracing the path of a packet is not always straightforward.

1. Clear the forwarding tables on all bridges, and clear the ARP cache on all hosts and IP routers.

2. Run *ethereal* on all PCs, and capture traffic on the *eth0* interface of each PC.

3. Issue the following set of `ping` commands. Use the output of *ethereal* to determine the path of the ICMP Echo Request and Reply packets. Note that not all `ping` commands will be successful.

   a. On PC1:

      ```
      PC1% ping -c 1 10.0.4.31
      ```

   b. On PC1:

      ```
      PC1% ping -c 1 10.0.4.41
      ```

   c. On PC4:

      ```
      PC4% ping -c 1 10.0.1.11
      ```

d. On PC1:

```
PC1% ping -c 1 10.0.3.21
```

- Determine which of the `ping` commands are successful and which fail.

- Use the data displayed by *ethereal* to determine the route of the ICMP Echo Request and Reply packets (e.g., PC1→Router1→Router2→Router4 → PC4).

- For each path, provide an explanation why a certain route is taken by the ICMP Echo Request and Reply packets.

4. Stop the packet capture with *ethereal* on all PCs. On each PC, save enough ICMP packets so that you can address the problems raised in Step 3.

Lab Report Describe which of the `ping` commands are successful and which fail. Use the data that you captured to determine the route of the ICMP Echo Request and Reply packets. For each route, provide an explanation why the path is taken for each of the `ping` commands.

CHECKLIST FORM FOR LAB 6

Complete this checklist as you work through the laboratory exercises and attach the form to your lab report.

Name (please print):_____

☐ Prelab 6 question sheet

☐ Checkoff for Part 1

☐ Checkoff for Part 2

☐ Checkoff for Part 3

☐ Checkoff for Part 4

☐ Checkoff for Part 5

☐ Checkoff for Part 6

☐ Checkoff for Part 7

☐ Feedback sheet

☐ Lab report

FEEDBACK FORM FOR LAB 6

- Complete this feedback form at the completion of the lab exercises and submit the form when submitting your lab report.

- The feedback is anonymous. *Do not put your name on this form* and keep it separate from your lab report.

- For each exercise, please record the following:

	Difficulty (–2, –1, 0, 1, 2)	Interest Level (–2, –1, 0, 1, 2)	Time to Complete (minutes)
	–2 = too easy	–2 = low interest	
	0 = just right	0 = just right	
	2 = too hard	2 = high interest	

Part 1.
Configuring a Linux PC
as a bridge

Part 2.
Configuring a Cisco
router as a bridge

Part 3.
The difference between an
Ethernet hub and an Ethernet
switch

Part 4.
Learning bridges

Part 5.
Spanning tree protocol

Part 6.
Reconfigurations of the
spanning tree

Part 7.
Mixed router and bridge
configuration

Please answer the following questions:

- What did you like about this lab?

- What did you dislike about this lab?

- Make a suggestion to improve the lab.

Network Address Translation (NAT)
Dynamic Host Configuration Protocol (DHCP)

OBJECTIVES

- How NAT (network address translation) works

- How DHCP (Dynamic Host Configuration Protocol) works

- How DHCP works together with NAT

CONTENTS

PRELAB 7

1. **Unix commands for NAT, DHCP:** Go to the online manual pages at

   `http://www.tcpip-lab.net/links/manual.html`

   and select the operating system version Red Hat Linux/i386 7.3. Read the manual pages of the following commands:

   a. `iptables`

   b. `dhcpd`

   c. `dhcpd.conf`

   d. `dhcp-options`

   e. `dhcpd.leases`

   Read the manual page of `dhclient` at

   `http://www.tcpip-lab.net/links/dhclient.html`

2. **Private IP addresses:** Read RFC 1918 on address allocation in private networks.

   `http://www.tcpip-lab.net/links/rfc1918.html`

3. **Network address translation (NAT):** Read the tutorial on NAT at

   `http://www.tcpip-lab.net/links/nat.html`

4. **Netfilter/`iptables`:** Read about *netfilter* and `iptables` at

   `http://www.tcpip-lab.net/links/netfilter.html`

5. **Dynamic Host Configuration Protocol (DHCP):** Read RFC 2131 on DHCP at

   `http://www.tcpip-lab.net/links/rfc2131.html`

QUESTION SHEET FOR PRELAB 7

Answer the questions in the space provided below each one. Use extra sheets of paper if needed and attach them to this document. Submit the answers to the prelab with your lab report.

Name (please print):_____

1. Explain why NAT is often mentioned as a solution to counteract the depletion of IP addresses on the global Internet. Which alternatives to NAT exist that address the scarcity of available IP addresses?

2. What does the following comment refer to: "NAT destroys the ability to do host-to-host communication over the Internet"?

3. Explain the following terms as used in the context of Network Address Translation:

   a.   Static NAT

   b.   Dynamic NAT

   c.   NAT with IP overload

   d.   Port address translations

   e.   IP masquerading

4. Refer to RFC 1918 and list the IP address blocks that are reserved for use in private networks. Why is there a need to specify IP addresses for private networks?

5. The utility *netfilter* and the command `iptables` provide support for NAT in Linux systems. Explain the relationship between the *netfilter* utility and the `iptables` command.

6. Describe the following terms that are used in the `iptables` command:

   a. Chain

   b. Postrouting

   c. Prerouting

7. Consider a NAT device between a private and the public network. Suppose the private network uses addresses in the range 10.0.1.0–10.0.1.255, and suppose that the interface of the NAT device to the public network has IP address 128.143.136.80.

   a. Write the `iptables` command so that the addresses in the private network are mapped to the public IP address 128.143.136.80.

   b. Write an IOS command so that the addresses in the private network are mapped to the public IP address 128.143.136.80.

8. Explain the meaning of the *magic cookie* in the DHCP protocol.

9. If the command `dhcpd` is issued (without arguments) on a Linux PC with multiple network interfaces, which network interfaces does the DHCP server listen on?

LAB 7

Figure 7.1 shows two private networks that are connected to a public network. Each private network is connected to the public network by a NAT device, which is either a PC or a Cisco router. On each NAT device, IP forwarding must be enabled.

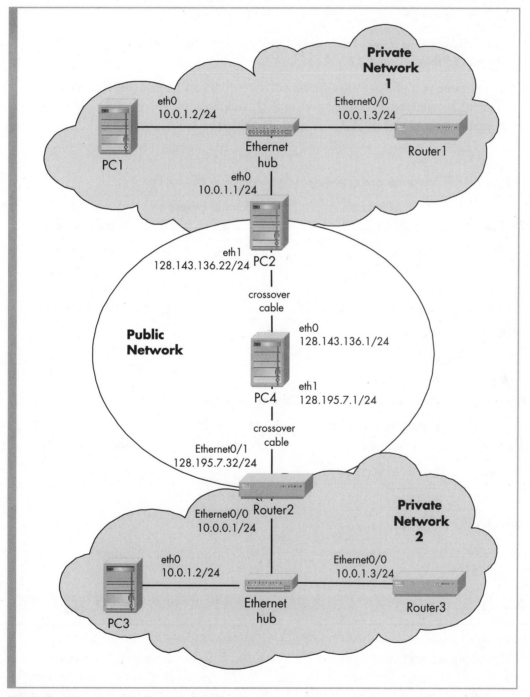

FIGURE 7.1.

Configuration for Part 1.

Note: In the private networks in Figure 7.1, Router1 and Router3 are used to mimic hosts (i.e., they are not configured to act as IP routers).

- In this lab PC2 and Router2 are routers that provide the gateways between the private and the public networks. Both PC2 and Router2 are configured as NAT devices.

- On PC2 the kernel is built with *netfilter*, an extension to the Linux kernel that provides the kernel with the ability to set IP packet filters, including NAT functions. On Router2, you will use Cisco IOS commands to configure NAT rules.

- PC4 runs as an IP router. (We use a Linux PC instead of a Cisco router so that *ethereal* can be used to capture traffic on the public network.)

- The assignment of IP addresses and default gateways for all PCs and routers are shown in Tables 7.1 and 7.2.

- The console port of Router1 is connected to a serial port of PC1; the console port of Router2 is connected to a serial port of PC2; and the console port of Router3 is connected to a serial port of PC3.

TABLE 7.1. IP addresses and gateway assignments of all PCs for Part 1.

Machine	IP Address of Interface (*eth0*)	IP Address of Private Network Interface (*eth1*)	Default Gateway
PC1	10.0.1.2/24	none	10.0.1.1
PC2	10.0.1.1/24	128.143.136.22/24	128.143.136.1
PC3	10.0.1.2/24	none	10.0.1.1
PC4	128.143.136.1/24	128.195.7.1/24	none

TABLE 7.2. IP addresses and gateway assignments of routers for Part 1.

Machine	IP Address of Interface (*Ethernet0/0*)	IP Address of Interface (*Ethernet0/1*)	Default Gateway
Router1	10.0.1.3/24	none	10.0.1.1
Router2	10.0.1.1/24	128.195.7.32/24	128.195.7.1
Router3	10.0.1.3/24	none	10.0.1.1

PART 1. NETWORK ADDRESS TRANSLATION (NAT)

Network address translation (NAT) refers to a function that replaces the IP addresses (and possibly the port numbers) of IP datagrams. NAT is run on routers that connect private networks to the public Internet, to replace the IP address-port pair of an IP packet with another IP address-port pair. Generally, the operations of NAT are specified in terms of a set of rules which determines how IP addresses are to be replaced.

Often, a NAT device is referred to as a *NAT box*. One of the reasons for using NAT is that it conserves IP addresses. NAT allows hosts in a private network to share public IP addresses or to limit the use of public IP addresses to a small number of hosts in the private network.

Private networks may have IP addresses that are non-Internet routable, as specified in RFC 1918. This means that regular IP routers do not have entries in their routing tables for these addresses.

In the network in Figure 7.1, both PC2 and Router2 will be configured as NAT devices. With NAT, the hosts in the private networks can access the public network (i.e., they are able to reach the addresses on the 128.143.136.0/24 and 128.195.7.0/24 networks).

EXERCISE 1(A).
Network setup.

Configure the network in Figure 7.1 with the IP address configuration shown in Tables 7.1 and 7.2. The following commands review the steps involved in the configuration.

1. On the Linux PCs, use `ifconfig` to configure the IP address of the interfaces. Add a default gateway on each PC with the command (shown for PC1):

   ```
   PC1% route add default gw 10.0.1.1
   ```

2. IP forwarding must be enabled on PC2 and PC4.

3. Use a serial cable to connect a serial port of a PC to the console port of a router. Use the `kermit` command to access the routers.

4. Configure the IP addresses of interfaces Ethernet0/0 and Ethernet0/1 on the routers, and set the default gateways as shown in Table 7.2. Following is the sample configuration for Router2, where the Ethernet interface is located in slot 0:

   ```
   Router2> enable
   Password: <enable secret>
   Router2# configure terminal
   Router2(config)# no ip routing
   Router2(config)# ip routing
   Router2(config)# ip route 0.0.0.0 0.0.0.0 128.195.7.1
   Router2(config)# interface Ethernet0/0
   Router2(config-if)# no shutdown
   Router2(config-if)# ip address 10.0.1.1 255.255.255.0
   Router2(config-if)# interface Ethernet0/1
   Router2(config-if)# no shutdown
   Router2(config-if)# ip address 128.195.7.32 255.255.255.0
   Router2(config-if)# end
   ```

   In the above commands `ip route 0.0.0.0 0.0.0.0 128.195.7.1` sets the default gateway of Router2.

   After completing the setup of the configuration you should be able to issue successful `ping` commands (between hosts in the private network and between hosts in the public network). However, `ping` commands across a private/public network boundary are not successful.

EXERCISE 1(B).
Configuration of NAT on a Cisco router.

A Cisco router can be set up to run as a NAT device.

In Cisco IOS, the private network is referred to as *inside,* and the public network is referred to as *outside.* An IP address that is seen by hosts on the inside is called a *local address,* and an IP address that is seen by hosts on the outside is called a *global address.* There are four different types of addresses:

* An *inside local address* is an address in the private network that is not visible in the public network.
* An *inside global address* can be used in the public network for devices in the private network.
* An *outside global address* is an address in the public network that is not made known in the private network.
* An *outside local address* is an IP address that is assigned in the private network to designate a host in the public network.

Using this terminology, a NAT device translates in outgoing packets inside local addresses to outside global addresses and in incoming packets translates outside global addresses to inside local addresses.

---

1. **Modify the NAT table of Router2:** Use the following commands to set up Router2 as a NAT device:

   a. A NAT rule is added so that the private IP address of PC3, 10.0.1.2, is translated to the public address 200.0.0.2. See Table 7.3.

TABLE 7.3. Private and public address of PC3.

Machine	Inside Local Address	Outside Global Address
PC3	10.0.1.2/24	200.0.0.2/24

The IOS commands are as follows

```
Router2> enable
Password: <enable secret>
Router2# show ip nat translations
Router2# configure terminal
Router2(config)# interface Ethernet0/0
Router2(config-if)# ip nat inside
Router2(config-if)# interface Ethernet0/1
Router2(config-if)# ip nat outside
```

```
Router2(config-if)# exit
Router2(config)# ip nat inside source static 10.0.1.2
     200.0.0.2
Router2(config)# end
Router2# show ip nat translations
```

b. After the preceding rule has been entered, display the content of the NAT table and save it to a file.

The commands used above are explained as follows.

IOS MODE: PRIVILEGED EXEC

`Show ip nat translations`
   Displays the content of the NAT table.

IOS MODE: INTERFACE CONFIGURATION

`ip nat inside`
   Specifies that an interface is connected to the private network.

`ip nat outside`
   Specifies that an interface is connected to the public network.

IOS MODE: GLOBAL CONFIGURATION

`ip nat inside source static IPaddr1 IPaddr2`
   Adds a rule so that the private IP address `IPaddr1` is mapped to a public IP address `IPaddr2`.

   For example, the command,

   `ip nat inside source static 10.0.1.2 200.0.0.2`

   maps the private address 10.0.1.2 to the public address 200.0.0.2.

Dynamic NAT is an alternative to the static NAT table entries used in this exercise. With dynamic NAT, a pool of global addresses is specified at the NAT device. Addresses from the pool are dynamically mapped to the private addresses whenever there is a demand for a new address.

2. **Update routing tables:** Add static routing entries to the routing table of PC4, so that traffic with destination IP address 200.0.0.0/24 is forwarded to Router2.

3. **Observe traffic at a NAT device:** To observe the IP address translation, issue `ping` commands between machines in the public and private network. Use *ethereal* to capture packets on the private and public interfaces of Router2.

   a. Start an *ethereal* session on PC3 to capture the traffic from Router2 on the private network.

   b. Start an *ethereal* session on interface *eth1* of PC4 to capture the traffic from Router2 on the public network.

c. Issue the following `ping` commands:

On PC3:

```
PC3% ping -c 3 10.0.1.3
PC3% ping -c 3 128.143.136.1
```

On Router3:

```
Router3# ping 10.0.1.2
Router3# ping 128.143.136.1
```

On PC4:

```
PC4% ping -c 3 10.0.1.2
PC4% ping -c 3 200.0.0.2
```

d. Save the *ethereal* data to files. Observe which `ping` commands succeed.

4. **Add additional NAT table entries:** Add NAT rules to Router2, so that Router2 and Router3 (on interface Ethernet0/0) are addressable from the public network. The private and public addresses are given in Table 7.4.

TABLE 7.4. Private and public addresses of Router2 and Router3.

Machine	Inside Local Address	Outside Global Address
Router2	10.0.1.1	200.0.0.1
Router3	10.0.1.3	200.0.0.3

Issue `ping` commands to verify that the IP addresses are correctly mapped.

Lab Report

- Include the NAT table of Router2 and provide an explanation of the columns of the table.

- For each of the preceding `ping` commands, provide an explanation of why the command succeeds or fails.

- Include the IP source address and IP destination address from the IP header data of an ICMP Echo Request and the corresponding ICMP Echo Reply packet before and after it passes through Router2.

EXERCISE 1(B).
IP masquerading with a Linux PC.

In this exercise we consider a special use of NAT that allows multiple private IP addresses to be mapped to a single public IP address. This use of NAT is called *IP masquerading, port address translation* (*PAT*), or *network address and port translation* (*NAPT*). Here, the private network has only a single public IP address but has multiple hosts in the private network. IP masquerading modifies the port number of packets so that the single public IP address can be overloaded.

In this exercise, PC2 will be configured to perform IP masquerading. The Linux kernel on all PCs has been built with *netfilter*, which adds the ability to set IP packet filters in a Linux system. IP packet filters are used to add firewalls as well as NAT functionality to a system. The `iptables` command is used to set up, maintain, and inspect IP packet filter rules to a Linux kernel.

On a Linux system, the configuration of NAT manipulates a set of rules of the *netfilter* utility, called the *NAT table*. The rules in the NAT table are grouped in so-called chains. Two of the built-in chains are called PREROUTING and POSTROUTING:

- PREROUTING: The rules in this chain are applied to incoming datagrams.
- POSTROUTING: The rules in this chain are applied to outgoing datagrams. The main rule is SNAT (source network address translation), which specifies how the source address of an outgoing IP datagram should be modified.

Commands that manipulate the NAT table start with

```
PC2% iptables -t nat
```

The following are some of the most important commands that manipulate the NAT table.

```
iptables -t nat -L
```
   Displays all rules in the NAT table.

```
iptables -t nat -D POSTROUTING 1
```
   Deletes the first rule in the POSTROUTING chain of the NAT table

```
iptables -t nat -F
```
   Deletes all entries in (flushes) the NAT table

```
iptables -t nat -A POSTROUTING -j SNAT --to IPAddr1 -s
IPAddr2/netmask
```
   Adds the following rule to the POSTROUTING chain of the NAT table:

   ```
   "in IP datagrams that go to the public network, the IP
   source address IPAddr2/netmask is changed to IPAddr1".
   ```

   For example, in the command

   ```
   iptables -t nat -A POSTROUTING -j SNAT --to 128.195.7.32
     -s 10.0.1.0/24
   ```

   the source address of outgoing IP datagrams that match 10.0.1.0/24 is changed to 128.195.7.32.

---

1. **Modify the NAT table of PC2:** On PC2, add a rule to the NAT table so that the IP source address of all outgoing IP datagrams are set to IP address 128.143.136.22.

   Display the content of the NAT table and save it to a file.

2. **Observe traffic at a NAT device:**

   a. To observe the IP address translation, observe traffic on both interfaces of PC2 that are between the private networks and the public network. On PC2, run *ethereal* on both *eth0* and *eth1*, and start to capture traffic.

b. Establish a set of *Telnet* sessions and log in to remote machines, using the following `telnet` commands:

On PC1:
```
PC1% telnet 10.0.1.3
PC1% telnet 128.143.136.1
```

On Router1:
```
Router1# telnet 10.0.1.2
Router1# telnet 128.143.136.1
```

On PC4:
```
PC4% telnet 10.0.1.2
```

When opening a *Telnet* session to a Cisco router, IOS asks for a login password. This password is generally not the same password as the enable secret, which is used to enter the privileged EXEC mode. However, in the Internet lab, the login password for *Telnet* sessions is set to use the same password as the enable secret.

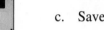

c. Save the *ethereal* data to files. Observe which `telnet` commands succeed.

d. For the successful *Telnet* sessions, observe how the IP addresses and port numbers are mapped.

3. **Observe mapping of ICMP packets:** The `ping` command sends out ICMP Echo Request messages and receives ICMP Echo Reply messages. Since ICMP messages do not contain a port number, it is not entirely obvious how a NAT device that performs IP masquerading can direct ICMP Echo Reply messages that return from the public network to the private network. In this exercise, you will explore how a NAT device handles ICMP messages.

a. On PC2, run *ethereal* on both *eth0* and *eth1*. Use the appropriate filters to capture the traffic generated by `ping` commands.

b. Issue the following `ping` commands:

On PC1:
```
PC1% ping -c 3 10.0.1.3
PC1% ping -c 3 128.143.136.1
```

On Router1:
```
Router1# ping 10.0.1.2
Router1# ping 128.143.136.1
```

On PC4:
```
PC4% ping -c 3 10.0.1.2
```

c. Save the *ethereal* output and the output of `ping` commands into files.

Lab Report

- For each of the preceding `telnet` and `ping` commands, provide an explanation why a command succeeds or fails.

- For each successful *Telnet* session, include the IP header data of an outgoing and an incoming packet header (with respect to the private network).

- For each successful `ping` command, include the IP header data of an outgoing ICMP Echo Request message and an incoming ICMP Echo Reply message (with respect to the private network).

- How does a PC know that a packet coming from the public network is destined to a host in the private network?

- Explain the steps performed by the Linux kernel during IP address translation.

EXERCISE 1(D).
NAT and *FTP*.

NAT can create problems for applications, which carry the IP addresses in the payload of an IP datagram. An example of such an application is the File Transfer Protocol (*FTP*).

In this exercise, you establish an *FTP* session from PC3 in the private network to PC2 in the public network and observe how *FTP* works with NAT.

1. Start *ethereal* on interface *eth0* of PC4 and on interface *eth0* of PC3.

2. *FTP* **session between two hosts in the public network:**

    a. Start an *FTP* sesion from PC4 to PC2 (the `-d` option prints out debug messages):

```
PC4% cd /root/labdata
PC4% ftp -d 128.143.136.22
```

    Log in with user name *root* and enter the root password.

    b. Download a file from the *FTP* server:

```
ftp> get fname
```

    where *fname* is a file on the remote server. (You can use the command `ls` to obtain a list of all files in the remote directory.)

    c. Use the traffic captured by *ethereal* to determine where the *payload* of *FTP* data carries information on IP addresses.

    d. Save the *ethereal* output and the *FTP* debug information output into files.

3. *FTP* **session from a private to the public network:**

    a. Use the same commands as previously to download a file from PC2 to PC3:

```
PC3% ftp -d 128.143.136.22
```

    Is the *FTP* session establishment successful?

    b. Save the traffic captured by *ethereal* and save the *FTP* debug information output. Make sure that you save enough data to answer the lab report questions.

Lab Report Use the captured data to explain the outcome of the *FTP* experiment. In particular, if the file was successfully *downloaded*, explain how the problem of sending the IP address as part of the data payload of the IP packet is solved.

PART 2. DYNAMIC HOST CONFIGURATION PROTOCOL (DHCP)

The Dynamic Host Configuration Protocol (DHCP) can be used to dynamically set and change configuration parameters of Internet hosts, including IP address, netmask, default router, and DNS server. DHCP is based on a client-server model. DHCP clients send requests to a DHCP server and the server responds with an allocation of IP addresses and other configuration parameters.

In this part of the lab, you will also learn about DHCP relay agents. When the DHCP client and DHCP server are not on the same IP network, DHCP relay agents can act as routers of DHCP messages. A DHCP relay agent can forward DHCP requests from a DHCP client to a DHCP server and it can forward the reply messages from the DHCP server to the DHCP client.

The network configuration for Part 2 is shown in Figure 7.2. PC1, PC3, and PC4 are set up as DHCP clients and initially do not have IP addresses. PC2 is configured as a DHCP server, which listens for DHCP requests on all of its interfaces and transmits network configuration parameters. Router1 acts as a DHCP relay agent, which forwards DHCP messages between different IP networks.

Table 7.5 lists the range of addresses that are associated at the DHCP server PC2 with each IP network.

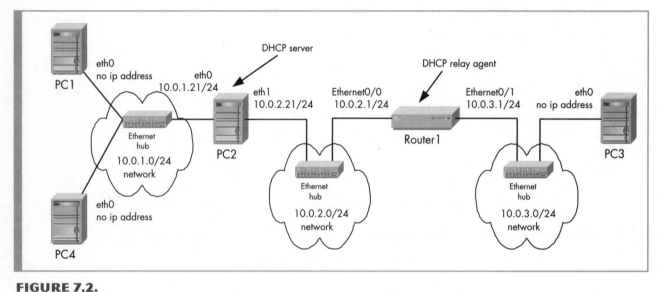

FIGURE 7.2.

Network configuration for Part 2.

TABLE 7.5. Configuration of the PCs in Part 2.

Machine	IP Address of Internet Interface (*eth0*)	IP Address of Private Network Interface (*eth1*)	Default Gateway
PC1	none	none	none
PC2	10.0.1.21/24	10.0.2.21/24	10.0.2.1
PC3	none	none	none
PC4	none	none	none

EXERCISE 2(A).

Network setup.

1. We strongly recommend that you reboot the PCs and the routers before you proceed.

2. Set up the network topology as shown in Figure 7.2. Configure the IP addresses of the PCs and Router1 as shown in Table 7.6 and 7.7.

TABLE 7.6. Router configuration in Part 2.

Machine	IP Address of Interface (*Ethernet0/0*)	IP Address of Interface (*Ethernet0/1*)	Default Gateway
Router1	10.0.2.1/24	10.0.3.1/24	10.0.2.21

TABLE 7.7. DHCP server configuration.

Subnet	Range of Addresses	Default Router
10.0.1.0/24	10.0.1.2 to 10.0.1.10	10.0.1.21
10.0.3.0/24	10.0.3.2 to 10.0.3.10	10.0.3.1

3. It is important that PC1, PC3, and PC4 do not have a default route and do not have an IP address associated with their respective interface *eth0*.

   Review the routing table and the interface configuration. On PC1, this is done with the commands

   ```
   PC1% netstat -rn
   PC1% ifconfig -a
   ```

In Linux, routing tables display the default route as an entry with destination 0.0.0.0. If the routing table shows a default route, you can delete this and all other routing table entries by setting the IP address to 0.0.0.0. This is done with the following command:

```
PC1% ifconfig eth0 0.0.0.0 up
```

EXERCISE 2(B).
Configuring and starting a DHCP server.

On a Linux system, a DHCP server is started with the command dhcpd. The DHCP server reads the configuration file */etc/dhcpd.conf*. The configuration file contains information on available IP addresses, as well as other configuration information. The following is an example of a configuration file for a DCHP server:

```
#dhcpd.conf file
ddns-update-style none;
default-lease-time 600;
subnet 10.0.1.0 netmask 255.255.255.0 {
   range 10.0.1.10 10.0.1.100;
   option routers 10.0.1.1;
   default-lease-time 120;
}
subnet 10.0.2.0 netmask 255.255.255.0 {
   range 10.0.2.101 10.0.2.200;
}
subnet 10.0.3.0 netmask 255.255.255.0 {
   range 10.0.3.6 10.0.3.10;
}
```

The DHCP client is assigned an IP address for a period of time that is known as a lease. The preceding configuration file assigns IP addresses for a lease time of 600 seconds (default-lease-time). For requests on network 10.0.1.0/24, the DHCP server assigns IP addresses in the range 10.0.1.10–10.0.1.100, assigns 10.0.1.1 as the default gateway, and limits the lease of addresses to 120 seconds, thus overruling the global limit of 600 seconds. For requests on network 10.0.2.0/24, the server assigns IP addresses in the range 10.0.2.101–10.0.2.200.

1. **Set the DHCP configuration file:** On PC2 set up the configuration file so that IP addresses are assigned as follows: On network 10.0.1.0/24, IP addresses are assigned in the range 10.0.1.2-10.0.1.10 with default gateway 10.0.1.21. On network 10.0.3.0/24, IP addresses are assigned in the range 10.0.3.2-10.0.3.10 with default gateway 10.0.3.1.

   Note that these assignments are similar to, but not identical with the configuration file shown above.

2. **Start the DHCP server:** On PC2, start the DHCP server by typing

```
PC2% dhcpd
```

The DHCP server listens for requests from DHCP clients on all its interfaces. In Linux, the DHCP server must be restarted each time the configuration file is modified. Since only one DHCP server can run at a time, you may need to terminate the current DHCP server process.

EXERCISE 2(C).
Starting a DHCP client.

The following steps start a DHCP client on PC1:

1. **Preparation:** On PC1, perform the following functions:

   a. Ensure that no default router entry exists in the routing table.

   b. A Linux DHCP client caches information from previous uses of DHCP. The cached information is stored in files

   ```
   /var/lib/dhcp/dhclient.leases
   /var/lib/dhcp/dhclient.leases~
   ```

   Since this cached information may interfere with your work, delete these files, if they exist.

   c. Start *ethereal* on interface *eth0* of PC2. (Set the display filter to `bootp.dhcp` so that only DHCP traffic is displayed in the window.)

2. **Start a DHCP client:** The DHCP client on PC1 is started with the command

   ```
   PC1% dhclient -d eth0
   ```

   Save the data that is captured by *ethereal* to a file. Save enough data to answer the following questions from the captured traffic:

   a. Which IP address is assigned to PC1?

   b. Observe the source and destination IP addresses of the packets that are sent between DHCP client and DHCP server.

   c. How is it possible that a host can send and receive DHCP packets, even though it does not have an IP address?

   d. Do you observe any ARP packets? If so, explain the function of ARP in this context.

   e. Observe and interpret the output of the DHCP packets. You should see the following packet types: DHCP Discover, DHCP Offer, DHCP Request, DHCP ACK.

   f. Identify and interpret all option fields in the DHCP packet types that you observe.

3. **Renewing leases of IP addresses:** The DHCP client is assigned an IP address for a limited period of time, which is called a *lease*. The maximum time of a lease is specified in the file *dhcpd.conf*. Information on current leases is stored at both the client side and the server side.

a. In Linux, information on the current leases is stored in the following files:

At the DHCP server: /var/lib/dhcp/dhcpd. leases

At the DHCP client: /var/lib/dhcp/dhclient. leases

b. To interpret the content of the files, refer to the manual pages of `dhcpd.conf`, `dhcp-options`, and `dhcpd.leases`.

c. Save the files that contain the information on current leases.

d. Observe how a DHCP client renews a lease and saves the captured traffic to a file.

  •   What type of DHCP message can be observed?

  •   How long does a DHCP client wait until it attempts to renew its lease?

e. Stop the process that runs the DHCP server by terminating the process *dhcpd* with the command

```
PC2% pkill dhcpd
```

Observe what the DHCP client does when it cannot reach the DHCP server. Use the command `ifconfig -a` to see how long the DHCP client waits until it releases the leased IP address.

f. Restart the DHCP server process by typing

```
PC2% dhcpd
```

4. **Starting more DHCP clients:** Repeat the instructions in Step 2 and start DHCP clients on PC3 and PC4.

a. The expected outcome is that PC4 receives an IP address but that PC3 is not successful. Why is the negative outcome for PC3 expected?

b. Compare the IP addresses assigned to PC1 and PC4. Is there a specific order in which IP addresses are assigned by the DHCP server?

Lab Report Answer the following questions using the *ethereal* output:

•   Use a figure to explain the packets that were exchanged by the DHCP client and the DHCP server as part of the process of acquiring an IP address.

•   Explain the entries in the lease file `dhcpd.leases`. How is the content of the lease file used when a DHCP client cannot contact the DHCP server?

•   In most client-server applications, the port number of a server is a well-known number (e.g., an *FTP* server uses port number 21, the *Telnet* server uses port number 23, etc.), while the client uses a currently available (ephemeral) port number. DHCP is different. Here, both the client and the server use a well-known port: UDP port 67 for the DHCP server and UDP port 68 for the DHCP client. Refer to RFC 2131 and provide an explanation for this protocol design choice.

EXERCISE 2(D).
DHCP relay agent.

A DHCP relay agent can forward DHCP packets when the DHCP server and the DHCP client are not on the same network. Note that the role of a DHCP relay agent is not entirely trivial, since it acts as a router for a host that does not have an IP address. Here you explore how packets from the client reach the server on another network and how the response from the server reaches the DHCP client.

The DHCP server is configured to allocate addresses as shown in Table 7.7.

Next we set up a Cisco router as a DHCP relay agent.

1. **Setting up a Cisco router as a DHCP relay agent:** The following commands set up Router1 as a DHCP relay agent. In essence, Router1 is configured to forward UDP packets.

    Start the DHCP relay agent on Router1 as follows:

    ```
    Router> enable
    Password: <enable secret>
    Router1# configure terminal
    Router1(config)# ip forward-protocol udp
    Router1(config)# interface Ethernet0/1
    Router1(config-if)# ip helper-address 10.0.2.21
    Router1(config-if)# end
    ```

    > **IOS MODE: GLOBAL CONFIGURATION**
    >
    > `ip forward-protocol udp`
    >   Enables UDP packet forwarding.

    > **IOS MODE: INTERFACE CONFIGURATION**
    >
    > `ip helper-address Ipadddr`
    >   Forwards DHCP request packets received on the current interface to IP address
    >   `IPaddr`, which should be the IP address of a DHCP server.

2. Start *ethereal* on PC2 and PC3.

3. Make sure that the DHCP server is running on PC2. If necessary, start a new DHCP server.

4. Start a DHCP client on PC3 with

    ```
    PC3% dhclient -d eth0
    ```

5. Verify that an IP address has been assigned to PC3.

    According to the configuration file, the DHCP configuration on network 10.0.2.0/24 does not set a default router. Verify that this is correct by inspecting the routing table.

6. Answer the following questions:

- Does the DHCP relay agent modify DHCP packets or the IP header? If so, what are the modifications?

- How does the relay agent redirect the replies from the DHCP server? Does it broadcast them or unicast them to the DHCP client?

- Is there a difference in the response of the DHCP server as compared to the DHCP configuration of PC1? If so, explain the difference.

- How does the DHCP server (PC2) know on which network PC3 is located when it receives the DHCP request?

- What is the destination IP address of the first DHCP packet that the DHCP server sends to PC3?

7. Save the DHCP packets that are captured by *ethereal* to a file.

Lab Report

- Include the *ethereal* data of the first three DHCP packets that are exchanged between PC3 and PC2.

- Provide answers to the questions in Exercise 2(D).

- What happens if a network has multiple DHCP servers?

PART 3. COMBINING NAT AND DHCP

Figure 7.3 shows a network configuration that can be found in many SOHO (small office, home office) networks.

- The SOHO network is a private network with multiple hosts (PC1 and PC4) and one IP router (PC2).

- The IP router of the SOHO network (SOHO router) provides access to the public Internet by connecting to a router of an Internet service provider. The SOHO router obtains a single IP address on the "public" interface of the SOHO network via DHCP from a DHCP server (PC3) of the Internet service provider.

- The SOHO router (PC2) works as a DHCP server and NAT server for the hosts in the SOHO network.

In this network setup, all SOHO hosts can share a single public IP address, which is dynamically assigned by the Internet service provider. Furthermore, the SOHO network requires minimal IP configuration. The hosts in the SOHO network obtain their IP addresses from the SOHO router. The SOHO router obtains its (public) IP address from the Internet service provider.

Your task is to set up the entire SOHO network, including the router and the DHCP server of the Internet service provider.

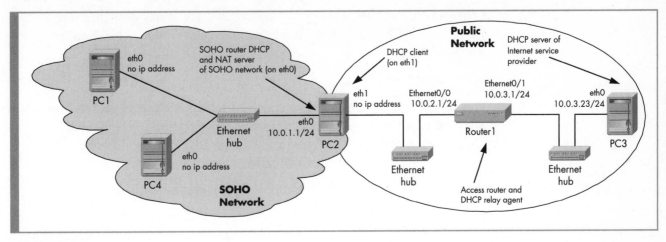

FIGURE 7.3.

Network configuration for Part 3.

EXERCISE 3:

The network configuration is shown in Figure 7.3. (The connections of the cables are identical to Figure 7.2). To reset the configuration of all machines, we recommend rebooting the PCs and the router.

1. DHCP server: PC3 is the DHCP server of the Internet service provider.

   a. Configure PC3 with IP address 10.0.3.23/24 on interface *eth0* and with default gateway 10.0.3.1.

   b. Configure and start a DHCP server on PC3. On PC3, set up the configuration file so that IP addresses in the range 10.0.2.2–10.0.2.10 are assigned for requests on network 10.0.2.0/24, and addresses in the range 10.0.3.2–10.0.3.10 are assigned for requests on network 10.0.3.0/24.

2. Router and DHCP relay agent: Router1 is the IP router to which the SOHO network sends its external traffic. Also, Router1 is a DHCP relay agent.

   a. Configure Router1 with IP addresses 10.0.2.1/24 on interface *Ethernet0/0* and 10.0.3.1/24 on interface Ethernet0/1.

   b. The routing table of Router1 should reflect that all traffic to network 10.0.2.0/24 is sent on interface *Ethernet0/0*, and all other traffic is sent on interface *Ethernet0/1*.

   c. Configure Router1 as a DHCP relay agent, so that requests from DHCP client PC2 reach DHCP server PC3.

3. SOHO router: PC2 is the SOHO router.

   a. Set up PC2 so that it is a DHCP client on interface *eth1*.

   b. Set up PC2 as an IP router. That is, IP forwarding must be enabled. The routing table entries must reflect that traffic to network 10.0.1.0/24 must be routed on interface *eth0*, and all other traffic must be sent to Router1 at 10.0.2.1.

    c.   Configure PC2 as DHCP server on interface *eth0* for addresses in the range 10.0.1.2–10.0.1.10. Execute the following command to start a DHCP server process on PC2:

```
PC2% dhcpd eth0
```

    d.   Start a NAT server on PC2 and set up a NAT table, which maps packets from the SOHO network with source IP address from network 10.0.1.0/24 to the IP address of interface *eth1*, PC2 obtained through DHCP protocol from PC3. The command for adding a rule that will achieve this is

```
iptables -t nat -A POSTROUTING -j MASQUERADE -o eth1 -s
10.0.1.0/24
```

4. Hosts in PCs: PC1 and PC4 are hosts in the SOHO network. Set up PC1 and PC4 as DHCP clients on interfaces *eth0*.

5. Collecting the results:

    a.   Display the routing tables from all PCs with `netstat -rn` and the IP configuration with `ifconfig -a` and save the results.

        What are the IP addresses assigned to PC1 and PC4? How are the IP addresses mapped to the public IP address defined on the NAT server PC2?

    b.   Display and save the NAT table of PC2.

    c.   Start *ethereal* on PC1 (*eth0*), PC2 (*eth1*), and PC3 (*eth0*).

    d.   Issue a `ping` command from PC1 to PC3:

```
PC1% ping -c 5 10.0.3.23
```

    e.   Save the traffic captured by *ethereal* on one of the PCs to a file.

Lab Report

- Include the *ethereal* data from the first ICMP Request and ICMP Reply messages.

- Include the routing table and the output of the `ifconfig` command from all PCs.

- Include the NAT table form PC2.

CHECKLIST FORM FOR LAB 7

Complete this checklist as you work through the laboratory exercises and attach the form to your lab report.

Name (please print):_____

☐ Prelab 7 question sheet

☐ Checkoff for Part 1

☐ Checkoff for Part 2

☐ Checkoff for Part 3

☐ Feedback sheet

☐ Lab report

FEEDBACK FORM FOR LAB 7

- Complete this feedback form at the completion of the lab exercises and submit the form when submitting your lab report.

- The feedback is anonymous. *Do not put your name on this form* and keep it separate from your lab report.

- For each exercise, please record the following:

	Difficulty (–2, –1, 0, 1, 2)	Interest Level (–2, –1, 0, 1, 2)	Time to Complete (minutes)
	–2 = too easy 0 = just right 2 = too hard	–2 = low interest 0 = just right 2 = high interest	

Part 1.
Network Address
Translation (NAT)

Part 2.
Dynamic Host
Configuration Protocol
(DHCP)

Part 3.
Combining NAT and
DHCP

Please answer the following questions:

- What did you like about this lab?

- What did you dislike about this lab?

- Make a suggestion to improve the lab.

The Domain Name System

OBJECTIVES

- How the Domain Name System (DNS) works

- How to set up a DNS server

- How the mapping from host names to IP addresses and vice versa is performed

CONTENTS

PRELAB 8

1. **Unix commands for DNS:** Go to the online manual pages at `http://www.tcpip-lab.net/links/manual.html` and select the operating system version Red Hat Linux/i386 7.3. Read the manual pages of the following commands:

   a. `host`

   b. `named`

   c. `nsswitch.conf`

2. **Domain Name System:** Read about the Domain Name System at

   `http://www.tcpip-lab.net/links/dns.html`

3. **DNS resolver:** Read about the client software of the Domain Name System, called *DNS resolver*, at

   `http://www.tcpip-lab.net/links/resolv_conf.html`

4. **Download configuration files:** The configuration of DNS servers requires a number of configuration files. Some of the configuration files needed in the lab are available online. You must download these files and save them to a single floppy disk. There is one set of files for each PC. The files are located in a directory with URL

   `http://www.tcpip-lab.net/links/conf/lab8`

   Download all of the files available at this URL to a floppy disk and bring the disk to the lab session.

QUESTION SHEET FOR PRELAB 8

Answer the questions in the space provided below each one. Use extra sheets of paper if needed and attach them to this document. Submit the answers to the prelab with your lab report.

Name (please print):_____

1. Briefly explain what the command host does.

2. Describe the following terms that are used in the Domain Name System.

   a. Top-level domain

   b. CNAME (canonical name)

   c. Resolver

   d. Name server

   e. Label

   f. FQDN (fully qualified domain name)

   g. BIND

   h. Inverse lookup

   i. RR (resource record)

   j. SOA (start of authority)

3. Explain the following types of DNS queries:

    a. Inverse queries

    b. Iterative queries

    c. Recursive queries

4. What is the difference between a DNS domain and a DNS zone?

5. What are some of the top-level domains in the DNS namespace?

6. Are domain names case sensitive? What, if any, is the constraint on the length of domain names?

7. Provide a list of the names and IP addresses of all root servers of the Internet.

8. What is the purpose of the top-level domain `arpa`?

9. From a command prompt on a Unix or Windows[1] machine, run the command `nslookup www.cnn.com`, which shows the IP addresses that are associated with the domain name `www.cnn.com`. When you access `www.cnn.com` using a web browser on your computer, which IP address is chosen by your computer?

---

[1]Windows NT 4.0 or later.

LAB 8

DNS is an Internet-wide distributed database, and all DNS servers on the Internet cooperate to perform the mapping of symbolic host names to Internet addresses.

The complexity of DNS is significant. This lab highlights only some of the main features of DNS and does not cover all of the rich functionality of DNS.

DNS uses a client-server style of interaction. A DNS client is also called a *DNS resolver* or simply a *resolver*, and a DNS server is also called a *name server*. On Linux systems, the DNS software is based on the BIND (Berkeley Internet Name Domain) software distribution, a widely used reference implementation of DNS.

The network configuration for this lab is shown in Figure 8.1. The IP addresses and configuration information of the PCs and routers are given in Tables 8.1 and 8.2.

This lab only uses interface Ethernet0/0. All other interfaces should be disabled.

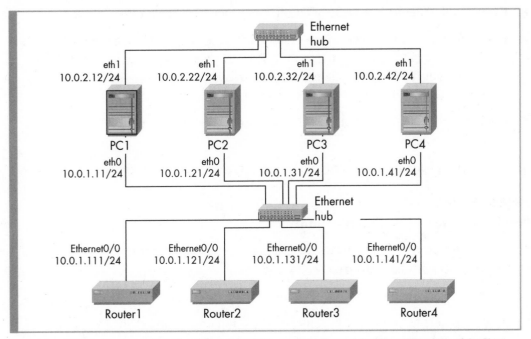

FIGURE 8.1.

Network configuration for Lab 8.

Note: When Ethernet interfaces of the Linux PCs (*eth0*, *eth1*) run at 100 Mbps and the Ethernet interfaces of the Cisco routers (*Ethernet0/0*, *Ethernet0/1*) run at 10 Mbps, you should avoid using dual-speed hubs if you connect two or more Cisco routers and one or more Linux PC to the same hub.

If you use dual speed hubs, in such a situation, the Linux PCs cannot observe the traffic between Cisco routers with *ethereal*.

TABLE 8.1. IP addresses of PCs for Lab 8.

Linux PC	Interface (*eth0*)	Interface (*eth1*)
PC1	10.0.1.11/24	10.0.2.12/24
PC2	10.0.1.21/24	10.0.2.22/24
PC3	10.0.1.31/24	10.0.2.32/24
PC4	10.0.1.41/24	10.0.2.42/24

TABLE 8.2. IP addresses of routers in Lab 8.

Cisco Router	Interface (*Ethernet0/0*)
Router1	10.0.1.111/24
Router2	10.0.1.121/24
Router3	10.0.1.131/24
Router4	10.0.1.141/24

PART 1.   NETWORK SETUP

EXERCISE 1(A).
Network setup.

1. Connect the Ethernet interfaces of the PCs and routers as shown in Figure 8.1.

2. Ensure that the console ports of the Cisco routers are connected to the serial port of a PC. Router1 should be connected to PC1, Router2 should be connected to PC2, and so on. Once the serial cables are connected, establish a *kermit* session from each PC to the connected router.

3. Configure the IP addresses of the PCs and routers as shown in Tables 8.1 and 8.2. No IP forwarding is used.

4. Use the `ping` command to verify that all interfaces are correctly connected.

EXERCISE 1(B).
Preparation for DNS configuration.

Perform the following tests to make sure that no name resolution scheme is currently active. The tests must be performed for each PC.

1. Make sure that the file */etc/resolv.conf* on each PC is empty.

2. Make sure that no process with name *named* is running on any of the PCs. If a process *named* is running, terminate the process with the command

   ```
   PC1% pkill named
   ```

3. Use the floppy with the downloaded files that were saved in the prelab assignment. Run a set of commands to install the configuration files on each PC. The commands for PC1 are as follows:

   a. Copy files *NamedConfPC1.tar.gz* and *named-installPC1* to the directory */root/namedpackage* on PC1.

   b. Execute the following commands:

   ```
   PC1% cd /root/namedpackage
   PC1% chmod 755 named-installPC1
   PC1% ./named-installPC1
   ```

These commands create directories with configuration files in

/var/named/part3
/var/named/part6

and, in addition, places the following files in directory */etc*:

/etc/named-part3.conf
/etc/named-part6.conf

c.   Verify that the directories and files are created.

PART 2.   NAME RESOLUTION WITHOUT DNS

This part of the lab reviews an exercise from Lab 2, which showed that the file */etc/hosts* can be used for static mapping of symbolic host names to IP addresses.

EXERCISE 2.
Static mapping of names to IP addresses via the */etc/hosts* file.

A simple method to associate IP addresses and symbolic names is to use the file */etc/hosts* on each PC. Each entry in the file establishes a static mapping of names and IP address. When a network command that includes a host name is issued, the local */etc/hosts* file is checked to translate the host name into an IP address.

1.   On PC1, delete the contents of file */etc/hosts*. Then, edit the file */etc/hosts* and associate names with IP addresses. The contents of the file */etc/hosts* should be as follows:

```
# loopback interface
127.0.0.1 localhost.localdomain localhost
# static configuration
10.0.1.21 myPC2.tcpip-lab.net     PC2
10.0.1.31 PC3+++
10.0.1.32 PC3--
10.0.1.41 PC4..tcpip-lab..net
```

The names are chosen to indicate that no specific format is required for the host names.

2.   On PC1, issue the commands:

```
PC1% ping -c 3 10.0.1.21
PC1% ping -c 3 PC2
PC1% ping -c 3 myPC2.tcpip-lab.net
PC1% ping -c 3 PC3+++
PC1% ping -c 3 PC3--
PC1% ping -c 3 PC4..tcpip-lab..net
```

• What happens if the same name is assigned to different IP addresses?

3. Delete the contents of */etc/hosts*. Verify that without entries in */etc/hosts*, the mapping does not work.

> **NOTE:**
>
> Even when DNS is used, the file */etc/hosts* should contain the symbolic names of the loopback interface. Thus, the following line should always be in file */etc/hosts* on all Linux systems:
>
> ```
> 127.0.0.1 localhost.localdomain localhost
> ```

Lab Report   Provide an answer to the question in Exercise 2.

PART 3.   CONFIGURING A DNS SERVER

In this part, PC4 is set up as a DNS server. PC1, PC2, and PC3 are run as regular hosts.

All PCs are assigned domain names so that they all belong to the domain `mylab.com`. The initial assignment of domain names to IP addresses is shown in Table 8.3.

TABLE 8.3.   Initial assignment of domain names to IP addresses.

Linux PC	Domain Name	IP Address
PC1	PC1.mylab.com	10.0.1.11/24
PC2	PC2.mylab.com	10.0.1.21/24
PC3	PC3.mylab.com	10.0.1.31/24
PC4	PC4.mylab.com	10.0.1.41/24

> **NOTE:**
>
> On some Linux systems we have observed problems with setting up a DNS server when the file */etc/resolv.conf* is present during bootup. When the system is booted, it tries to contact the DNS servers listed in the */etc/resolv.conf* file and stall for a long time, if the servers are not responding. We recommend you rename the file */etc/resolv.conf* before rebooting a PC that runs a DNS server and rename it back to */etc/resolv.conf* when the boot completes.

Note that, since the Internet Lab is not connected to the public Internet, we can assign any name that complies with the formatting rules of DNS. On the Internet, one needs to register domains with authorized domain name registries. Actually, the domain *mylab.com* is currently not available in the public Internet.

EXERCISE 3(A).
Configure a DNS server on a Linux PC.

The DNS server program on Linux systems is called *named*. The configuration of *named* for the domain *mylab.com* on PC4 requires you to organize a set of configuration files, which includes a set of so-called *zone data files* and the file */etc/named.conf*. The role of these files is explained in the following paragraphs. All files are included on the floppy disk that you created in the prelab and were copied to PC4 in Part 1 of this lab.

Zone data files: The zone data files contain the database records for the DNS domain. The directory where the zone data files are located on a system is specified in the file */etc/named.conf*. By convention, on many Linux systems, the zone data files are kept in directory */var/named* or in one of its subdirectories. The records in the files, called *resource records*, must be in a specific format. To set up the database records for PC4 as the DNS server for the domain *mylab.com*, a total of five zone data files must be created, of which the last two are specific for BIND DNS servers.

1. One zone data file is needed to define the DNS zone *mylab.com* and to map host names in the zone to IP addresses. We name the file *db.mylab.com*.[2] The contents of the file is shown in Figure 8.2.

```
$TTL 86400
mylab.com. IN SOA PC4.mylab.com. hostmaster.mylab.com. (
                1 ; serial
                28800 ; refresh
                7200 ; retry
                604800 ; expire
                86400 ; ttl
                )

;
mylab.com.       IN    NS    PC4.mylab.com.
;
localhost        A     127.0.0.1
PC4.mylab.com.   A     10.0.1.41
PC3.mylab.com.   A     10.0.1.31
PC2.mylab.com.   A     10.0.1.21
PC1.mylab.com.   A     10.0.1.11
```

FIGURE 8.2.

Contents of file *db.mylab.com*.

2. The second zone data file is needed for the inverse lookup (i.e., address-to-name) mapping, which maps the IP addresses in *mylab.com* to host names. We name the file *db.10.0.1*. The contents of the file is given in Figure 8.3.

3. The third and fourth zone data files maps the loopback address of PC4 to the host name of PC4, and vice versa. We name these files *db.127.0.0*. The files are shown in Figures 8.4 and 8.5.

4. The last zone data file contains a pointer to a *root name server*. We name this file *db.cache*. Since the equipment in the Internet Lab is not connected to the Internet, all entries in this file are commented out by having a semicolon (;) at the beginning of each line. If the DNS server was connected to the Internet, the address of one or several root servers listed in the file would not be commented out.

---

[2]The names of the zone data files can be selected arbitrarily. Since the number of zone files can be large, adopting a convention for naming zone files has advantages. Here, we use the naming convention proposed in *DNS and BIND*, P. Albitz and C. Liu, 4th ed., O'Reilly & Associates, Inc., 2001.

```
$TTL 86400
1.0.10.in-addr.arpa. IN SOA PC4.mylab.com.
hostmaster.mylab.com. (
                1 ; serial
                28800 ; refresh
                7200 ; retry
                604800 ; expire
                86400 ; ttl
                )


1.0.10.in-addr.arpa. IN     NS      PC4.mylab.com.

11 IN     PTR     PC1.mylab.com.
21 IN     PTR     PC2.mylab.com.
31 IN     PTR     PC3.mylab.com.
41 IN     PTR     PC4.mylab.com.
```

FIGURE 8.3.

Contents of file
db.10.0.1.

```
$TTL 86400
localhost. IN SOA    localhost   root.localhost (
                1 ; serial
                28800 ; refresh
                7200 ; retry
                604800 ; expire
                86400 ; ttl
                )


localhost.      IN     NS     PC4.mylab.com.


localhost.      IN     A      127.0.0.1
```

FIGURE 8.4.

Contents of file
db.localhost.

```
$TTL 86400
0.0.127.in-addr.arpa. IN SOA       PC4.mylab.com.
hostmaster.mylab.com. (
                1 ; serial
                28800 ; refresh
                7200 ; retry
                604800 ; expire
                86400 ; ttl
                )

0.0.127.in-addr.arpa. IN     NS    PC4.mylab.com.


127.0.0.1        IN     PTR     localhost.
```

FIGURE 8.5.

Contents of file
db.127.0.0.

BIND configuration file: The configuration of the BIND software is given in the file */etc/named.conf*. The configuration file specifies the role and the location of zone data files.

```
;        This file holds the information on root name servers needed to
;        initialize cache of Internet domain name servers
;        (e.g. reference this file in the "cache  .   <file>"
;        configuration file of BIND domain name servers).
;
;        This file is made available by InterNIC registration services
;        under anonymous FTP as
;        file                    /domain/named.root
;        on server               FTP.RS.INTERNIC.NET
;        -OR- under Gopher at     RS.INTERNIC.NET
;        under menu               InterNIC Registration Services (NSI)
;        submenu                  InterNIC Registration Archives
;        file                     named.root
;
;        last update:    Aug 22, 1997
;        related version of root zone:   1997082200
;
;;
;.                          3600000    IN   NS    A.ROOT-SERVERS.EDU.
;;;;;A.ROOT-SERVERS.EDU.    3600000         A     10.0.2.32
;;
; formerly NS.INTERNIC.NET
;;
;.                          3600000    IN   NS    A.ROOT-SERVERS.NET.
;A.ROOT-SERVERS.NET.        3600000         A     198.41.0.4
;;
;; formerly NS1.ISI.EDU
;;
;.                          3600000         NS    B.ROOT-SERVERS.NET.
;B.ROOT-SERVERS.NET.        3600000         A     128.9.0.107
;;
;; formerly C.PSI.NET
;;
;.                          3600000         NS    C.ROOT-SERVERS.NET.
;C.ROOT-SERVERS.NET.        3600000         A     192.33.4.12
;;
;; formerly TERP.UMD.EDU
;;
;.                          3600000         NS    D.ROOT-SERVERS.NET.
;D.ROOT-SERVERS.NET.        3600000         A     128.8.10.90
;;
;; formerly NS.NASA.GOV
;;
;.                          3600000         NS    E.ROOT-SERVERS.NET.
;E.ROOT-SERVERS.NET.        3600000         A     192.203.230.10
;;
;; formerly NS.ISC.ORG
;;
;.                          3600000         NS    F.ROOT-SERVERS.NET.
;F.ROOT-SERVERS.NET.        3600000         A     192.5.5.241
;;
;; formerly NS.NIC.DDN.MIL
;;
;.                          3600000         NS    G.ROOT-SERVERS.NET.
;G.ROOT-SERVERS.NET.        3600000         A     192.112.36.4
;;
;; formerly AOS.ARL.ARMY.MIL
;;
```

FIGURE 8.6.

Contents of file *db.cache*.

```
;.                            3600000    NS    H.ROOT-SERVERS.NET.
;H.ROOT-SERVERS.NET.          3600000    A     128.63.2.53
;;
;;  formerly NIC.NORDU.NET
;;
;.                            3600000    NS    I.ROOT-SERVERS.NET.
;I.ROOT-SERVERS.NET.          3600000    A     192.36.148.17
;;
;;  temporarily housed at NSI (InterNIC)
;;
;.                            3600000    NS    J.ROOT-SERVERS.NET.
;J.ROOT-SERVERS.NET.          3600000    A     198.41.0.10
;;
;;  housed in LINX, operated by RIPE NCC
;;
;.                            3600000    NS    K.ROOT-SERVERS.NET.
;K.ROOT-SERVERS.NET.          3600000    A     193.0.14.129
;;
;;  temporarily housed at ISI (IANA)
;;
;.                            3600000    NS    L.ROOT-SERVERS.NET.
;L.ROOT-SERVERS.NET.          3600000    A     198.32.64.12
;;
;;  housed in Japan, operated by WIDE
;;
;.                            3600000    NS    M.ROOT-SERVERS.NET.
;M.ROOT-SERVERS.NET.          3600000    A     202.12.27.33
;;  End of File
```

FIGURE 8.7.

Contents of file *db.cache* (continued).

1. On PC4, after completing the last task of Part 1, the following files should have been created and put in the directories */etc* and */var/named/part3*.

   /var/named/part3/db.mylab.com
   /var/named/part3/db.10.0.1
   /var/named/part3/db.cache
   /var/named/part3/db.127.0.0
   /var/named/part3/db.localhost
   /etc/named-part3.conf

   These files are the zone data files and the BIND configuration files for PC4.

2. Review and verify the contents of the zone data files and the configuration file.

Lab Report Explain the role of each resource record in file *db.mylab.com* shown in Figure 8.2. Explain the line $TTL 86400?

```
## named.conf - configuration for bind

options {
      directory "/var/named/";
};

zone    "." {
      type hint;
      file   "part3/db.cache";
};

zone    "0.0.127.in-addr.arpa" {
      type master;
      file   "part3/db.127.0.0";
};

zone    "localhost" {
      type master;
      file   "part3/db.localhost";
};

zone    "mylab.com" {
      type master;
      file   "part3/db.mylab.com";
};

zone    "1.0.10.in-addr.arpa" {
      type master;
      file   "part3/db.10.0.1";
};
```

FIGURE 8.8.

Contents of file /etc/named.conf.

EXERCISE 3(B).

Configuring a DNS resolver.

The *resolver* is a set of procedures that are used by all programs that must resolve domain names to IP addresses and vice versa. On Linux systems, the configuration of a DNS resolver involves three files:

- */etc/nsswitch.conf*: This file contains configuration information for a program called the *name service switch*. The name service switch controls a variety of naming services on a Linux system, including DNS. For DNS functions, the file needs to contain a line

```
hosts: dns files
```

  With this line, name resolution will first invoke DNS and, if that is unsuccessful, do a lookup in the file */etc/hosts*.

- */etc/resolv.conf*: The resolver configuration file *resolv.conf* specifies the IP address of a name server. If the file does not exist or if the file is empty, the system assumes that the local system is running a name server. For our purposes, the file merely needs to contain a single line, which is the IP address of the name server. The format of this entry is:

```
nameserver 10.0.1.41
```

If a host uses multiple name servers, one line is needed for each name server.

- **/etc/hosts:** This is the host file with static mapping as discussed in Part 1. The file should have at least one entry that resolves the name of the loopback interface. This entry has the following format:

```
127.0.0.1 localhost.localdomain localhost
```

Your task is to configure the DNS resolvers on PC1, PC2, and PC3. Verify that the files */etc/nsswitch.conf*, */etc/resolv.conf*, and */etc/hosts* are correctly configured. If the file */etc/nsswitch.conf* is updated, you need to execute the following command to put any change into effect:

```
PC1% /etc/rc.d/init.d/network restart
```

EXERCISE 3(C).
Running a DNS name server.

With the configuration files, PC4 is ready to run a DNS server. The following is a list of commands to control the DNS server:

```
/etc/rc.d/init.d/named start
    starts the DNS server.
pkill named
    stops the DNS server.
```
Note: On Linux Redhat 9.0, the command /etc/rc.d/init.d/named stop does not work.

1. **Start the server:** Copy the file */etc/named-part3.conf* to */etc/named.conf* so that the BIND configuration file is in the correct location.

   ```
   PC4% cp /etc/named-part3.conf /etc/named.conf
   ```

   On PC4, run the following command to start the *named* DNS server:

   ```
   PC4% /etc/rc.d/init.d/named start
   ```

2. **DNS at the server:** On PC4, execute the following commands:

   ```
   PC4% host -v PC3.mylab.com
   PC4% host -v 10.0.1.21
   PC4% host -v localhost
   PC4% host -v tcpip-lab.net
   ```

   Save the output of the commands to a file.

3. **DNS at the clients:** Test the name resolution by running the following commands on PC1, PC2, or PC3:

```
PC1% host -v PC3.mylab.com
PC1% host -v 10.0.1.21
PC1% host -v localhost
PC1% host -v tcpip-lab.net
```

Save the output of the commands to a file.

4. Verify that you can run applications, such as *FTP*, *Telnet*, and so on, using domain names.

Lab Report Include the output on PC4 from commands host -v PC3.mylab.com and host -v 10.0.1.21 and provide an interpretation of the output.

EXERCISE 3(D).
Modifying the name server (Part 1).

1. Extend the name server at PC4 so that it provides a DNS service for the names in the domain lab8.net. The assignment of names to IP addresses in this domain is given in Table 8.4.

TABLE 8.4. Assignment of domain names to IP addresses for Exercise 3(D).

Linux PC	Domain Name	IP Address
PC1	PC1.lab8.net	10.0.2.12/24
PC2	PC2.lab8.net	10.0.2.22/24
PC3	PC3.lab8.net	10.0.2.32/24
PC4	PC4.lab8.net	10.0.2.42/24

This involves the following steps:

a. Add new zone data files with names *db.lab8.net* and *db.10.0.2*, which are, respectively, responsible for name queries and reverse queries for the domain *lab8.net*. Place the files in directory */var/named/part3*. The assignment of domain names is as shown in Table 8.4.

b. Add statements to the configuration file */etc/named.conf* for the domains *lab8.net* and *2.0.10.in-addr.arpa*.

c. Restart the name server.

2. Save the modified configuration file and zone data files.

3. On PC1, run the following command and save the output:

```
PC1% host -v PC3.lab8.net
```

Lab Report Include the saved zone data files and the output of the command host in the lab report.

EXERCISE 3(E).
Modifying the name server (Part 2).

With DNS it is possible to assign more than one name to an IP address. Also, the same name can be assigned to different IP addresses.

1. Extend the name server at PC4 so that it provides a DNS service for the domains *mylab.com* and *lab8.net*. The assignment of names to IP addresses in this domain is given in Table 8.5.

TABLE 8.5. Assignment of domain names to IP addresses for Exercise 3(E).

Domain Name	IP Address
PC1.mylab.com	10.0.1.11/24
PC2.mylab.com	10.0.1.21/24
PC3.mylab.com	10.0.1.31/24
PC4.mylab.com	10.0.1.41/24
PC1.lab8.net PC1.mylab.com	10.0.2.12/24
PC2.lab8.net PC2.mylab.com	10.0.2.22/24
PC3.lab8.net PC3.mylab.com	10.0.2.32/24
PC4.lab8.net PC4.mylab.com	10.0.2.42/24

This involves the following steps:

a. Update the following zone data files with an assignment of domain names as shown in Table 8.5:

   /var/named/part3/db.mylab.com
   /var/named/part3/db.lab8.net
   /var/named/part3/db.10.0.1
   /var/named/part3/db.10.0.2

b. Restart the name server.

2. Save the modified zone data files.

3. On PC1, run the following commands and save the output:

   ```
   PC1% host -v PC3.lab8.net
   PC1% host -v PC3.mylab.com
   ```

Lab Report Include the saved zone data files and the output of the command host in the lab report.

PART 4.   DNS TRAFFIC

In Part 4, you explore the exchange of DNS messages between DNS resolvers and DNS servers. This part of the lab continues with the configurations of Part 3, and assumes that you have completed Part 3.

EXERCISE 4.
Observe traffic of DNS queries.

1.   On PC1, start *ethereal* sessions on interfaces *eth0* and *eth1*.

> To prevent *ethereal* from contacting a DNS server and causing DNS traffic to be sent, make sure the following settings in *ethereal* are unselected:
>
> In the *ethereal* main window, select the *Display : Options*:
> *   Unselect *Enable MAC name resolution.*
> *   Unselect *Enable network name resolution.*
> *   Unselect *Enable transport name resolution.*
>
> In the *ethereal* main window, select the window *Capture : Start*:
> *   Unselect *Enable MAC name resolution.*
> *   Unselect *Enable network name resolution.*
> *   Unselect *Enable transport name resolution.*

2.   Make sure that the DNS server is running on PC4.

Does the DNS server generate traffic when there are no DNS requests?

3.   On PC1, observe the network traffic caused by issuing the following sequence of commands:

```
PC1% ping -c 3 PC3.mylab.com
PC1% ping -c 3 localhost
PC1% ping -c 3 tcpip-lab.net
```

4.   Save the DNS traffic generated by these commands as captured by *ethereal*. (You need to save the details of the messages.)

5.   Observe the traffic and take note of the message contents so that you can answer the following questions:

*   Do all commands generate a DNS message?

*   Determine how domain names and IP addresses are encoded in DNS messages.

*   What happens if a DNS query that cannot be resolved is issued?

*   If you repeat one of the commands, does PC1 issue another request or does PC1 cache the previous response?

*   DNS queries are either recursive or iterative. Use the data captured by *ethereal* to determine if DNS queries are generated by issuing the `ping` commands.

Lab Report

- Include answers to the questions listed in Step 5 of Exercise 4.

- Include the captured DNS packet header from the DNS query and response for PC3.mylab.com.

- Select a single DNS query or response, and explain all fields in the flags field.

- Determine how domain names and IP addresses are encoded in the DNS messages.

PART 5. CACHING-ONLY SERVERS

An alternative method to set up DNS is to start a DNS server (*named*) on each host, but run these DNS servers as *caching-only* servers. These servers are not authoritative for any zones with the exception of the loopback address.

Since DNS servers cache the results from previous DNS requests, caching-only DNS servers may reduce DNS traffic. Whenever a DNS resolver tries to resolve a domain name, it contacts its local caching-only DNS server. The DNS server checks the local cache and, if the data is found, responds without generating any DNS traffic. If no match is found in the cache, the DNS server contacts another DNS server.

Caching-only DNS servers can be configured as shown in Figures 8.9 and 8.10. As the files indicate, the only zone data files are the files with the root server information and the file that resolves the loopback IP address. In the configuration shown, IP address 10.0.1.41 is given as the root server for the domain ".". Therefore, whenever a domain cannot be resolved, the caching-only DNS server contacts 10.0.1.41.

FIGURE 8.9.

Contents of file
/etc/named.conf in
Part 5.

```
## named.conf - configuration for bind

options {
directory "/var/named/";
};

zone   "." {
type hint;
file  "part3/db.cache";
};

zone   "0.0.127.in-addr.arpa" {
   type master;
   file   "part3/db.127.0.0";
};
```

FIGURE 8.10.

Contents of file
db.cache in Part 5.

```
.3600000   IN   NS     A.ROOT-SERVERS.EDU.
A.ROOT-SERVERS.EDU. 3600000   A   10.0.1.41
```

EXERCISE 5.
Run a caching-only DNS server.

Your task is to set up PC2 as a caching-only DNS server and observe the difference between a name resolution of a caching-only DNS server to that of a "regular" DNS server.

1. Start *ethereal* sessions on interfaces *eth0* and *eth1* of PC2.

2. **Configure a caching DNS server:** On PC2, set up the following files:

   a. Set up the file */etc/named.conf* and */var/named/part3/db.cache* with the contents shown in Figures 8.9 and 8.10.

   b. Set up files */var/named/part3/db.localhost* and */var/named/part3/db.127.0.0*, with the same contents as the files shown in Figures 8.4 and 8.5.

   c. Verify that the file */etc/resolv.conf* is empty.

3. **Start the server:** Start a DNS server on PC2 with the command

   ```
   PC2% /etc/rc.d/init.d/named start
   ```

4. **Using DNS at the clients:**

   a. On PC2, run the following command:

   ```
   PC2% host -v PC1.mylab.com
   ```

   Save the output of the command and also save the DNS traffic generated by this command as captured by *ethereal*.

   b. On PC2, execute the following commands:

   ```
   PC2% ping -c 3 PC3.mylab.com
   PC2% ping -c 3 PC3.mylab.com
   PC2% ping -c 3 localhost
   ```

   c. Save the DNS traffic generated by these commands as captured by *ethereal*.

5. **Answer the following questions:**

   - Which commands generate a DNS message?

   - Are any DNS queries issued when you repeat the query to resolve `PC3.mylab.com`?

   - Do you observe any difference with the queries captured in Part 4? Specifically, if you run `ping -c 3 PC3.mylab.com` on PC1 (which runs a DNS resolver, but no caching-only DNS server) and PC2 (which runs a caching-only DNS server) do you observe any difference in the outgoing DNS messages?

   - What happens on PC2 if a DNS query that cannot be resolved is issued? Is there any difference as compared to PC1?

Lab Report

- Provide answers to the questions in the preceding exercises.

- Suggest an advantage and a disadvantage of running a caching-only DNS server at each host?

PART 6. HIERARCHY OF DNS SERVERS

In this part of the lab you set up a hierarchy of DNS servers, complete with a root server. When the local DNS server does not know the answer to a DNS query, it forwards the query to another DNS server to get the answer.

This lab is about observing how DNS queries are processed in the hierarchy of DNS servers. You will observe the difference between iterative and recursive queries.

The hierarchy of the namespace in this part of the lab is shown in Figure 8.11. All PCs are set up as name servers. The assignment of servers to domains is shown in Tables 8.6 and 8.7.

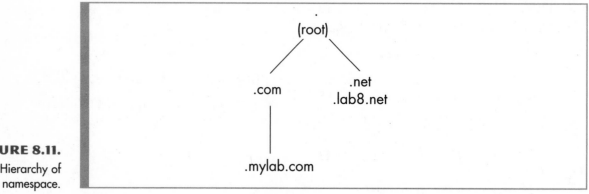

FIGURE 8.11.
Hierarchy of namespace.

TABLE 8.6. Assignment of domain names to IP addresses for Part 6 (Linux PCs).

Linux PC	IP Address of *eth0*	Domains	Domain Server for DNS Zones
PC1	10.0.1.11	root-server.net	.(*root server*)
PC2	10.0.1.21	top-server.com	.com(*top level domain*)
PC3	10.0.1.31	top-server.net	.net(*top level domain*) lab8.net
PC4	10.0.1.41	nameserver.mylab.com	mylab.com

TABLE 8.7. Assignment of domain names to IP addresses for Part 6 (Routers).

Cisco Router	IP Address	Domain Names	Name Server
Router1	10.0.1.111	R1.mylab.com	10.0.1.41/24 (PC4)
Router2	10.0.1.121	R2.mylab.com	10.0.1.41/24 (PC4)
Router3	10.0.1.131	R3.lab8.net	10.0.1.31/24 (PC3)
Router4	10.0.1.141	Router4.com	10.0.1.21/24 (PC2)

EXERCISE 6(A).
Network setup.

1. The network topology is as shown in Figure 8.1, and the IP address assignment is as given Tables 8.1 and 8.2.

2. **DNS configuration of PCs:**

   a. First clean up the files from the previous exercises. Delete or comment out all lines in the file */etc/hosts*. Make sure that the file */etc/resolv.conf is empty*.

   b. The DNS configuration for this part of the lab is included on the floppy that you generated in the prelab. After completing Part 1 of the lab, the configuration files for the subsequent exercises have been copied into directory */var/named/part6* and in the file */etc/named-part6.conf* of each PC.

   c. On each PC, copy the file */etc/named-part6.conf* to */etc/named.conf*, and restart the DNS server *named*. The following are the commands for PC1. Repeat the corresponding commands on the other PCs.

   ```
   PC1% cp /etc/named-part6.conf /etc/named.conf
   PC1%pkill named
   PC1% /etc/rc.d/init.d/named start
   ```

3. **Enabling DNS on Cisco routers:** The next step is to enable DNS on the Cisco routers. By default, DNS is enabled in IOS with default address 255.255.255.255 (broadcast) as the address of the name server. Here, we need to specify 10.0.1.41 as the name server. The following are the commands for Router1. Repeat the corresponding commands on the other routers.

```
Router1> enable
Password: <enable secret>
Router1# configure terminal
Router1(config)# ip name-server 10.0.1.41
Router1(config)# end
Router1# show hosts
Router1# clear host *
```

Below are some explanations and comments on the DNS-related commands.

IOS MODE: GLOBAL CONFIGURATION

`ip name-server IPaddr`

Specifies a DNS name server with IP address *IPaddr*.

`no ip domain-lookup`

Disables DNS name resolution.

`ip domain-lookup`

Enables DNS name resolution. DNS resolution is enabled by default with the broadcast address 255.255.255.255 as name server.

IOS MODE: PRIVILEGED EXEC

`Router1# show hosts`

Displays the contents of DNS cache. If DNS is enabled, a Cisco router runs a DNS cache.

`clear host *`

Cleans up the DNS cache.

EXERCISE 6(B).
Exploring the DNS configuration files of the DNS name servers.

Explore the DNS configuration files on the PCs.

- Save all configuration files for PC1. Recall that PC1 is the root server. Compare the file */var/named/part6/db.cache* on the PCs and describe the differences. What is the difference of the file *db.cache* to the file *db.cache* used earlier (shown in Figures 8.6 and 8.7)?

- Compare the entry for zone `.` in file */etc/named.conf* at PC1 (the root server) and the other PCs. Explain the differences.

- In the DNS hierarchy, the root server has resource records in the zone data file so that it can delegate DNS queries to the servers of the `.com` and the `.net` zone. Likewise, the server for `.com` has resource records that delegate DNS queries to the server for *mylab.com*. These resource records are called *glue records*. Identify the glue records at the DNS servers for zones `.`, `.com`, and `.net`. Are there any other glue records?

Lab Report

- Include the configuration files for PC1.

- Provide the answers to the questions in the preceding exercises.

EXERCISE 6(C).
Resolution of DNS queries in a hierarchical system of DNS servers.

Now, you will execute a set of DNS queries. Capture and observe the resulting DNS traffic. Determine how the DNS queries are resolved.

1. On PC1, start an *ethereal* session on *eth0*.

2. Run the following `ping` commands from the routers and save the output of *ethereal* into files (save the details of the output).

   On Router1:

   ```
   Router1# ping R2.mylab.com
   Router1# ping R3.lab8.net
   Router1# ping Router4.com
   ```

   On Router3:

   ```
   Router3# ping R1.mylab.com
   Router3# ping Router4.com
   Router3# ping root-server.net
   ```

   On Router4:

   ```
   Router4# ping R3.lab8.net
   ```

3. Stop the root server on PC1. Then issue the following command on Router2:

   ```
   Router2# ping R3.lab8.net
   ```

   Which DNS queries succeed and which DNS queries fail?

Lab Report

- For each command explain how the observed DNS queries are resolved.

- For each command, provide a list of the observed DNS messages. For each DNS message, include only the following fields: source IP address, destination IP address, flags in the DNS message, and all resource records in the DNS message.

- Which queries have the recursion-desired flag set?

- List the authoritative servers for the `.net` domain and `.com` domain.

- Do you observe recursive or iterative DNS queries, or both? What is the main advantage/disadvantage of recursive DNS queries? What is the main advantage/disadvantage of iterative DNS queries?

CHECKLIST FORM FOR LAB 8

Complete this checklist as you work through the laboratory exercises and attach the form to your lab report.

Name (please print):_____

☐ Prelab 8 question sheet

☐ Checkoff for Part 1   ☐ Checkoff for Part 5

☐ Checkoff for Part 2   ☐ Checkoff for Part 6

☐ Checkoff for Part 3   ☐ Feedback sheet

☐ Checkoff for Part 4   ☐ Lab Report

FEEDBACK FORM FOR LAB 8

- Complete this feedback form at the completion of the lab exercises and submit the form when submitting your lab report.

- The feedback is anonymous. *Do not put your name on this form* and keep it separate from your lab report.

- For each exercise, please record the following:

	Difficulty (−2, −1, 0, 1, 2)	Interest Level (−2, −1, 0, 1, 2)	Time to Complete (minutes)
	−2 = too easy 0 = just right 2 = too hard	−2 = low interest 0 = just right 2 = high interest	

Part 1.
Network setup

Part 2.
Name resolution
without DNS

Part 3.
Configuring a DNS
server

Part 4.
DNS Traffic

Part 5.
Caching-Only servers

Part 6.
Hierarchy of DNS
servers

Please answer the following questions:

- What did you like about this lab?

- What did you dislike about this lab?

- Make a suggestion to improve the lab.

Simple Network Management Protocol (SNMP)

PRELAB 9

1. **NET-SNMP tools:** Read about the *NET-SNMP* software tools at http://www.cs. virginia.edu/~itlab/book/links/netsnmp.html. Read about the following commands, which are used throughout this lab:

   a. `snmpd`

   b. `snmpget`

   c. `snmpgetnext`

   d. `snmpwalk`

   e. `snmptrapd`

   f. `snmptranslate`

   g. `snmpset`

2. **SNMP overview:** Read the overviews of SNMP at

   `http://www.cs.virginia.edu/~itlab/book/links/snmp.html`

   and

   `http://www.cs.virginia.edu/~itlab/book/links/snmpios.html`

3. Download the file *snmpd.conf* that is available at URL

   `http://www.tcpip-lab.net/links/conf/lab9`

   Save the file to a floppy disk. This is a configuration file for an SNMP agent on a Linux PC. *Bring the floppy to the laboratory!*

4. **Security features of SNMPv3:** Read about the security features of SNMPv3 at

   `http://www.net-snmp.org/tutorial-5/commands/snmpv3.html`

   In the manual page of *snmpd.conf*, which is available at

   `http://www.cs.virginia.edu/~itlab/book/links/snmpdconf.html`

   read about the View-based Access Control Model (VACM) configuration tables.

QUESTION SHEET FOR PRELAB 9

Answer the questions in the space provided below each one. Use extra sheets of paper if needed and attach them to this document. Submit the answers to the prelab with your lab report.

Name (please print):_____

1. Provide a brief definition of the following SNMP terms, and explain which role they play in SNMP:

   a. SNMP manager

   b. SNMP agent

   c. Management Information Base (MIB)

   d. Object identifier (OID)

2. Describe the function of the following *NET-SNMP* tools in one sentence each:
   `snmpd, snmpget, snmpgetnext, snmpwalk, snmptranslate, snmpset.`

3. Which port does the *snmpd* program (SNMP agent) use to listen to SNMP messages? Which port does the *snmptrapd* program use to listen to SNMP trap messages?

4. Relate textual and numerical description of object identifiers by answering the following questions:

   a. Which object is referred to by the object identifier 1.3.6.1.2.1.4.2?

   b. What is the numerical description of object `tcpRetransSegs` in the `tcp` group of MIB-II?

    c.   What is the object identifier of the Internet?

5.   What is an SNMP trap? Which SNMP entity issues traps and which SNMP entity handles traps?

6.   Describe the main differences between the SNMP versions SNMPv1, SNMPv2c, and SNMPv3?

7.   Refer to the configuration file *snmpd.conf* that you downloaded from `http://www.tcpip-lab.net/links/conf/lab9`. Describe the VACM access control that is specified in this file.

8.   Use the VACM commands given in the downloaded *snmpd.conf* (`com2sec`, `group`, `view`, and `access`) to define the following access control rules:

    a.   The SNMP agent grants read authority to the MIB subtree that starts at node *iso.org.dod.internet.mgmt.mib-2.system*, and

    b.   The SNMP manager sending the request has network address 10.10.0.0/16, and

    c.   The SNMP manager provides the community string `public`, and

    d.   The SNMP protocol version of messages is SNMPv1.

LAB 9

The Simple Network Management Protocol (SNMP) framework provides facilities for managing and monitoring network resources on the Internet. The SNMP framework consists of SNMP agents, SNMP managers, Management Information Bases (MIBs), and the SNMP protocol itself. An SNMP agent is software that runs on a piece of network equipment (host, router, printer, or others) and that maintains information about its configuration and current state in a database. An SNMP manager is an application program that contacts an SNMP agent to query or modify the database at the agent. The organization of information in the database is described by so-called Management Information Bases (MIBs). Finally, the SNMP protocol is the application layer protocol used by SNMP agents and managers to send and receive data.

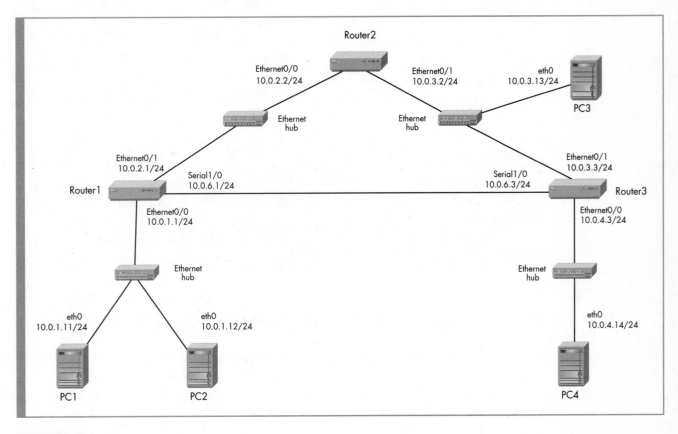

FIGURE 9.1.

Network configuration for Lab 9.

The network configuration for Lab 9 is shown in Figure 9.1. The IP configuration of PCs and routers is given in Tables 9.1 and 9.2.

TABLE 9.1. IP addresses and gateway assignments of PCs for Lab 9.

Linux PC	Ethernet Interface *eth0*	Ethernet Interface *eth0*	Default Gateway
PC1	10.0.1.11/24	Not used	10.0.1.1
PC2	10.0.1.12/24	Not used	10.0.1.1
PC3	10.0.3.13/24	Not used	10.0.3.2
PC4	10.0.4.14/24	Not used	10.0.4.3

TABLE 9.2. IP address assignments of routers for Lab 9.

Cisco Router	Interface Ethernet0/0	Interface Ethernet0/1	Interface Serial1/0
Router1	10.0.1.1/24	10.0.2.1/24	10.0.6.1/24
Router2	10.0.2.2/24	10.0.3.2/24	Not used
Router3	10.0.4.3/24	10.0.3.3/24	10.0.6.3/24

RECALL:

- Before you get started, please reboot the Linux PCs.
- During the lab, you need to save data to files. Save all files in the directory /labdata.
- Save your files to a floppy disk before the end of the lab. You will need the files when you prepare your lab report.

PART 1.   MANAGEMENT INFORMATION BASE (MIB)

The managed objects maintained by an agent are specified in a Management Information Base (MIB). A MIB file is a text file that describes managed objects using the syntax of ASN.1 (Abstract Syntax Notation 1), a formal language for describing data and its properties. A network device may have multiple MIB files. All current Internet devices support MIB-II, which specifies about 170 MIB objects.

In a MIB, each object is assigned an *object identifier* (OID), which is used to name the object. An OID is a unique sequence of integers separated by decimal points. An example of an OID is 1.3.6.1.2.1.4.6. Each OID has a textual description. For example, the textual description of OID 1.3.6.1.2.1.4.6 is *iso.org.dod.internet.mgmt.mib-2.ip.ipForwDatagrams*, or simply *ipForwDatagrams*. In MIB-II, the *ipForwDatagrams* object is described as an integer counter that stores the number of forwarded datagrams at a router. When an SNMP manager requests an object, it sends the OID of an instantiation of this object to the SNMP agent.

Managed objects are organized in a treelike hierarchy and the OIDs reflect the structure of the hierarchy. Each OID represents a node in the tree. For example, the OID 1.3.6.1.2.1.4.6 is a child node of OID 1.3.6.1.2.1.4. The OID 1.3.6.1.2.1 (*iso.org.dod.internet.mgmt.mib-2*) is at the top of the hierarchy for all managed objects of the MIB-II. Manufacturers of networking equipment can add product-specific objects to the hierarchy. The object hierarchy of the MIB tree is illustrated in Figure 9.2.

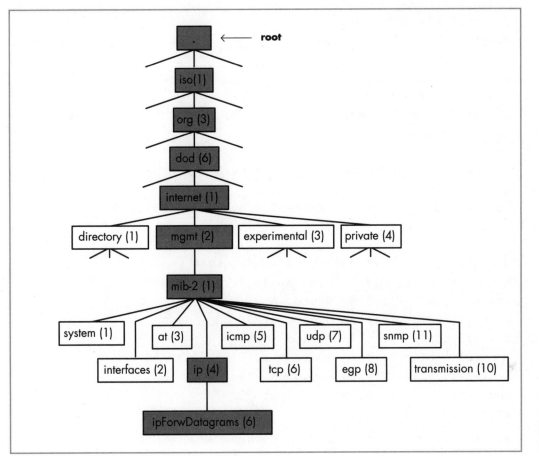

FIGURE 9.2.
Hierarchy of the MIB tree.

EXERCISE 1(A).
Network setup.

1. Connect the network equipment of the Linux PCs and the Cisco routers as shown in Figure 9.1. With the exception of the serial WAN link between Router1 and Router3, the PCs and routers are connected via Ethernet hubs.

2. Verify that the serial interfaces of the PCs are connected to the console port of the routers. As usual, PC1 should be connected to Router1, PC2 to Router2, and so on. Once the serial cables are connected, establish a *kermit* session from each PC to the connected router.

3. Configure the IP addresses of the PCs and routers as shown in Tables 9.1 and 9.2. For the Linux PCs, also configure a default gateway.

4. On each PC, copy the file *snmpd.conf* you downloaded during the Prelab to the directory */usr/share/snmp*.

5. Start the OSPF routing protocol on each router. Make sure that there are no statically configured routes in the routing table. On all routers, set the cost of each interface to 10. The following commands are needed for Router1:

```
Router1> enable
Password: <enable secret>
Router1# clear ip route *
Router1# configure terminal
Router1(config)# no ip routing
Router1(config)# ip routing
Router1(config)# router ospf 1
Router1(config-router)# network 10.0.0.0 0.255.255.255 area 0
Router1(config-router)# exit

Router1(config)# interface Ethernet0/0
Router1(config-if)# no shutdown
Router1(config-if)# ip address 10.0.1.1 255.255.255.0
Router1(config-if)# ip ospf cost 10

Router1(config-if)# interface Ethernet0/1
Router1(config-if)# ip address 10.0.2.1 255.255.255.0
Router1(config-if)# no shutdown
Router1(config-if)# ip ospf cost 10
Router1(config-if)# interface Serial1/0
Router1(config-if)# ip address 10.0.6.1 255.255.255.0
Router1(config-if)# no shutdown
Router1(config-if)# ip ospf cost 10
Router1(config-if)# end
```

You are done when you can issue `ping` commands between all PCs and Cisco routers.

EXERCISE 1(B).
Definition of managed objects in a MIB.

In this exercise, you explore how managed objects are defined in MIB files and how MIB files and objects are organized. On the Linux PCs, the MIB files are stored in the directory */usr/share/snmp/mibs*. When an SNMP agent starts, the MIB files are analyzed and loaded into a database.

Each MIB file specifies a set of managed objects. The objects are specified following the SMI format (Structure of Management Information), which defines, for each managed object, the OID, the textual descriptor for the OID, and the data type in ASN.1 syntax.

1. On PC1, go to directory */usr/share/snmp/mibs/* and explore the MIB files that are relevant to this lab:

   a. *RFC1155-SMI.txt*

   b. *RFC1213-MIB.txt*

   c. *IF-MIB.txt*

   d. *INET-ADDRESS-MIB.txt*

   e. *IP-FORWARD-MIB.txt*

   f. *IP-MIB.txt*

   g. *TCP-MIB.txt*

   h. *UDP-MIB.txt*

2. Find and save the definitions of the following managed objects:

   a. *ipForwarding*

   b. *sysName*

   c. *at*

   d. *ipRouteTable*

   e. *tcpRtoAlgorithm*

   f. *tcpConnState*

   For each object, answer the following questions:

   - What is the numerical OID?

   - What is the full textual descriptor?

   - Does this object have children in the MIB hierarchy? If so, give the names of the children.

   - Characterize the data type of the object.

Lab Report

- Include the saved descriptions of the managed objects.

- From the saved data, draw a tree that, starting at node *iso*, includes all of the managed objects mentioned previously.

- Include the answers to the questions in this exercise.

EXERCISE 1(C).
View MIB structure using `snmptranslate`.

You can use the command `snmptranslate` to explore the structure of a MIB tree. The command `snmptranslate` can translate between numerical and textual representation of objects. In addition, the command can display the tree hierarchy in textual form.

1. On PC1, run the following commands and save the output to a file:

   ```
   PC1% snmptranslate .1.3.6.1.2.1.7.4
   PC1% snmptranslate -On -IR icmp
   PC1% snmptranslate -Tp -IR -OS tcp
   ```

   The first command displays the textual representation of an OID (note the leading period (.)). The second command performs the opposite translation. By default, snmptranslate adds the prefix *.iso.org.dod.internet.mgmt.mib-2* (or *.1.3.6.1.2.1*) to the argument. The third command prints a diagram of the portion of the MIB hierarchy rooted at node tcp.

2. Display and save the MIB hierarchy rooted at nodes interfaces and ip.

Lab Report

- Include the saved data in your lab report.

- With the data, answer the following questions:

  — What are the routing protocols recognized by SNMP?

  — List the states of a TCP connection?

  — What are the feasible states of the object ipForwarding?

PART 2.   SNMP AGENTS AND MANAGERS: RETRIEVING MIB OBJECTS

In this part of the lab, you explore the interactions between an SNMP agent and an SNMP manager. You start SNMP agents on the Linux PCs and Cisco routers, and you run an SNMP manager on a Linux PC.

An SNMP manager and an SNMP agent communicate using the SNMP protocol. Figure 9.3 shows the message exchange between a manager and an agent. There are three versions of the protocol that are in use today: SNMPv1, SNMPv2c, and SNMPv3. SNMPv3 is relatively new, and the older versions, SNMPv1 and SNMPv2c, are still widely used. Many SNMP agents and managers support all three versions of the protocol.

The SNMP message types used in this lab, shown in Figure 9.3, are supported in all three versions of SNMP. For the most part of this lab, we work with SNMPv1, the most basic version of SNMP. SNMPv2c and SNMPv3 have additional message formats and richer functionality.

With the exception of trap messages, the exchange in SNMP is initiated by an SNMP manager by sending a request to an SNMP agent. The SNMP agent replies in a response message. The message types are as follows:

1. **Get-request:** Requests the values of one or more objects from an SNMP agent.

2. **Get-next-request:** Requests the value of the next object, according to a lexicographical ordering of OIDs.

3. **Set-request:** A request to modify the value of one or more objects at the agent.

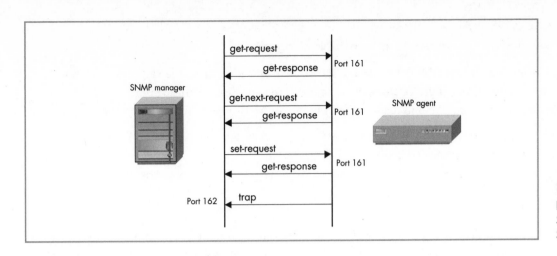

FIGURE 9.3.

Interaction between SNMP manager and SNMP agent.

4. **Get-response:** Sent by an SNMP agent in response to a get-request, get-next-request, or set-request message.

5. **Trap:** An SNMP trap is a notification sent by an SNMP agent to an SNMP manager, which is triggered by certain events at the agent.

In this part of the lab, you enable and access SNMP agents on a Linux PC and on a Cisco router and learn to interpret SNMP messages exchanged between the SNMP manager and the SNMP agent.

The Linux PCs support SNMP through the *NET-SNMP* software (version 5.0.6 or later), which is part of Red Hat 9.0. *NET-SNMP* includes software for an SNMP agent (*snmpd*) and several SNMP manager commands (`snmpget`, `snmpgetnext`, `snmpwalk`, and `snmpset`). On Cisco routers, SNMP support is integrated in IOS.

The general syntax of the SNMP manager commands of the *NET-SNMP* software is as follows:

`snmpcmd [-v version] agent -c community objectid`

where

snmpcmd is the name of an SNMP manager command (`snmpget`, `snmpgetnext`, `snmpwalk`, and `snmpset`).

version is the version number of SNMP, where version is 1, 2c, or 3. By default, SNMPv3 is used. In SNMPv3, additional options need to be provided for authentication purposes (see Part 4).

agent is the IP address or host name of an SNMP agent.

community is what SNMP calls a community string and which, in versions 1 and 2c, serves as a password between an SNMP agent and an SNMP manager. An SNMP manager puts the community string into each request message. An SNMP agent knows three community access moves: *read-only*, *read-write*, and *trap*. The read-only community can retrieve values of managed objects but cannot modify them. The read-write community can modify managed objects. The trap community is used by an SNMP manager to authenticate trap messages.

objectid is the OID or descriptor of a managed object.

EXERCISE 2(A).
Send SNMP requests to a local SNMP agent.

In this exercise the SNMP agent and SNMP manager are run on the same system. You run the SNMP manager commands `snmpget`, `snmpgetnext`, `snmptranslate`, and `snmpwalk` to retrieve and display the contents of MIB objects managed by the local SNMP agent.

The following exercises are done on PC1.

1. Start an SNMP agent on PC1 by invoking the command:

   ```
   PC1% snmpd
   ```

   This command starts an SNMP agent. The command loads the management database with the MIB files in directory */usr/share/snmp/mibs* and configures the agent with file */usr/share/snmp/snmpd.conf*.

 2. Execute the following commands to access scalar variables and record the output:

   ```
   PC1% snmpget localhost -v1 -c public system.sysDescr.0
   PC1% snmpget localhost -v1 -c public udp.udpOutDatagrams.0
   PC1% snmpget localhost -v1 -c public udp.udpInDatagrams.0
   ```

> **NOTE:**
>
> - Note the `.0` suffix at the end of the OID. This suffix is a reference to an instantiation of the referred object that stores the value. We will refer to the instantiations as variables. For example, 1.3.6.1.2.1.7.4.0 refers to the variable that contains the value for object `udp.udpOutDatagrams`. Variables that store a single value are called *scalar variables*. If an object consists of a sequence of values, then the suffix indicates the index in the sequence. For example, `interfaces.ifTable.ifEntry.ifDescr.2`, refers to the second entry of the sequence of values in `interfaces.ifTable.ifEntry.ifDescr`.
> - The community string of the agent is set to `public`. This is often the default community string for the read-only community.

 3. Execute the following commands to access nonscalar variables and save the output:

   ```
   PC1% snmpget localhost -v1 -c public \
        interfaces.ifTable.ifEntry.ifDescr.1
   PC1% snmpget localhost -v1 -c public \
        interfaces.ifTable.ifEntry.ifDescr.2
   ```

   - Continue to increase the index until you get an error message. Save the output of all commands.

   - What happens if you query the value as a scalar value, that is, `interfaces.ifTable.ifEntry.ifDescr.0`

4. Use the command `snmpget` to request multiple object values with the same command. Save the output.

```
PC1% snmpget localhost -v1 -c public system.sysUpTime.0 \
    system.sysName.0
```

5. The command `snmpgetnext` retrieves the value of the next variable according to the lexicographical ordering of OIDs. In the object hierarchy tree, the command retrieves the next object in the tree.

Use the command `snmpgetnext` to retrieve all objects under the node `at` (address translation) in the MIB tree. The object `at` defines a group of objects that store the ARP table of the local system. Start with the command

```
PC1% snmpgetnext localhost -v1 -c public at
```

This value retrieves the variable name of the first entry of the ARP table, as well as its contents.

    a. Issue an `snmpgetnext` command that retrieves the second entry of the ARP table. (The output of the preceding command displayed the identifier that stores the first ARP table entry. Provide this identifier as the argument of the `snmgetnext` command). Repeat until the entire table is displayed. Save the output.

    b. How can you know that you have reached the end of the group *at*?

6. The command `snmpwalk` can be used to retrieve the values of all objects under a particular location in the MIB object hierarchy tree. The retrieval of a complete subtree is referred to as *walking the MIB*. Use `snmpwalk` to obtain the values of all the objects under the nodes *system* and *interfaces*.

```
PC1% snmpwalk localhost -v1 -c public system
PC1% snmpwalk localhost -v1 -c public interfaces
```

Save the output to a file.

Lab Report Include the saved data and the answers to the questions in your lab report.

EXERCISE 2(B).
Send SNMP requests to a remote PC.

Next, the SNMP manager and SNMP agent are run on different systems. PC1 acts as the SNMP manager and PC4 runs an agent. You are asked to run the same commands as before. The emphasis of this exercise is to observe SNMP messages that are exchanged between the SNMP manager and the SNMP agent.

1. On PC1, start to capture traffic with *ethereal* on interface *eth0*. You may set a capture filter or display filter so that only SNMP messages are displayed.

2. On PC4, start an SNMP agent by invoking the command

```
PC4% snmpd
```

3. On PC1, execute the following commands:

```
PC1% snmpget 10.0.4.14 -v1 -c public system.sysDescr.0
PC1% snmpget 10.0.4.14 -v1 -c public udp.udpOutDatagrams.0
PC1% snmpget 10.0.4.14 -v1 -c public udp.udpInDatagrams.0
PC1% snmpget 10.0.4.14 -v1 -c public system.sysContact.0
PC1% snmpget 10.0.4.14 -v1 -c public \
    interfaces.ifTable.ifEntry.ifDescr.1
PC1% snmpget 10.0.4.14 -v1 -c public \
    interfaces.ifTable.ifEntry.ifDescr.2
PC1% snmpget localhost -v1 -c public system.sysUpTime.0 \
    system.sysName.0
PC1% snmpgetnext 10.0.4.14 -v1 -c public at
PC1% snmpwalk 10.0.4.14 -v1 -c public system
PC1% snmpwalk 10.0.4.14 -v1 -c public interfaces
```

Save the captured SNMP packets. You need to set the *Print detail* option.

Observe and interpret the SNMP payload of the messages. Answer the following questions:

- Verify the version number of SNMP messages and the UDP port numbers used by the SNMP manager and the SNMP agent.

- Describe the format of an SNMP message and the fields of an SNMP header.

- Explain how the community string is transmitted in the SNMP messages.

- Describe how data is transmitted when the manager issues an `snmpwalk` command. What is the maximum size of the payload?

- How is textual data represented? How are an IP address and a MAC address represented?

- Describe how SNMP transmits the content of a table (e.g., ARP table).

Lab Report   Include the saved data and the answers to the questions in your lab report.

EXERCISE 2(C).
Send SNMP requests to a Cisco router.

All Cisco routers support SNMP. In most scenarios, routers play the role of an SNMP agent, but SNMP manager commands may be run on a router. The set of IOS commands to configure SNMP is quite large, and this lab uses only the listed basic commands.

IOS MODE: GLOBAL CONFIGURATION

```
snmp-server community ComString [ ro | rw ]
```
Starts an SNMP agent if it is not already running and assigns a community string *ComString*. The options `ro` and `rw`, respectively, assign a read-only and read-write community. (The default setting is `ro`.)

```
no snmp-server community ComString
```
Deletes the community *ComString*.

```
no snmp-server
```
Disables the SNMP agent.

In this exercise you start an SNMP agent in IOS and access the MIB of a router from an SNMP manager running on one of the Linux PCs. You use *ethereal* to capture the SNMP traffic between the SNMP manager and the SNMP agent.

1. From PC1, establish a *kermit* session and connect to Router1.

2. On Router1, execute the following commands to enable an SNMP agent:

```
Router1> enable
Password: <enable secret>
Router1# configure terminal
Router1(config)#     snmp-server community public
Router1(config)# end
```

These commands start an SNMP agent and set the community string to `public`. By default, access to the MIB of the router is read-only. With this command, the SNMP agent responds to the SNMP manager that provides the community string `public`.

3. Use the command `show running-config` to display the communities that are configured at the router:

```
Router1# show running-config
```

4. On PC1, start to capture traffic on interface *eth0* with *ethereal*. Set a capture or display filter to limit the displayed packets to SNMP messages.

5. On PC1, query the SNMP agent on Router1 using `snmpget` (with option `-v1`) to obtain the values of the following object identifiers:

  a. `system.sysDescr.0`

  b. `icmp.icmpInRedirects.0`

  c. `icmp.icmpInSrcQuenchs.0`

  d. `udp.udpInDatagrams.0`

  e. `udp.udpNoPorts.0`

6. On PC1, use the `snmpwalk` command to obtain the values of all objects under the nodes *icmp* and *udp*. Use the *snmptranslate* command to obtain the OIDs of the objects occurring in the previous SNMP manager commands.

7. Observe the SNMP traffic sent between PC1 and Router1. Are there any differences between the SNMP traffic seen in this exercise and the SNMP traffic seen in Exercise 2(B)? Record the differences.

8. Save the output of the commands and save the SNMP messages captured by *ethereal*.

Lab Report

*   Include the save output of the `snmpget` commands and the *ethereal* data.

*   Match the output of the commands with the payload of the SNMP messages.

*   Answer the question posed in the exercise.

PART 3.   MODIFYING MIB OBJECTS

Next, you use SNMP to modify the value of managed objects at an agent. Before modifying an object at an SNMP agent, you must create a community string on a Linux PC and a Cisco router. Community-based access control is a mechanism implemented in SNMPv1 and SNMPv2c.

The SNMP manager command on the Linux PCs is `snmpset`. The command supplies the required community string. For modifying the values of objects, a community string for the read-write community is needed.

This community string must be configured at the SNMP agent. On the Linux PCs, the community string for the read-write community is configured by editing the configuration file */usr/share/snmp/snmpd.conf*. By default, the NET-SNMP software configures only the read-only community string `public`. On the Cisco routers, a community string is set with the `snmp-server` command.

EXERCISE 3(A).
Modify the values of MIB objects on a Linux PC.

The main problem is to configure a read-write community string at the SNMP agent. As before, PC1 acts as the SNMP manager and PC4 runs an SNMP agent.

1. On PC4, terminate the SNMP agent daemon program started in Part 2 by typing

    ```
    PC4% pkill snmpd
    ```

2. On PC4, edit the file */usr/share/snmp/snmpd.conf* and add the following lines:

    ```
    com2sec newuser 10.0.0.0/16 private
    group MyRWGroup any newuser
    view mib2view included .iso.org.dod.internet.mgmt.mib-2
    access MyRWGroup "" any noauth exact mib2view mib2view none
    ```

The interpretation of the configuration is discussed in Part 4.

3. On PC4, restart the SNMP agent with the command

   ```
   PC4% snmpd
   ```

4. On PC1, start to capture traffic with *ethereal* on interface *eth0*. You may want to set a capture filter or display filter to show only SNMP messages.

5. On PC1, execute the following commands. First, observe what happens when you try to change a MIB object but supply the wrong community string.

   ```
   PC1% snmpset 10.0.4.14 -v1 -C WrongCommunity system.sysName.
     0 s XYZ
   ```

   The argument s XYZ in the snmpset command tries to set the string variable to value XYZ.

   • What is the output of the command?

   • How does the SNMP agent tell the SNMP manager when the community string is not correct?

6. Next, on PC1, change the value of the object with the community string private and observe the output of the commands

   ```
   PC1% snmpget 10.0.4.14 -v1 -c private system.sysName.0
   PC1% snmpset -v1 -c private 10.0.4.14 system.sysName.0 s XYZ
   PC1% snmpget 10.0.4.14 -v1 -c private system.sysName.0
   PC1% snmpset -v1 -c private 10.0.4.14 system.sysName.0 s PC4
   ```

7. Save the SNMP manager commands and the corresponding output into a file. Save the *ethereal* output into a file. You need to select the *Print detail* option.

8. On PC4, edit the file */usr/share/snmp/snmpd.conf* and delete the lines that were added in Step 2.

Lab Report

• Include the captured data of the SNMP commands and the *ethereal* output in the lab report. Describe your observations.

• Answer the question in Step 5.

EXERCISE 3(C).
Modify the values of MIB objects on a Cisco router.

Next, modify the value of a MIB object on a Cisco router. The SNMP manager program snmpset is used to disconnect an existing TCP connection by modifying the value of the object *tcp.tcpConnTable.tcpConnEntry.tcpConnState*, which holds the state of the current TCP connections, for a particular TCP connection. To achieve this, use the community string private, which has read-write permissions.

Creating a read-write community string on a Cisco router is relatively simple. The following IOS commands create a new community string on Router1 and give it read-write permissions on the whole MIB tree.

1. On Router1, execute the following commands to set up an SNMP agent with read-write community string private.

```
Router1> enable
Password: <enable secret>
Router1# configure terminal
Router1(config)# snmp-server community private rw
Router1(config)# end
```

2. On PC1, start *ethereal* on interface *eth0*. You can set a capture or display filter to just display SNMP messages.

3. On PC1, set up a *Telnet* session to Router1 by typing

```
PC1% telnet 10.0.1.1
```

Log in to Router1. (In general, in IOS, the password for creating a *Telnet* session can be different from the `enable secret`. In the Internet Lab, the passwords should be set to the same value.). Note that a *Telnet* session establishes a TCP connection.

4. On PC1, execute the following command to find the entry in the `tcpConnTable` which records the status of TCP connections:

```
PC1% snmpwalk 10.0.1.1 -v1 -c private \
    tcp.tcpConnTable.tcpConnEntry.tcpConnState
```

The form of the output looks like this:

```
tcp.tcpConnTable.tcpConnEntry.tcpConnState.
  LocalIP.LocalPort.RemoteIP.RemotePort = value
```

where `LocalIP` and `LocalPort` are the IP address and port number of the local system, and `RemoteIP` and `RemotePort` are the IP address and port number of the remote connection of a TCP connection. (Find the record where `RemoteIP` is set to 10.0.1.11. There should be only one TCP connection.)

5. On PC1, execute the following command:

```
PC1% snmpset -v1 -c private 10.0.1.1\
    tcp.tcpConnTable.tcpConnEntry.tcpConnState.LocalIP.
    LocalPort.RemoteIP.RemotePort i 12
```

where `LocalIP`, `LocalPort`, `RemoteIP`, and `RemotePort` are as discussed earlier. The meaning of i 12 is that the command sets an integer variable to value 12.

Observe what happens. Is the *Telnet* session terminated?

6. Find out what the meaning of `TCP connection state = 12` is. Can the SNMP manager set the state of the connection to any value?

7. Save the *ethereal* output of the SNMP traffic, selecting the *Print detail* option.

Lab Report

- Include the output from *ethereal* in your answers.

- Explain the fields in the captured packets. Observe the community string; what is the disadvantage of a community-based security mechanism?

- Explain the `snmpset` command, which disconnected the preceding TCP connection.

PART 4. SNMPV3 SECURITY

As you have observed, SNMPv1 uses plain text community strings for authentication. Clearly, this makes network management with SNMP highly insecure. SNMPv2 was supposed to fix the security problems, but SNMPv2c, the only widely adopted version of SNMPv2, still uses community strings for access control.

SNMPv3 has solved most of the security problems of the earlier versions. SNMPv3 can ensure that a packet has not been tampered with (*integrity*), that a message is from a valid source (*authentication*), and that a message cannot be read by unauthorized users (*privacy*).

The security model of SNMPv3 has two components. First, instead of granting access rights to a community, SNMPv3 grants access to users. Second, SNMPv3 allows restricting sections of the MIB tree that can be accessed by a user. The latter is called View-based Access Control Module (VACM). The following two exercises explore each of the components in turn.

EXERCISE 4(A).
Community-based and user-based security in SNMP.

The following is a list of the types of security provided by SNMPv1, SNMPv2c, and SNMPv3. SNMPv1 and SNMPv2 offer the same type of security, and SNMPv3 has three security levels:

- **SNMPv1, SNMPv2:** Authentication with matching a community string

- **SNMPv3 (Level noAuthNoPriv):** Authentication with matching a user name

- **SNMPv3 (Level authNoPriv):** Authentication with MD5 or SHA message digests

- **SNMPv3 (Level authPriv):** Authentication with MD5 or SHA message digests and encryption with DES encryption

In this part of the lab, you study how security levels are invoked and how they improve the security of SNMP traffic.

Throughout all lab exercises, PC1 is used as an SNMP manager and PC4 runs an SNMP agent.

1. On PC1, start to capture traffic with *ethereal* on interface *eth0*. Set a capture filter or display filter so that only SNMP messages are displayed. Capture all SNMP traffic until this exercise is completed.

2. On PC4, terminate the SNMP agent program (if there is one running) by typing

   `PC4% pkill snmpd`

3. **Community-based security in SNMPv1 and SNMPv2c:**

   a. On PC4, start an SNMP agent by invoking the command

   `PC4% snmpd`

   b. On PC1, start to execute the following commands:

   ```
   PC1% snmpget -v 1 10.0.4.14 -c public sysUpTime.0
   PC1% snmpget -v 2c 10.0.4.14 -c public sysUpTime.0
   ```

   What is the difference between the SNMP messages (Request and Response) of the two versions?

   c. Verify that the wrong community string results in an error message. For example,

   `PC1% snmpget -v 1 10.0.4.14 -c WrongCommunity sysUpTime.0`

4. **User-based security in SNMPv3:** Since SNMPv3 has a user-based security model, you need to configure a user at the SNMP agent.

   a. To configure a new user at PC4, the SNMP agent on PC4 needs to be stopped:

   `PC4% pkill snmpd`

   b. Create a new user at the SNMP agent as follows. Edit the file */usr/share/snmp/snmpd.conf* and add the following line:

   `rwuser user1 noauth`

   c. Add passwords for `user1` by editing the file */var/net-snmp/snmpd.conf* and adding the following line:

   `createuser user1 MD5 MyPassword DES MyPassword`

   This line adds two passwords, an *authentication password* and a *privacy password*. The authentication password is used to build MD5 message digests, and the privacy password is used for encrypting the payload of the SNMP message using DES encryption. Here, both passwords are set to `MyPassword`.

   d. On PC4, restart the SNMP agent with the command

   `PC4% snmpd`

   e. **SNMPv3 (Level noAuthNoPriv):** On PC1, execute the following SNMP manager command:

   ```
   PC1% snmpget -v 3 -u user1 -l noAuthNoPriv \
       10.0.4.14 sysUpTime.0
   ```

   Observe the SNMP messages and compare them to SNMPv1 and SNMPv2 messages.

f. **SNMPv3 (Level `authNoPriv`):** Next, on PC1, execute the same command with user authorization:

```
PC1% snmpget -v 3 -u user1 -l authNoPriv \
    -A MyPassword 10.0.4.14 sysUpTime.0
```

Here, a digital signature is added to the SNMP message.

Which field(s) in the SNMP message is (are) affected by the authentication?

g. **SNMPv3 (Level `authPriv`):** Next, run a command with the highest security level on PC1:

```
PC1% snmpget -v 3 -u user1 -l authPriv \
    -A MyPassword \
    -X MyPassword 10.0.4.14 sysUpTime.0
```

Here, a digital signature is added and the payload of the SNMP message is encrypted.

- Which parts of the SNMP messages are encrypted? Consider both the Request and the Response message.

- Do you notice increased delays due to the encryption algorithms?

5. Save the *ethereal* output into a file. You need to set the *Print detail* option. Also, terminate the SNMP agent running on PC4:

```
PC4% pkill snmpd
```

6. Delete the lines that you added in Step 4(b) in file */usr/share/snmpd.conf* and in Step 4(c) in file */var/net-snmp/snmpd.conf*.

Lab Report

- For each security level—SNMPv1 and SNMPv2c, SNMPv3 (`noAuthNoPriv` `authNoPriv`, `authPriv`)—include the saved SNMP messages.

- Include your answers to the questions in this exercise, and answer the following questions:

  — Compared to community strings, what additional security do user names provide?

  — What type of security is provided by using message digests?

  — What type of security is provided by encrypting the payload?

  — To which type of security attack is SNMP vulnerable even with the highest level of security?

EXERCISE 4(B).
View-based Access Control Module (VACM).

The View-based Access Control Module (VACM) of SNMPv3 permits an SNMP agent to limit the access rights of users and communities that access the agent. The access rights can be limited by specifying a range of valid IP addresses for a user or community, and by specifying the part of the MIB tree that can be accessed.

Even though VACM was introduced with SNMPv3, in the NET-SNMP package on the Linux PCs VCAM is used to configure the community-based access control of SNMPv1 and SNMPv2. The access rights are specified in *snmpd.conf*. Note that you modified this file in Part 3, adding a community and giving the community the right to modify MIB objects.

The following exercise uses the VACM model of SNMPv3 but applies it to SNMPv1 messages. The objective of this exercise is to define a new community (`Mycommunity`), which has read-write access to the TCP portion of the MIB-II subtree (`1.3.6.1.2.1.6`). In addition, SNMP managers with the correct community string are restricted to the 10.0.1.0/24 network.

1. On PC4, terminate the SNMP agent program on PC4:

   ```
   PC4% pkill snmpd
   ```

2. On PC1, start to capture traffic with *ethereal* on interface *eth0*, with a capture filter or display filter set so that only SNMP messages are displayed.

3. On PC4, add the access rights for the new community, as given earlier. This is done by editing the file */usr/share/snmp/snmpd.conf* and adding the following lines:

   ```
   rwcommunity    MyCommunity    10.0.1.0/24
   com2sec        NewSecName     10.0.1.0/24            Mycommunity
   group          MyGroup        any                   NewSecName
   view           NewView        included              .1.3.6.1.2.1.6
   access         MyGroup        "" any noauth exact NewView NewView
                                 none
   ```

   The first line creates a read-write community with name `MyCommunity`, which is limited to IP addresses in `10.0.1.0/24`. The second line associates a name `NewSecName` and the IP address range `10.0.1.0/24` with the community string `Mycommunity`. The third line maps the name to the group name `MyGroup`. The fourth line defines the scope of access to group .1.3.6.1.2.1.6, which designates the group *tcp*. The last line specifies read and write access rights to the defined view. The options are explained in more detail in the man page of *snmpd.conf*.

   - Explain why these commands achieve the objective stated at the beginning of this exercise.

4. On PC4, start an SNMP agent by invoking the command

   ```
   PC4% snmpd
   ```

5. On PC1, execute an SNMP manager command that accesses a value from the tcp group of the MIB.

```
PC1% snmpget 10.0.4.14 -v1 -c MyCommunity tcpRtoMax.0
```

Save the preceding SNMP manager commands and the corresponding output into a file. Save the *ethereal* output into a file (using *Print detail*).

Verify that this command is not successful if you (1) use a different community and (2) run an SNMP manager on a network different from 10.0.1.0/24.

Save the output of the SNMP manager commands in these cases.

Lab Report

- Include your answers to the questions in this exercise.

- Provide a detailed explanation of how the commands in Step 3 realize the desired access rights.

- Include the saved output and saved SNMP packets in the lab report.

PART 5.   SNMP TRAPS

A trap is a notification mechanism in which the occurrence of certain events at an SNMP agent triggers the transmission of an SNMP trap message to an SNMP manager. SNMP has several predefined traps that include events when the system is rebooted, an SNMP agent is started, a link goes up or down, and an unauthorized access has been attempted.

In this part of the lab, we use the SNMP manager program *snmptrapd* to handle traps. The manager listens on UDP port 162 for SNMP trap messages and logs SNMP trap messages that are received.

EXERCISE 5(A).
Configure SNMP traps on a Linux PC.

On Linux PCs, traps are enabled and configured using the configuration file */usr/share/ snmp/snmpd.conf*. On the Linux PCs with the NET-SNMP software, the predefined set of traps for NET-SNMP does not include the events of a link failure or recovery.

The following steps configure the SNMP agent at PC4 to send trap messages to PC1.

1. On PC4, terminate the SNMP agent program by typing

```
PC4% pkill snmpd
```

2. On PC4, edit the configuration file */usr/share/snmp/snmpd.conf* and add the following lines:

```
trapcommunity public
trapsink 10.0.1.11
authtrapenable 1
```

The first line sets the trap community string to `public`. The next line sets PC1 as the receiver of trap messages. The line `authtrapenable 1` enables trap messages to be sent when an unauthorized access occurs.

EXERCISE 5(B).
Configure SNMP traps on a Cisco router.

Next, enable traps on one of the Cisco routers. The commands needed to enable the predefined set of traps are listed.

IOS MODE: GLOBAL CONFIGURATION

`snmp-server enable traps`

   Enables the ability to issue traps for notifications.

`snmp host IPaddr traps [version 1 | version 2c] ComString`

   Sets IP address *IPaddr* as the destination for trap messages with community string *ComString*. The version specifies the types of SNMP messages transmitted. The default is SNMPv1.

---

1. On Router3, enable SNMP traps and have all SNMP traps sent to PC1 by typing the following commands:

```
Router3> enable
Password: <enable secret>
Router3# configure terminal
Router3(config)# snmp-server host 10.0.1.11 traps public
Router3(config)# snmp-server enable traps
Router3(config)# end
```

2. Run the command

```
Router3# show running-config
```

From the output, find the defined traps and save them into a file.

EXERCISE 5(C).
Capture and handle SNMP trap messages.

Here, you set up PC1 as the SNMP manager that collects and displays trap messages. You will create two type of traps. First, you disconnect one of the interfaces on Router3. When the link goes down, the router will generate a trap. Then, you terminate the SNMP agent on PC4. When the agent shuts down, a trap is sent to PC1.

1. On PC1, start to capture traffic on interface *eth0* with *ethereal*. Set a display filter to capture only SNMP messages.

2. On PC1, run *snmptrapd* SNMP manager with the option -P. This option specifies that messages are printed in a terminal window.

```
PC1% snmptrapd -P
```

Save the output of the command to a file.

3. On PC4, start an SNMP agent with the command

```
PC4% snmpd
```

After a few minutes, stop the agent with the command

```
PC4% pkill snmpd
```

Terminating the agent program triggers a trap message. When you restart the agent you should observe another trap message.

4. On Router3, disconnect the cable on interface *Serial1/0*. After a few minutes, reconnect the cable. For each event you should observe a trap.

5. Save the output of *snmptrapd* and the SNMP packets captured by *ethereal* to a file. For *ethereal*, you need to select *Print detail*.

Lab Report

- Include the SNMP trap messages captured by *ethereal* and the output of *snmptrapd* in your report.

- Which trap types do you observe in the experiment?

- How many trap messages are sent each time an event is triggered?

- Which OID values are transmitted in the trap messages? What is their textual interpretation?

PART 6. APPLICATIONS OF SNMP

In this part of the lab, you perform three network management tasks with SNMP. The first task is to query the status of network connections on a remote PC; the second task is to determine the path between two hosts.

EXERCISE 6(A).
Observe TCP connections on a remote Linux PC.

A network administrator can use the SNMP manager to observe the status of TCP connections on remote hosts where an SNMP agent is running. The collected information can be used to monitor the activities on remote systems.

1. On PC4, start an SNMP agent by typing

```
PC4% snmpd
```

2. Set up *Telnet* sessions from PC2 and PC3 to PC4 by typing the following commands:

```
PC2% telnet 10.0.4.14
PC3% telnet 10.0.4.14
```

Log in to PC4 as the root user.

3. On PC1, query the TCP portion of the MIB at PC4 with the command

```
PC1% snmpwalk 10.0.4.14 -vi -c public tcp
```

4. Save the output into a file.

5. Close the *Telnet* sessions.

Lab Report

- In the saved output, find the records that relate to the *Telnet* sessions and include them in the lab report.

- How can this information be used by a network administrator?

EXERCISE 6(B).

Determine the path between two hosts.

The command `traceroute` determines the forwarding path taken by a packet from a source to a destination. With SNMP it is possible to determine the path between any pair of hosts.

In this exercise, you use SNMP to find the forwarding path from PC4 (10.0.4.14) to PC2 (10.0.1.12).

1. Make sure that SNMP agents are running on all routers and on all PCs. Start an SNMP agent on each Cisco router. The SNMP agent should provide read-only access for requests that use the community string `public`.

   The commands for Router3 are as follows:

```
Router3> enable
Password: <enable secret>
Router3# configure terminal
Router3(config)# snmp-server community public
Router3(config)# end
```

   The command for PC4 is:

```
PC4% snmpd
```

2. On PC1, execute the following command to find the next hop of PC4 on the path from PC4 to PC2:

```
PC1% snmpwalk 10.0.4.14 -v1 -c public \
    ip.ipRouteTable.ipRouteEntry.ipRouteNextHop
```

   The output of the command consists of entries of the form

```
ip.ipRouteTable.ipRouteEntry.ipRouteINextHop.NetIPAddress =
    IpAddress: NextHopIPAddress
```

   There is one line for each routing table entry. *NetIPAddress* is the destination address and *NextHopIPAddress* is the IP address of the next-hop router to destination *NetIPAddress*. Determine the matching routing table for destination 10.0.1.12 from the output, and obtain the corresponding *NextHopIPAddress*.

3. Repeat the process described before, but replace IP address 10.0.4.14 in the snmpwalk command with the IP address of the next hop, *NextHopIPAddress*, you obtained then. Repeat these steps, until a router that is directly connected to PC2 is reached. Save the output of the snmpwalk commands to a file.

   • How does this process determine the path from PC4 to PC2?

4. On Router3 and Router1, change the cost of interface *Serial1/0* to 40. The following commands are for Router3:

```
Router3# configure terminal
Router3(config)# interface Serial1/0
Router3(config-if)# ip ospf cost 40
Router3(config-if)# end
```

5. Repeat Steps 2–4, and determine the new path from PC4 to PC2.

   • Has the path from PC4 to PC2 changed? If so, what is the new path?

Lab Report

• Use the saved data to discuss how you can use SNMP to infer the path between PC4 and PC2.

• Answer the questions in this part of lab.

CHECKLIST FORM FOR LAB 9

Complete this checklist as you work through the laboratory exercises and attach the form to your lab report.

Name (please print):_____

☐ Prelab 9 question sheet

☐ Checkoff for Part 1   ☐ Checkoff for Part 5

☐ Checkoff for Part 2   ☐ Checkoff for Part 6

☐ Checkoff for Part 3   ☐ Feedback sheet

☐ Checkoff for Part 4   ☐ Lab report

FEEDBACK FORM FOR LAB 9

- Complete this feedback form at the completion of the lab exercises and submit the form when submitting your lab report.

- The feedback is anonymous. *Do not put your name on this form* and keep it separate from your lab report.

- For each exercise, please record the following:

	Difficulty (–2, –1, 0, 1, 2) −2 = too easy 0 = just right 2 = too hard	**Interest Level** (–2, –1, 0, 1, 2) −2 = low interest 0 = just right 2 = high interest	**Time to Complete** (minutes)
Part 1. Management Information Base (MIB)			
Part 2. SNMP agents and managers: retrieving MIB objects			
Part 3. Modifying MIB objects			
Part 4. SNMPv3 security			
Part 5. SNMP traps			
Part 6. Applications of SNMP			

Please answer the following questions:

- What did you like about this lab?

- What did you dislike about this lab?

- Make a suggestion to improve the lab.

IP Multicast

- How IP multicast datagrams reach multiple destinations with a single packet

- How IGMP is used to set the membership of an IP multicast group

- How multicast routing protocols set up distribution trees that connect multicast sources and receivers

CONTENTS

PRELAB 10

1. **IP Multicast commands in Unix:** Go to the online manual pages at
   `http://www.tcpip-lab.net/links/manual.html`, and select the operating
   system version Redhat Linux/i386 7.3. Read about the multicasting options in the
   man pages for the commands `netstat` and `ping`:

   - For `netstat`, read about the `-g` option.

   - For `ping`, read which options are available when a `ping` is issued to a multicast
     address.

   Read the Linux man pages of the following commands, available at the given web
   link:

   - `mtrace` (available at `http://www.tcpip-lab.net/links/mtrace.html`)

   - `mrinfo` (available at `http://www.tcpip-lab.net/links/mrinfo.html`)

   - `map-mbone` (available at `http://www.tcpip-lab.net/links/`
     `map-mbone.html`)

2. **IP Multicast:** Review the following specifications of the three versions of IGMP:

   - IGMPv1: RFC 1112: Host Extensions for IP Multicasting, 1989

     (available at: `http://www.tcpip-lab.net/links/igmpv1.html`)

   - IGMPv2: RFC 2236: Internet Group Management Protocol, Version 2, 1997

     (available at: `http://www.tcpip-lab.net/links/igmpv2.html`)

   - IGMPv3: RFC 3376: Internet Group Management Protocol, Version 3, 2002

     (available at: `http://www.tcpip-lab.net/links/igmpv3.html`)

     Read about the assignment of permanent multicast addresses by the IANA at

     `http://www.tcpip-lab.net/links/mcassign.html`

3. **IP Multicast Routing:** Visit the following URLs:

   - Review the specification of PIM-DM, which is available at
     `http://www.tcpip-lab.net/links/pimdm.html`

   - Review the specification of PIM-SM, which is available at
     `http://www.tcpip-lab.net/links/pimsm.html`

4. **Msend/mreceive commands:** Visit the following URLs

   - `http://www.tcpip-lab.net/links/msend.html`

   - `http://www.tcpip-lab.net/links/mreceive.html`

   and read about the man pages of the `msend` and `mreceive` commands.

QUESTION SHEET FOR PRELAB 10

Answer the questions in the space provided below each one. Use extra sheets of paper if needed and attach them to this document. Submit the answers with your lab report.

Name (please print):_____

1. What range of IP addresses is reserved for IP multicasting?

2. What are the multicast addresses in the range 224.0.0.0 through 224.0.0.255 used for? How do multicast routers treat packets with destination addresses in that range?

3. What are the multicast addresses 224.0.0.5 and 224.0.0.6 reserved for?

4. How is the TTL field interpreted in IP multicast packets?

5. Write the following `msend` and `mreceive` commands:
   a. The syntax of a multicast receiver that listens to multicast packets for group 224.1.1.1 on interface *eth1*

   b. The syntax of an `msend` command that starts a multicast sender for group 224.1.1.1, which sends multicast packets to interface *eth0*, with a TTL value of 10

6. What are the main differences between IGMP version 1 (IGMPv1), IGMP version 2 (IGMPv2), and IGMP version 3 (IGMPv3)?

7. What is the syntax for the `mtrace` command to display the multicast path for multi-cast group address 224.12.0.1 from source address 192.0.1.1 to destination address 192.0.2.1?

8. What is the Ethernet MAC address that corresponds to the IP address 224.1.1.39?

9. Explain the implications of the fact that the mapping between multicast IP addresses and MAC addresses is not a one-to-one mapping.

10. List the different message types of the PIM multicast routing protocol and briefly explain their function.

11. In PIM, there is one message type for join and prune messages, called *PIM Join/Prune*. How do routers determine if a PIM Join/Prune message indicates a join or a prune, or both?

12. According to the specification of PIM-SM, a router on a LAN can perform three different functions. Depending on the function performed, a router may act as a querier, as a forwarder, and/or as a designated router. Explain the difference between these functions.

13. Is it possible, in PIM-SM, for the rendezvous point tree (RPT) and the shortest-path tree (SPT) to be identical? Provide an example or counterexample.

LAB 10

This lab has several configurations, shown in the figures throughout.

SETUP FOR LAB 10

In this lab you will set up the machines with the IP address configuration shown in Tables 10.1 and 10.2.

TABLE 10.1. IP addresses of PCs for Figures 10.1–10.4.

Linux PC	Interface *eth0*	Interface *eth1*
PC1	10.0.1.11/24	10.0.2.12/24
PC2	10.0.1.21/24	10.0.2.22/24
PC3	10.0.1.31/24	10.0.2.32/24
PC4	10.0.1.41/24	10.0.2.42/24

TABLE 10.2. IP addresses of Router1 for Figures 10.2–10.4.

Cisco Router	Interface *Ethernet0/0*	Interface *Ethernet0/1*
Router1	10.0.1.1/24	10.0.2.1/24

NOTE:

Before you get started, please reboot your machine.

RECALL:

- During the lab, you need to save data to files. Save all files in the directory /labdata.
- Save your files to a floppy disk before the end of the lab. You will need the files when you prepare your lab report.

PART 1.   MULTICAST ON A SINGLE SEGMENT

In the first part of the lab, you explore the basics of IP multicast and the IGMP protocol. You observe how hosts join a multicast group using the IGMP protocol. Also, you will observe how IP multicast addresses are mapped to MAC addresses.

Throughout this lab, you will work with the Linux commands `msend` and `mreceive`, which send traffic to and receive traffic from an IP multicast group.

- **msend:** Periodically transmits UDP datagrams to a given multicast group. The *msend* program does not join the multicast group, unless the option `-join` is given as an argument.

- **mreceive:** Joins a multicast group and displays the payload of received multicast messages to the standard output.

For example, the command

```
PC1% msend -g 224.1.1.1 -p 4444 -text "PC1"
```

sends UDP datagrams that contain the string `"PC1"` to multicast group 224.1.1.1 at port number 4444. A multicast receiver is started with the command

```
PC2% mreceive -g 224.1.1.1 -p 4444
```

This command displays all data sent to multicast address 224.1.1.1 at port number 4444 to the standard output.

The default values of `msend` and `mreceive` can be modified using various options.

EXERCISE 1(A).
Network setup.

1. Set the network up as shown in Figure 10.1, where the *eth0* interfaces of the PCs are connected to an Ethernet hub. On each PC, ensure that the *eth1* interface is disabled.

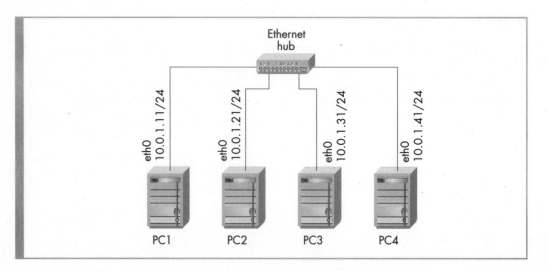

FIGURE 10.1.

Configuration for Part 1.

2. Verify that the PCs are connected to the console ports of routers. PC1 should be connected to Router1, PC2 to Router 2, and so on. Verify that you can connect to the routers using the `kermit` command.

3. Use the `ping` command to verify that all interfaces are correctly configured.

EXERCISE 1(B).
Observe IP multicast traffic.

1. On each PC, add a route to network address 224.0.0.0/8 for interface *eth0*. For example:

   ```
   PC1% route add -net 224.0.0.0/8 dev eth0
   ```

2. Start *ethereal* to capture traffic on interface *eth0* of PC1.

3. Start a multicast sender on PC1 by typing

   ```
   PC1% msend -i eth0 -g 224.1.2.3 -p 4444 -text "PC1"
   ```

4. Observe the traffic in *ethereal*.

   - What are the MAC address and the IP destination address of the transmitted packets?

   - What is the value of the TTL field in the IP headers?

   - What is the transport protocol used?

   - Which IGMP messages do you observe? How many IGMP packets do you observe?

5. Start a multicast receiver application on PC2 and PC3:

   ```
   PC2% mreceive -g 224.1.2.3 -p 4444
   PC3% mreceive -g 224.1.2.3 -p 4444
   ```

   - What is the impact of adding receivers?

   - What, if any, extra packets do PC2 and PC3 generate?

6. Now start a new multicast sender on PC 4:

   ```
   PC4% msend -g 224.1.2.3 -p 4444 -text "PC4"
   ```

   - How do the receivers handle the transmissions from multiple senders?

7. Stop the receiver applications on PC2 and PC3. Observe the impact on the traffic and any extra packets captured by *ethereal*.

8. Set a display filter on *ethereal* to show only IGMP packets. Save the summary capture to a plain text file.

   Match the IGMP messages with the events of starting and stopping the multicast senders and receivers.

Lab Report Use the saved data from *ethereal* to answer the following questions:

- Include your answers to the questions in Exercise 1(B).

- Only UDP datagrams can be sent to IP multicast. There is no IP multicast support for TCP. What are the implications? Speculate why there is no multicast version for TCP.

- What is the impact of adding and deleting additional multicast senders and receivers to a multicast group?

PART 2. IGMP

The Internet Group Management Protocol (IGMP) involves multicast routers and hosts on the same IP network. In Part 1 of the lab, you already observed some IGMP packets on a network without a router. Since the main role of IGMP is to help a multicast router keep track of multicast groups on the network, we now add a multicast router, Router1, to the network configuration. For this part of the lab, the PCs are configured on one Ethernet segment as shown in Figure 10.2. Throughout this lab, you will work with IGMP version 2 (IGMPv2).

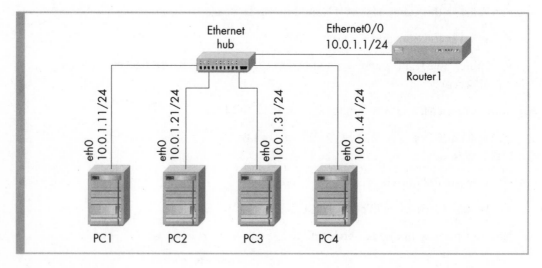

FIGURE 10.2.

Configuration for Part 2.

EXERCISE 2(A).
Network setup.

1. Set the network up as shown in Figure 10.2.

2. Configure the IP addresses of Router1 as shown in Table 10.2.

3. For each PC, add a default route to Router1. Recall that routing table entries are set using the command `route`, for example:

    `PC1% route add default gw 10.0.1.1`

4. Use the `ping` command to verify that all interfaces are correctly configured.

EXERCISE 2(B).
Enabling IGMP at a router.

Set up Router1 so that it uses the IGMP protocol. However, for now, do not enable multicast packet forwarding, since there is only one IP network segment. The listed IOS commands are needed.

IOS MODE: GLOBAL CONFIGURATION

```
ip multicast-routing
no ip multicast-routing
```
> The first command enables IP multicast forwarding, and the second command disables multicast forwarding.

IOS MODE: PRIVILEGED EXEC MODE

```
show ip mroute
```
> Displays the multicast routing table for all groups.

```
clear ip mroute *
```
> Deletes all multicast routing table entries.

```
show ip igmp groups
show ip igmp interface interface
```
> Displays the multicast groups that have group members on the interfaces of the router. The first command displays information on all multicast groups that have members. The second command displays multicast groups that have group members on the network attached to the given interface.

IOS MODE: INTERFACE CONFIGURATION

```
ip pim dense-mode
ip pim sparse-mode
ip pim sparse-dense-mode
```
> Enables the multicast routing protocols PIM-DM or PIM-SM for an interface. The option sparse-dense-mode uses PIM-SM if a rendezvous point is known and PIM-DM when a rendezvous point is not known.

Enter the following commands for Router1:

```
Router1> enable
Password : <enable secret>
Router1# configure terminal
Router1(config)# no ip routing
Router1(config)# ip routing
Router1(config)# no ip multicast-routing
Router1(config)# interface Ethernet0/0
Router1(config-if)# no shutdown
Router1(config-if)# ip pim dense-mode
Router1(config-if)# end
```

EXERCISE 2(C).
IGMP packets.

Create several multicast groups, and, using *ethereal*, observe the IGMP packets that are exchanged between hosts and the router.

1. Start an *ethereal* session on PC4 that captures data on interface *eth0*.

2. Start multiple multicast senders and/or receivers on the PCs as shown. Start each multicast sender and receiver command in a separate window.

   ```
   PC1% msend -g 224.1.1.1 -p 1111 -t 8 -text "PC1"
   PC1% msend -g 224.2.2.2 -p 2222 -t 8 -text "PC1"
   PC1% mreceive -g 224.3.3.3 -p 3333

   PC2% msend -g 224.3.3.3 -p 3333 -t 8 -text "PC2"
   PC2% msend -g 224.1.1.1 -p 1111 -t 8 -text "PC2"

   PC3% msend -g 224.2.2.2 -p 2222 -t 8 -text "PC3"
   PC3% msend -g 224.3.3.3 -p 3333 -t 8 -text "PC3"

   PC4% mreceive -g 224.1.1.1 -p 1111
   PC4% mreceive -g 224.2.2.2 -p 2222
   PC4% mreceive -g 224.3.3.3 -p 3333
   ```

   • For each PC and each multicast group, determine which PC is receiving data from which other PC. Explain the outcome.

3. In *ethereal*, set a display filter so that only IGMP packets are displayed. Save the IGMP packets to a file.

4. Terminate all `msend` and `mreceive` programs.

5. Save the IGMP packets to a file. Save the details of these packets.

Lab Report Answer the following questions using the *ethereal* data that you saved. Include the relevant portion of data with each answer.

• From the saved *ethereal* data, prepare a table that lists the different IGMP message types observed on the network. For each IGMP message, include only the timestamp (from *ethereal*), the IP destination address, the IP source address, the type of the IGMP packet, and the group address in the IGMP payload.

• Which type of IGMP messages do you observe? What are their TTL values? What is the destination IP address of an IGMP Membership Report? What is the destination IP address of IGMP Leave messages?

EXERCISE 2(D).
Commands to query IP multicast group membership.

1. Start an *ethereal* session on PC1.

2. On PC4, issue a `ping` command to a multicast group address:

   ```
   PC4% ping -c 5 224.0.0.1
   ```

   Multicast group 224.0.0.1 is a special multicast group, in that all IP interfaces that
   are IP multicast enabled join this group. How many hosts respond to the query?

3. Establish three IP multicast senders as follows:

   ```
   PC1% msend -g 224.3.3.3 -p 3333 -join
   ```

   ```
   PC2% msend -g 224.3.3.3 -p 3333 -join
   PC2% mreceive -g 224.3.3.3 -p 3333
   ```

   ```
   PC3% msend -g 224.3.3.3 -p 3333 -join
   PC3% mreceive -g 224.3.3.3 -p 3333
   ```

4. From PC4, issue a `ping` command to the IP multicast group *224.3.3.3*:

   ```
   PC4% ping -c 5 224.3.3.3
   ```

   Observe how many hosts respond to the query.

5. Terminate all `msend` and `mreceive` programs.

6. Record the answers to the questions in this exercise for the lab report.

Lab Report

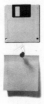

- Include your answers to the questions posed in this exercise.

- Did you observe multiple replies from a node in which multiple multicast applications are joined in the same multicast group?

PART 3. MULTICAST ON MULTIPLE SEGMENTS

This part of the lab explores how IP multicasting works on a network with multiple IP
networks. Here, two segments are connected by a multicast-enabled router. For each segment, the router keeps track of which hosts have joined a multicast group.

For this part of the lab, the PCs are arranged in two segments as shown in Figure 10.3.

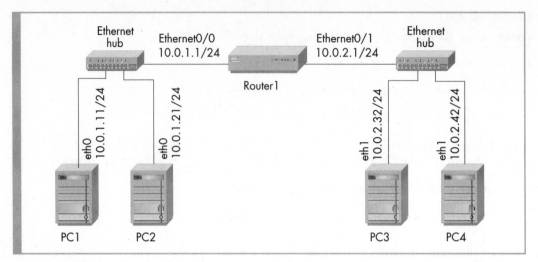

FIGURE 10.3.

Configuration for Part 3.

EXERCISE 3(A).
Network setup.

1. Set the network up as shown in Figure 10.3. Note that PC1 and PC2 are connected to the hub via interface *eth0*, and PC3 and PC4 are connected to the hub via interface *eth1*.

2. Configure the IP addresses of Router1 as given in Table 10.2.

3. For each PC, add a default route to Router1. For PC1 and PC2, a default route is set to 10.0.1.1, and for PC3 and PC4, a default route is set to 10.0.2.1.

4. On each PC, add a second route for the network 224.0.0.0/8. On PC1 and PC2, type:

   ```
   PC1% route add -net 224.0.0.0/8 dev eth0
   ```

   On PC3 and PC4, type:

   ```
   PC3% route add -net 224.0.0.0/8 dev eth1
   ```

5. Disable the unused interfaces on each PC. For PC1 and PC2, disable interface *eth1*, and for PC3 and PC4, disable interface *eth0*.

6. Use the `ping` command to verify that all interfaces are correctly configured.

EXERCISE 3(B).
Enabling IGMP at a router.

Set up Router1 so that it runs IGMP protocol on both interfaces *Ethernet0/0* and *Ethernet0/1*, but IP multicast forwarding remains disabled on the router. Refer to Exercise 2(B) for the required commands.

EXERCISE 3(C).
IGMP packets.

1. Verify that unicast traffic is going across the router by issuing a `ping` command to a PC on the other side of the router—e.g.,

   ```
   PC1% ping 10.0.2.32
   ```

2. Start an *ethereal* session on PC1 that captures data on the interface *eth0*, and start an *ethereal* session on PC3 that captures data on the interface *eth1*.

3. Start multicast senders and receivers on the hosts as follows. (These are exactly the same commands as used in Exercise 2(C).)

   ```
   PC1% msend -g 224.1.1.1 -p 1111 -t 8 -text "PC1"
   PC1% msend -g 224.2.2.2 -p 2222 -t 8 -text "PC1"
   PC1% mreceive -g 224.3.3.3 -p 3333

   PC2% msend -g 224.3.3.3 -p 3333 -t 8 -text "PC2"
   PC2% msend -g 224.1.1.1 -p 1111 -t 8 -text "PC2"

   PC3% msend -g 224.2.2.2 -p 2222 -t 8 -text "PC3"
   PC3% msend -g 224.3.3.3 -p 3333 -t 8 -text "PC3"

   PC4% mreceive -g 224.1.1.1 -p 1111
   PC4% mreceive -g 224.2.2.2 -p 2222
   PC4% mreceive -g 224.3.3.3 -p 3333
   ```

   - For each PC, take note of which transmissions are received. Explain the outcome.

4. Set the display filter of the *ethereal* programs running on PC1 and PC3 so that only IGMP packets are displayed, and save the IGMP packets. Save the details of these packets.

   - Pay attention to the IGMP messages exchanged between the PCs and the routers.

   - For each IGMP query, how many reports are generated? Is a report generated by every PC for each group that it joins?

   - How often are IGMP messages exchanged? Which PCs are involved?

5. Type the commands `show ip igmp groups Ethernet0/0` and `show ip igmp groups Ethernet0/1` on Router1. Does the router maintain a list of the group membership for individual PCs? If not, then do the routers maintain the number of hosts that have joined groups?

6. Terminate all `msend` and `mreceive` programs.

EXERCISE 3(D).
Enabling multicast forwarding.

This exercise repeats the steps of the previous exercise, but with multicast forwarding enabled on Router1.

1. Make sure that PIM-DM is enabled on the Ethernet interfaces of Router 1. Enable IP multicast forwarding on Router 1 with the following global configuration command:

```
Router1(config) ip multicast-routing
```

2. Start an *ethereal* session on PC1 that captures data on the *eth0* interface, and start an *ethereal* session on PC3 that captures data on the *eth1* interface.

3. Repeat the commands from Part 1 that start multicast senders and receivers on the PCs:

```
PC1% msend -g 224.1.1.1 -p 1111 -t 8 -text "PC1"
PC1% msend -g 224.2.2.2 -p 2222 -t 8 -text "PC1"
PC1% mreceive -g 224.3.3.3 -p 3333

PC2% msend -g 224.3.3.3 -p 3333 -t 8 -text "PC2"
PC2% msend -g 224.1.1.1 -p 1111 -t 8 -text "PC2"

PC3% msend -g 224.2.2.2 -p 2222 -t 8 -text "PC3"
PC3% msend -g 224.3.3.3 -p 3333 -t 8 -text "PC3"

PC4% mreceive -g 224.1.1.1 -p 1111
PC4% mreceive -g 224.2.2.2 -p 2222
PC4% mreceive -g 224.3.3.3 -p 3333
```

- For each PC, take note of which transmissions are received. Note the differences from the outcome in the previous exercise. Explain the outcome.

4. Terminate the *mreceive* program `mreceive -g 224.1.1.1 -p 1111` on PC4. Do you still observe traffic with destination IP address 224.1.1.1 on the IP network segment of PC3 and PC4?

5. Terminate all *msend* and *mreceive* programs.

6. Save the IGMP packets saved by *ethereal*. Save the details of these packets. Save the details of the IGMP packets.

Lab Report

Answer the following questions using the *ethereal* capture data that you obtained:

- What are the destination IP addresses of IGMP queries from the multicast router? What is the destination IP address of an IGMP report? What does this imply about the behavior of the multicast router that receives the IGMP report?

- For each IGMP query, how many reports are generated? Is a report generated by every host for each group that it joins?

EXERCISE 3(E).
Designated routers.

On a network with more than one router, only one router, the *querier*, issues IGMP queries. Also, only one router, the *forwarder*, forwards IP multicast packets to the network. (In addition to the querier and the forwarder, the multicast routing protocol PIM designates one router as the *designated router*.) In this exercise, you explore the rules that determine the querier and forwarder on a network with multiple routers.

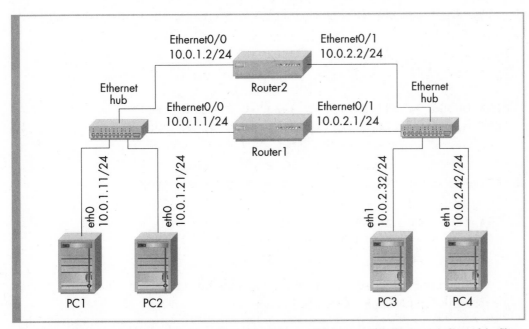

FIGURE 10.4.

Configuration for Part 3, Exercise 3(E).

Note: When the Ethernet interfaces of the Linux PCs (*eth0*, *eth1*) run at 100 Mbps and the Ethernet interfaces of the Cisco routers (*Ethernet0/0*, *Ethernet0/1*) run at 10 Mbps, you should avoid using dual speed hubs, when you connect two or more Cisco routers and one or more Linux PCs to the same hub.

If you use dual-speed hubs in such a situation, the Linux PCs cannot observe the traffic between Cisco routers with *ethereal*.

1. Set the network up as shown in Figure 10.4. This is the same setup as in Figure 10.3, with the addition of Router2.

   a. Configure the IP addresses of Router2 as shown in Table 10.3.

TABLE 10.3. IP addresses of Router2 for Figure 10.4.

Cisco Router	Interface Ethernet0/0	Interface Ethernet0/1
Router2	10.0.1.2/24	10.0.2.2/24

    b. For PC1 and PC2, the default route is set to 10.0.1.1, and for PC3 and PC4, the default route is set to 10.0.2.1. Recall that routing table entries are set using the command `route`:

```
PC1% route add default gw 10.0.1.1
```

    c. Use the `ping` command to verify that all interfaces are correctly configured.

2. Repeat the commands from Part 1 that start multicast senders and receivers on the PCs:

```
PC1% msend -g 224.1.1.1 -p 1111 -t 8 -text "PC1"

PC1% msend -g 224.2.2.2 -p 2222 -t 8 -text "PC1"
PC1% mreceive -g 224.3.3.3 -p 3333

PC2% msend -g 224.3.3.3 -p 3333 -t 8 -text "PC2"
PC2% msend -g 224.1.1.1 -p 1111 -t 8 -text "PC2"

PC3% msend -g 224.2.2.2 -p 2222 -t 8 -text "PC3"
PC3% msend -g 224.3.3.3 -p 3333 -t 8 -text "PC3"

PC4% mreceive -g 224.1.1.1 -p 1111
PC4% mreceive -g 224.2.2.2 -p 2222
PC4% mreceive -g 224.3.3.3 -p 3333
```

 There is no need to save data to an output file. Find out and record which router is the forwarder and which router is the querier.

- Determine the router that sends IGMP queries. This is the IGMP querier.

- Determine the router that forwards multicast packets. This is the forwarder.

3. Change the IP address of *Ethernet0/0* on Router1 to 10.0.1.100/24.

- Determine if this change has an impact on the assignment of the querier and the forwarder on the networks.

- Determine if your observation is consistent with the rules used to designate a router as querier or forwarder on a network.

4. Terminate all *msend* and *mreceive* programs.

 Lab Report Include the answers to the questions in this exercise.

PART 4. MULTICAST ROUTING WITH PIM-DM

In this part of the lab, you observe how IP multicast routers exchange group membership information using a multicast routing protocol. All multicast routing protocols build a distribution tree of routers that connect the multicast senders to the multicast receivers. Lab 10 uses the routing protocol PIM (Protocol Independent Multicast). PIM implements two routing schemes: dense mode (PIM-DM) and sparse mode (PIM-SM).

In this part of the lab, you explore the operations of the PIM-DM protocol. PIM-DM builds one distribution tree for each multicast source. In PIM-DM, the distribution tree is a shortest-path tree (SPT), which is established using a flood-and-prune approach.

A multicast router has multicast routing table entries, which give a list of next-hop addresses for a source IP address and a multicast IP address. These entries are called a *source-group address pair*, or *(S,G) address pair*. In the PIM-DM routing protocol, all routing table entries are (S,G) address pairs. In the PIM-SM, where multiple sources can share the same distribution tree, it is sufficient to have one routing table entry for all sources. We use (*, G) to denote the corresponding source-group address pair, where * stands for *all sources*.

The network configuration for this lab is shown in Figure 10.5.

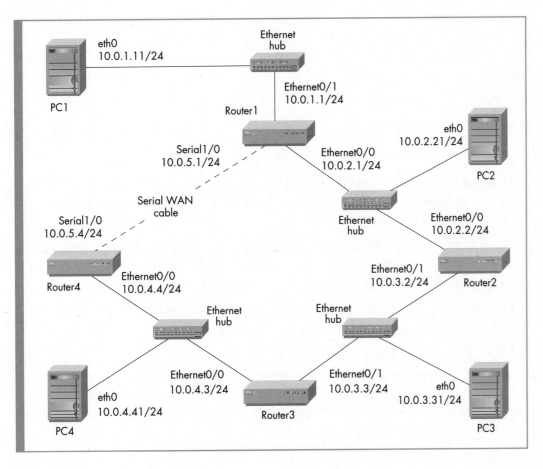

FIGURE 10.5.

Network topology for Parts 4 and 5.

EXERCISE 4(A).

Network setup.

Set the network configuration up as shown in Figure 10.5. Use the configuration information from Tables 10.4 and 10.5.

TABLE 10.4. Configuration of PCs for Part 4.

Linux PC	Interface *eth0*	Interface *eth1*	Default Gateway
PC1	10.0.1.11/24	Disabled	10.0.1.1
PC2	10.0.2.21/24	Disabled	10.0.2.2
PC3	10.0.3.31/24	Disabled	10.0.3.3
PC4	10.0.4.41/24	Disabled	10.0.4.4

TABLE 10.5. Configuration of routers for Part 4.

Cisco Router	Interface *Ethernet0/0*	Interface *Ethernet0/1*	Interface *Serial1/0*
Router1	10.0.2.1/24	10.0.1.1/24	10.0.5.1/24
Router2	10.0.2.2/24	10.0.3.2/24	Disabled
Router3	10.0.4.3/24	10.0.3.3/24	Disabled
Router4	10.0.4.4/24	Disabled	10.0.5.4/24

1. **Connecting cables:** Connect the routers, PCs, and Ethernet hubs as shown in Figure 10.5. Connect the serial WAN interfaces (Serial1/0) of Router1 and Router 4 with DB-60-to-DB-60 crossover cable.

2. **Setup of PCs:** On each PC, enable interface *eth0* and set the IP address as shown in Table 10.4. Disable interface *eth1*, for example, by issuing the command `ifconfig eth1 down` on each PC.

   On each PC, add a default gateway to the routing tables of the PCs as given in Table 10.4. Add the routing table entry with the `route add` command.

3. **Setup of Cisco routers:** On each Cisco router, enable unicast and multicast forwarding. Also start the unicast routing protocol RIP. The multicast commands are explained in Part 2 of this lab. The commands that must be executed on Router1 are as follows:

```
Router1> enable
Password: <enable password>
Router1# configure terminal
Router1(config)# no ip routing
Router1(config)# ip routing
Router1(config)# ip multicast-routing
Router1(config)# router rip
Router1(config-router)# version 2
Router1(config-router)# network 10.0.0.0
Router1(config-router)# exit
```

Configure the IP addresses of the interfaces of the routers according to Table 10.5, and enable the multicast routing protocol PIM-DM on each interface. Here are the configuration commands for Router1:

```
Router1(config)# interface Ethernet0/0
Router1(config-if)# no shutdown
Router1(config-if)# ip address 10.0.2.1 255.255.255.0
Router1(config-if)# ip pim dense-mode
Router1(config-if)# interface Ethernet0/1
Router1(config-if)# no shutdown
Router1(config-if)# ip address 10.0.1.1 255.255.255.0
Router1(config-if)# ip pim dense-mode

Router1(config-if)# interface Serial1/0
Router1(config-if)# no shutdown
Router1(config-if)# ip address 10.0.5.1 255.255.255.0
Router1(config-if)# ip pim dense-mode
Router1(config-if)# end
Router1# clear ip route *
Router1# clear ip mroute *
```

4. When the serial WAN interfaces of Router1 and Router4 are directly connected by a serial WAN cable as in Figure 10.5, one interface functions as DCE and the other as DTE. In IOS, a clock rate must be set on the serial interfaces that function as DCE. Whether an interface functions as DCE or DTE is determined by the serial WAN cable.

   a. **Determine the DCE end:** To check whether a cable connected to a serial interface of a router is a DCE or DTE, type the following command:

   ```
   Router3# show controllers Serial 1/0
   ```

   The command displays low-level information on the serial interface, including whether an interface functions as DTE or DCE. Look for the statement V.35 DTE cable or V.35 DCE cable in the output of the command.

   b. **Set the clock rate at the DCE end:** Once the DCE has been identified, you must set the clock rate. Assuming that the serial interface of Router1 functions as DCE, type the following commands:

   ```
   Router1# configure terminal
   Router1(config)# interface Serial1/0
   Router1(config-if)# clock rate 64000
   ```

   This sets the clock rate to 64 kbps.

NOTE:

Since executing the command clock rate on a DTE interface has no effect and merely results in the display of an error message, it is safe to execute the command on both Router1 and Router4. In this case, you need not determine which interface is the DCE.

5. **Verify setup:** Verify the correctness of the network configuration. The following commands may help to determine if the network is correctly configured.

   a. On the PCs:

   - `ping IPaddr`: Tests connectivity to destination `IPaddr`.

   - `traceroute IPaddr`: Displays the route of a unicast packet to destination `IPaddr`.

   - `netstat -rn`: Displays the IP routing table.

   - `map-mbone -f -n IPaddr`: Where `IPaddr` is the IP address of a multi-cast router close to the PC. The command `map-mbone` displays all multicast routers that are reachable from `IPaddr`. A PC that runs this command must be on the same IP network as `IPaddr`.

   b. On the routers:

   - `show ip route`: Displays the IP unicast routing table.

   - `show ip mroute`: Displays the IP multicast routing table.

   - `Mrinfo`: Displays multicast configuration parameters.

6. **Collect data:**

   a. Run `map-mbone` on all PCs, and save the output to a file.

   b. For each router and on each interface, record the IP multicast groups that a router is aware of. For Router1, the command is

   `Router1# show ip igmp interface Ifname`

   where `Ifname` is the name of an interface of the router (*Ethernet0/0*, *Ethernet0/1*, *Serial1/0*).

   - Which multicast groups are shown at the routers?

   - Determine the designated router and querier for each network (10.0.1.0/24, 10.0.2.0/24, 10.0.3.0/24, 10.0.4.0/24, 10.0.5.0/24).

Lab Report

- Include the answers to the questions in Step 6(B).

- Try to explain which hosts and routers are members of the multicast groups detected in Step 5(B).

- Include the output of `map-mbone` to draw a map of how the multicast routers are connected. Can you use the output to determine the topology of a multicast distribution tree?

EXERCISE 4(B).
Flood and prune and graft messages in PIM-DM.

Now you explore how PIM-DM builds a multicast distribution tree, using the flood-and-prune approach.

Flood-and-prune: PIM-DM implements a flood-and-prune approach to set up a shortest-path distribution tree (SPT) for each source. This means that multicast packets from a source to a multicast group are periodically flooded to all multicast routers. Routers that do not have any members in a group send *prune* messages on the interface for that group to the upstream neighbor in the distribution tree. If a router receives a prune message on an interface for a group, then the router does not forward multicast packets for that group on that interface.

Graft message: If a network has no members of a particular group and one of its hosts wants to join that group, then the router for that network sends a graft message in the direction of the source of the router. When a router with a pruned routing entry receives a graft message, it activates the corresponding routing table entry and starts to forward multicast packets on the interface on which it received the graft message. Multicast routers use prune and graft messages to update their state information about the membership of groups.

1. Start *ethereal* session on all PCs, and start to capture traffic on interface *eth0*.

2. Stop all multicast senders and receivers that may still be running.

   - Do you observe PIM routing messages in a network without multicast senders and receivers? If you do, which PIM message types do you observe?

3. Start a multicast sender on PC1 with no receivers:

   ```
   PC1% msend -g 224.1.1.1 -p 1111 -t 64 -text "PC1"
   ```

   - Observe the IGMP messages. Which hosts and routers send IGMP messages. Which IGMP message types do you observe?

   - Observe the PIM messages that are transmitted as a result. Which types of PIM messages do you observe?

   - Note the destination addresses of the PIM messages. Although some PIM messages have a multicast address as destination address, a router that receives such a PIM message does not forward the PIM message on its outgoing interfaces. Why?

   - Do routers forward traffic sent to the multicast address?

   - Save the details of one packet for each IGMP and PIM message type to a file.

4. Start multicast receivers on PC2, PC3, and PC4:

   ```
   PC3% mreceive -g 224.1.1.1 -p 1111
   PC2% mreceive -g 224.1.1.1 -p 1111
   PC4% mreceive -g 224.1.1.1 -p 1111
   ```

- Which PIM message, that you did not see in Step 2 do you observe now? Pay specific attention to the prune and graft messages that are transmitted.

- Let the system run for a few minutes. How often are multicast packets flooded to all multicast routers? How often are prune messages transmitted?

- Save the details of one packet for each PIM message type (not saved before) to a file.

5. Use the display window of *ethereal* to determine the route on which multicast traffic from PC1 is flowing to the receivers.

  - Disconnect the Ethernet connection on interface *Ethernet0/0* of Router4. How does the flow of traffic change? How long does it take until PC4 again receives multicast packets from PC1.

6. Reconnect the Ethernet connection to the interface *Ethernet0/0* of Router4.

Lab Report

- List the IGMP and PIM message types that you observed. For each packet type, include one sample (include only the IGMP and PIM fields. Do not include any other headers.)

- Use the captured prune and graft messages to explain how the multicast distribution tree is built. For each router that sends PIM Prune messages, provide an explanation why the prune message is sent.

EXERCISE 4(C).
IP multicast routing tables and teverse path forwarding.

Here, you access the routers and interpret the multicast routing tables of the routers. Your task is to determine how the multicast routing tables are derived from the unicast routing tables.

In PIM-DM, there is a separate (S, G) routing table entry for each sender in a multicast group. You need to determine the multicast distribution tree for each (S,G) entry and the upstream and downstream routers for an (S,G) entry. You can determine the distribution tree from the RPF neighbor information, the incoming interfaces, and the outgoing interface lists of the routing table.

1. Resume with the settings of Exercise 4(B) with PC1 a multicast sender for group 224.1.1.1 and PC2, PC3, and PC4 multicast receivers for that group.

2. Start two new multicast senders on PC2 and PC4:

```
PC2% msend -g 224.1.1.1 -p 1111 -t 64 -text "PC2"
PC4% msend -g 224.1.1.1 -p 2222 -t 64 -text "PC4"
```

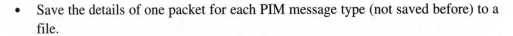

3. At each router, use the command show ip mroute to display the multicast routing tables. Save the output to a file. Observe that there is an (S, G) entry for each source. Each entry specifies the incoming interface and the set of outgoing interfaces for a sender in an IP multicast group.

Sketch the multicast distribution tree for the source-group pairs (10.0.1.11, 224.1.1.1), (10.0.2.21, 224.1.1.1), and (10.0.4.41, 224.1.1.1).

4. The routing tables of PIM-DM are derived from the unicast routing tables, using reverse path forwarding. Use the command `show ip route` to display the unicast routing tables of all routers. Save the output to a file. In the lab report you will discuss the relationship between unicast and multicast routing tables.

Lab Report

- Select a router, and include its multicast routing table. Explain the content of the routing table. Explain the meaning of the flags.

- Select an (S,G) entry from the collected data, and use its unicast routing table and the multicast routing tables of all routers to explain the concept of reverse path forwarding. Explain how the multicast routing tables are derived from the unicast routing tables.

- Draw a directed graph for the (S, G) entries (10.0.2.21, 224.1.1.1), and (10.0.1.11, 224.1.1.1).

EXERCISE 4(D).
Tools for displaying the status of a multicast network.

This exercise provides some of the available commands, in addition to those from Exercise 4(B) that can be used to determine the state of a multicast network.

> **LINUX OR IOS:**
>
> `mtrace IPsrc [IPrecv] [IPgroup]`
>
> The `mtrace` command, executed from a Linux PC or a Cisco router, traces a multicast route from a receiver with IP address `IPrecv` to a multicast group sender with IP address `IPsrc` for the multicast group `IPgroup`. The arguments `IPrecv` and `IPgroup` are optional. The default value for `IPrecv` is the IP address of the local host and the default for `IPgroup` is 224.2.0.1.
>
> `mrinfo McastRouter`
>
> The `mrinfo` command can be used to query the neighbors of a multicast router with IP address `McastRouter`.

Use the output of the `mtrace` and `mrinfo` commands to determine the multicast distribution tree for the source-group pair (10.0.2.21, 224.1.1.1).

1. Select a router, and run the `mrinfo` command. Save the output to a file.

2. Select a multicast receiver and a multicast source for group 224.1.1.1 and trace the path of multicast traffic using the `mtrace` command. Issue the `mtrace` command on a PC that is a receiver. Save the output to a file.

3. Select a router and run the following commands. Save the output to a file.

   a. `show ip igmp groups`

   b. `show ip pim neighbor`

       c. `show ip pim interface`

       d. `show ip rpf`

Lab Report

- Include the `mrinfo` and `mtrace` output.

- Explain how you can determine the multicast distribution tree from the output of `mtrace`.

- Do any of the commands in Step 3 display information that is not obtainable from `show ip mroute` or `mrinfo`? If so, which additional information do these commands provide?

PART 5. MULTICAST ROUTING WITH PIM-SM

In this part of the lab, you explore the operations of the PIM-SM protocol. In the dense mode of the PIM protocol, there is a source-specific shortest-path tree (SPT) for each source in the multicast group. In PIM sparse mode, all routers build a shared tree for a group, called a *rendezvous point tree* (RPT), which is rooted at a specific router, called the *rendezvous point* (RP). In Cisco IOS, a rendezvous point can be statically configured, or it can be dynamically determined using a special protocol to designate and advertise the rendezvous point. In this lab, we consider only a statically configured rendezvous point.

PIM-SM operates as follows. When a new receiver joins a group, multicast routers build a path to the RPT. This is similar to the graft messages seen in Part 4 of the lab. Each source of multicast traffic sends the traffic to the rendezvous point. When the rendezvous point receives a multicast datagram, it forwards the datagram downstream to the RPT. In PIM-SM, receivers switch from an RPT to an SPT, if the traffic from a source exceeds a certain threshold, called the *spt-threshold*.

When a new source starts sending multicast traffic, the designated router of the source sends *PIM Register* messages to the RPT and attaches its multicast packets to the PIM Register messages. Interestingly, the PIM Register messages are sent as a unicast datagram to the rendezvous point. When the rendezvous point receives the first packet from a new source, it sends a *PIM Join/Prune* message toward that source. What follows is an interaction between the rendezvous point and the designated router of the source, in which the designated router stops putting multicast packets in PIM Register messages and starts sending regular multicast packets to the rendezvous point.

Enabling PIM-SM involves two steps: (1) Setting the multicast protocol, in our case, from PIM dense mode to PIM sparse mode and (2) selecting and setting a rendezvous point. As an additional step—(3)—we force PIM-SM to only use the RPT (and not switch over to an SPT).

1. **Enable PIM-SM:** On each router, and for each interface of the routers with an IP
   address, change the routing protocol from PIM dense mode to PIM sparse mode.
   This is done with the command

   ```
   Router1(config-if)# ip pim sparse-mode
   ```

2. **Set the rendezvous point:** Fix Router2 as the rendezvous point. The rendezvous
   point must be configured at each router. For Router1, the command is

   ```
   Router1(config)# ip pim rp-address 10.0.3.2
   ```

   You can verify that the rendezvous point is set correctly by issuing the command

   ```
   Router1# show ip pim rp mapping
   ```

3. **Enforcing the use of the shared tree:** Normally, PIM-SM switches eventually from
   an RPT to an SPT. To study the RPT, you need to disable this feature. You can pre-
   vent the establishment of SPTs with the following command:

   ```
   Router1(config)# ip pim spt-threshold infinity
   ```

   If `spt-threshold` is followed by a number, the routers will switch over to an SPT
   when the traffic it receives reaches the traffic threshold given by that number in kilo-
   bits per second. By setting the threshold to `infinity`, you ensure that the threshold
   is never exceeded.

EXERCISE 5(A).
Setup and preparation.

The network configuration is the same as in Part 4 and as shown in Figure 10.5.

1. Make sure that all multicast senders and multicast receivers (`msend` and `mreceive`
   commands) are terminated.

2. On each router, purge the routing tables with the `clear ip mroute *` command.

EXERCISE 5(B).
Enabling the PIM-SM multicast routing protocol.

1. Enable PIM-SM on all interfaces of all routers. For the *Ethernet0/0* interface of
   Router1, the commands are

   ```
   Router1# configure terminal
   Router1(config)# interface Ethernet0/0
   Router1(config-if)# ip pim sparse-mode
   ```

2. On each router, set the rendezvous point to IP address *10.0.3.2*. Also, configure PIM-
   SM so that it does not switch from an RPT to an SPT. On Router1, this is done with
   the following commands:

   ```
   Router1# configure terminal
   Router1(config)# ip pim rp-address 10.0.3.2
   Router1(config)# ip pim spt-threshold infinity
   ```

3. On each PC, start *ethereal* to capture traffic.

4. Start a set of multicast senders and receivers:

- PC1 sends to group 224.1.1.1 at port 1111.

- PC2, PC3, and PC4 receive from group 224.1.1.1 at port 1111.

5. Record the current content of the multicast routing tables with `show ip mroute`. Save the output to a file.

6. Observe and record the transmission of PIM protocol messages.

- Which PIM message types that you did not see in Exercise 4(B) do you observe? Save one packet of each type.

- Pay specific attention to the PIM Register and PIM Register-Stop messages that are sent between the source and the rendezvous point. Observe that the multicast packet is attached to a register message.

7. Start two new multicast senders:

- PC4 sends to group 224.1.1.1 at port 2222

- PC2 sends to group 224.1.1.1 at port 1111.

8. At each router, record the content of the multicast routing tables with `show ip mroute`.

- Do you observe (*,G) or (S,G) entries or both? Explain your answer.

- Construct the RPT for group 224.1.1.1.

Lab Report

- List the PIM message types that you observed. For each packet type, include one sample. (Include only the PIM fields and file IP source address. Do not include any other headers.)

- Select one router, and include the contents of the multicast routing table for this router.

- Provide a drawing that shows the structure of the RPT for group 224.1.1.1.

EXERCISE 5(C).
PIM-SM: Switch from RPT to SPT.

Now, modify the threshold so that PIM switches from an RPT to an SPT.

- Use the same set of multicast senders and receivers as in Exercise 5(B).

- Restart the *ethereal* sessions on all PCs.

- On each router, set the `spt-threshold` value to 0 with the command

    ```
    Router1(config)# ip pim spt-threshold 0
    ```

NOTE:

By default, a Cisco router switches to a source-based tree immediately after receiving the first packet on the shared tree for a given (S,G) address pair. The preceding configuration has the same effect.

1. Observe and record that the distribution tree for 224.1.1.1 switches to an SPT. The switch involves a number of steps. Make sure that you record the corresponding PIM packets.

   a. When the first data packet from PC1 arrives at Router2, the rendezvous point, it creates a multicast table entry for the address pair (10.0.1.2, 224.1.1.3). This first packet is a unicast packet that is encapsulated in a PIM Register message.

   b. Router2 sends a PIM Join/Prune message to Router1, since it is on the reverse path toward IP address PC1. Router1 creates a multicast table entry for the (S,G) address pair.

      • When Router2 receives a multicast message from PC1, it knows that the SPT is established at least partially from PC1 to Router2. Next, Router2 sends a PIM Register-Stop message to Router1, to tell the router to stop sending packets in PIM Register messages.

      • All routers switch to the source-based tree as soon as they receive a multicast packet from PC1. They will send PIM Join/Prune messages to change the route.

2. After the SPT has been built, display the content of the multicast routing tables with `show ip route`. Determine the route of the packets from senders to all the receivers.

3. Save the *ethereal* outputs of the PIM packets that you saved. Save the contents of multicast routing tables on all routers.

Lab Report Based on the captured outputs, explain the events that occurred in the network when the distribution tree switched from an RPT to an SPT.

CHECKLIST FORM FOR LAB 10

Complete this checklist as you work through the laboratory exercises and attach the form to your lab report.

Name (please print):_____

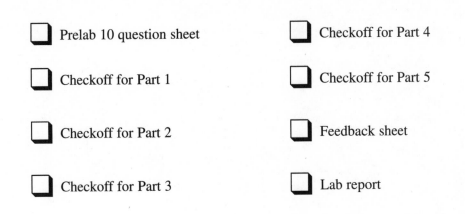

☐ Prelab 10 question sheet

☐ Checkoff for Part 1

☐ Checkoff for Part 2

☐ Checkoff for Part 3

☐ Checkoff for Part 4

☐ Checkoff for Part 5

☐ Feedback sheet

☐ Lab report

FEEDBACK FORM FOR LAB 10

- Complete this feedback form at the completion of the lab exercises and submit the form when submitting your lab report.

- The feedback is anonymous. *Do not put your name on this form* and keep it separate from your lab report.

- For each exercise, please record the following:

	Difficulty (−2, −1, 0, 1, 2) −2 = too easy 0 = just right 2 = too hard	Interest Level (−2, −1, 0, 1, 2) −2 = low interest 0 = just right 2 = high interest	Time to Complete (minutes)
Part 1. Multicast on a single segment			
Part 2. IGMP			
Part 3. Multicast on multiple segments			
Part 4. Multicast routing with PIM-DM			
Part 5. Multicast routing with PIM-SM			

Please answer the following questions:

- What did you like about this lab?

- What did you dislike about this lab?

- Make a suggestion to improve the lab.

Index

\#, 35
%, 16
&, 20
*, 18
?, 18, 35, 42
., 14
.., 14
/, 13
/dev, 15–16
/etc/dhcpd.conf file, 268
/etc/hosts file, 88–89, 287, 294
/etc/named.conf file, 289–290, 293, 298
/etc/nsswitch.conf file, 293
/etc/re.d/init.d directory, 139
/etc/resolv.conf file, 293–294
/home, 13
/labdata, 55, 59, 77, 103, 134, 218, 349
>, 35, 105

A

ABR. *see* Area Border Router
access permissions, 15
access to Cisco router, via console port with
    kermit, 107–108
acknowledgments (ACKs), 187
  cumulative, 187
  delayed, 187
  segments, 175
  selective, 200
Add Bridge, 219
Add Interface, 220
Address Resolution Protocol (ARP), 82–84
  ARP requests for non existing address, 84
  common uses of ARP command, 82
  matching IP addresses and MAC addresses, 83
  refreshing ARP cache, 82
  time-outs in ARP cache, 82
ageing value, 230
AIX operating system, 10
algorithms
  Karn's, 200
  learning, 230–231
  Nagle's, 187, 192
applications of SNMP, 335–337
  determining path between two hosts, 336–337

observing TCP connections on remote Linux
    PC, 335–336
Area Border Router (ABR), 153, 157
arp, 113
arp -a, 82
arp -d, 82
arp -s, 82
ARP cache, refreshing, 82
ARP command
  common uses of, 82
  manipulations to cache, 113
  requests for non existing address, 84
AS. *see* autonomous system
ASBR (Autonomous System Boundary Router),
  153
ascii, 23
ASN.1 (Abstract Syntax Notation 1) language,
  316
assignment of domain names to IP addresses,
  295–296
  for Linux PCs, 300
  for routers, 301
Asynchronous Transfer Mode (ATM) interface,
  38
AUI/RJ-45 transceivers, 7
authentication, 329
autonomous system (AS), 133, 160
Autonomous System Boundary Router (ASBR),
  153

B

background processes, 20
bash shell, 139
Bell Laboratories, 10
bg, 21
BGP. *see* Border Gateway Protocol
binary, 23
BIND (Berkeley Internet Name Domain)
  /etc/named.conf file, 293
  configuration file, 290–293
  software distribution, 285
Blocking state, 238–239
Border Gateway Protocol (BGP), 38, 129
  basic configuration, 161–163
  path convergence, 163–164

S